IMAGES
of America

WEST ORANGE REVISITED

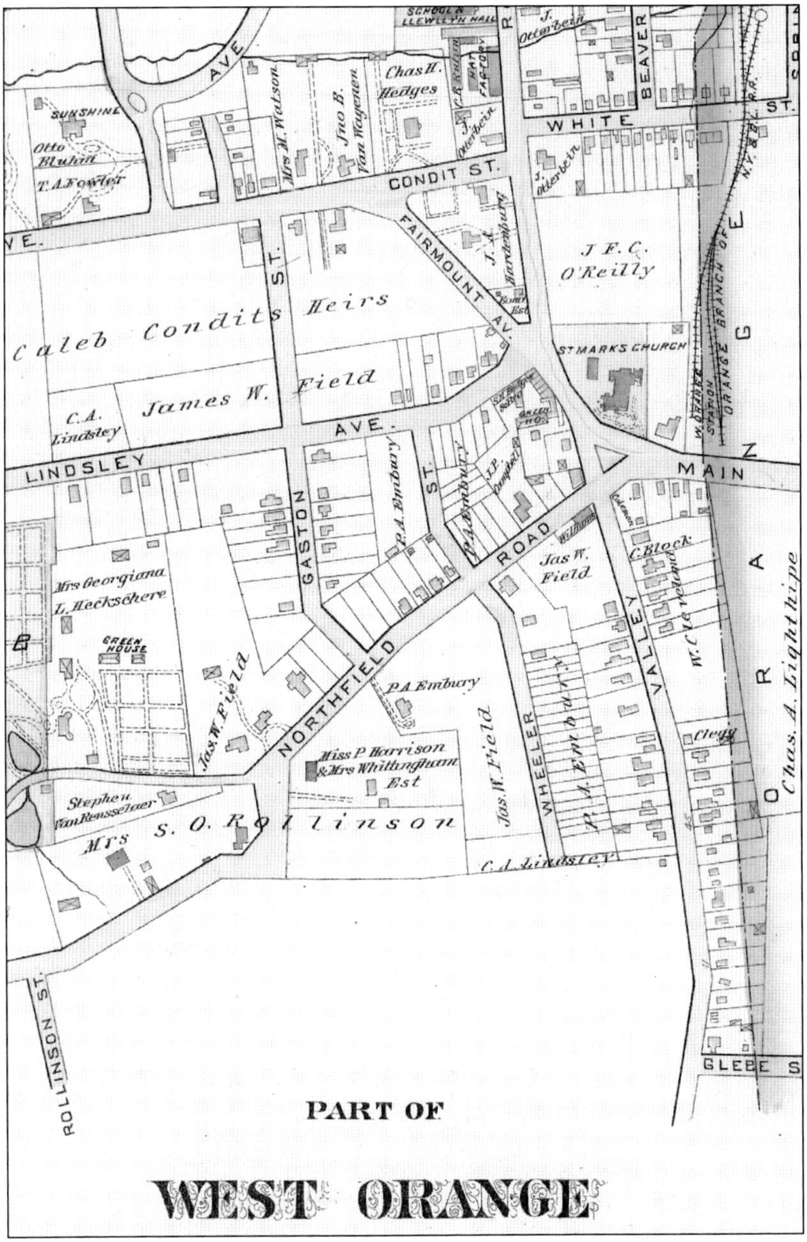

St. Mark's Episcopal Church, seen here on an 1890 map, was the oldest landmark in West Orange and was gutted by fire on January 1, 2016. The church opened in 1827 and later additions were completed in 1861. The map also shows a triangular plot of land formed by Condit Place, Fairmount Avenue, and what is today Main Street, where the current-day town hall was erected and opened in 1937. (Author's collection.)

On the Cover: Mike Gillen is seen giving girls a ride to Colgate Field during the 1950s. He was born in County Roscommon, Ireland, in 1922 and emigrated directly to West Orange. After graduation from St. John Grammar School in Orange, he worked with his three brothers at Thomas Edison's factory. Gillen began working for the recreation department full-time in 1950 and continued until 1976, when he retired; he passed away in February 1996. (Author's collection.)

IMAGES
of America

WEST ORANGE REVISITED

Joseph Fagan

ARCADIA
PUBLISHING

ISBN 978-1-4671-1594-0

Published by Arcadia Publishing
Charleston, South Carolina

Printed in the United States of America

Library of Congress Control Number: 2015950596

For all general information, please contact Arcadia Publishing:
Telephone 843-853-2070
Fax 843-853-0044
E-mail sales@arcadiapublishing.com
For customer service and orders:
Toll-Free 1-888-313-2665

Visit us on the Internet at www.arcadiapublishing.com

To my grandfather James J. Fagan Sr., who unknowingly inspired me as a child in ways we never could have imagined or dreamed

Contents

Acknowledgments

I would like to thank the countless individuals who for the last 15 years have given me various maps, atlases, vintage photographs and negatives, old documents and books, early newspapers and magazines, and all other memorabilia relevant to West Orange history. It has allowed me to acquire a vast and concise collection to help both preserve and promote local history for past, present, and future generations. Individually, any one of these items may seem unimportant, but collectively, they have become an invaluable archival resource to help tell the story of West Orange. Unless otherwise noted, the photographs in this book come from that private collection. Other images appear courtesy of Bob Rourke (BR), Detroit Public Library (DPL), Fred Magliacane (FM), Frank Seifiert (FS), Gregory School (GS), Ira Deutsch (ID), Robert Stagg (RS), Roz Moskovitz Bielski (RMB), and the Stott family (SF).

I would like to acknowledge the West Orange Public Library for continually granting me unlimited access to its resource material. It has allowed me to fill in many missing pieces in terms of dates and biographical information about former town officials. I would like to thank West Orange mayor Robert Parisi and the West Orange Town Council for bestowing upon me in 2012 the honorary title of official town historian, which has validated the importance of town history for all to know. I would also like to thank John McElroy, chairman, and Megan Brill, executive director, and the entire Downtown West Orange Alliance Board of Directors for their support in allowing me the opportunity to promote West Orange history.

It should be noted that every effort possible has been undertaken to present all the information contained within this book as accurate, reliable, and up to date. But I am not infallible and should not be considered the ultimate authority or only expert on town history, since many have important contributions to make.

Finally, by the deepest measure possible, I would like to extend a heartfelt thank-you to my wife, Debbie, and son, Joseph, and countless family and friends with whose continued love, support, and encouragement make life a worthy journey.

INTRODUCTION

I have always contended that there is so much more to West Orange history than the town's iconic image of Thomas Edison. He deserves his rightful place in history, but there were over two centuries of history before he arrived in the area now encompassing West Orange. The first settlers came in May 1666 when Robert Treat and a small group of Puritans from Milford, Connecticut, first sailed into what is now called Newark Bay and came ashore. Subsequent land purchases from the Lenni-Lenape whom they encountered eventually resulted in the settlement and formation of most of current-day Essex County, where West Orange is located.

On March 11, 1862, the New Jersey Legislature formed the township of Fairmount from existing parts of Orange, Caldwell, and Livingston. The western boundary between the new township of Fairmount and Orange was what is present-day Prospect Avenue in West Orange. But in 1862, West Orange as we know it today did not yet exist. A little over a year later, on March 14, 1863, the New Jersey Legislature created the township of West Orange by combining all of the land of the existing Fairmount Township formed only a year earlier with another section of neighboring Orange to create West Orange as it still is today.

This is important to note because subsequent celebrations of West Orange's founding have used the year of Fairmount Township's founding to commemorate when West Orange began. The town clearly did not exist in 1862, therefore creating a historically inaccurate dilemma requiring an explanation. Using the year 1862 was perhaps considered to represent the year the original portion of the town as we now know it was formed that eventually became all of West Orange in 1863. I think a more plausible explanation is that town officials chose 1862 to coincide with the opening of current-day West Orange Town Hall in 1937 as part of a 75th year celebration. The new town hall was a major source of profound community pride for West Orange and understandably a cause for celebration. Perhaps, little though was given at the time to the tradition this started since both the centennial and sesquicentennial followed suite in their respective celebrations using 1862 as the founding year. So it should be known for clarification purposes that the first part of the current town was established in 1862 as Fairmount Township then with further expansion became known as West Orange in 1863.

It would be difficult for this book to represent a concise chronological order of all events in West Orange history. It rather tells a story using narratives with available photographs to present a wide-ranging cross-sectional view of people, places, and events that make up the town's rich and sometimes overlooked history. Each individual picture will help advance the story in ways words cannot by adding a unique layer of historical texture. This history is also presented with a random sampling of many past individuals who have called West Orange home. But the general history is governed by the availability of photographs and somewhat limits the ability to tell a complete history in terms of the topics covered. Omission of certain places or people should not be seen as unimportant or overlooked. There is no limitation however to appreciate the local history that is seen here in a wide spectrum of photographs that will show a West Orange most never knew. Hopefully it will bring renewed meaning to the lives and locations seen here. This collection spans from the 1870s to the 1970s, which will allow the reader to explore and discover, or in some cases rediscover, a streaming confluence of people, places, and past events. Special attention to detail has been made with each photograph to provide exact dates and locations with points of references. In most cases additional relevant facts have been presented with each picture to further advance the story.

Some of the photographs come from my own family photo album, and many were given to me by current and former town residents who all have done their due diligence in preserving history and passing it forward. The understood boundaries that divide, the past and the present have respectfully been disregarded as stories buried deep within the treasure chest of time come alive. Hopefully the reader will feel history's beating pulse as the author has to see beyond what these pictures show. To further imagine what can't be seen to gain more insight to bridge the gap between today and the West Orange of yesteryear. For everything old will become new again to teach, enlighten and guide us all on the road of our own self-discovery as a people. To help better understand who we are and from where we came because every tomorrow includes a little piece of yesterday.

It should be further noted that all towns mentioned in this book are in New Jersey unless otherwise stated. In addition, all references to past or present West Orange locations are made using their current-day street names. This was done to avoid lengthy and unnecessary repetitiveness in describing many of the locations. Identifying present-day Main Street in West Orange has often caused confusion because it was once known as Valley Road before the name was changed sometime in the 1920s.

My personal family history spans nearly 150 years in the Oranges. Although I am the fourth generation of my family to have grown up in West Orange my situation should not be considered unique. Countless families in West Orange have family roots that run deep and have lived in town for generations. Others like myself may have moved a short distance away but still consider West Orange their hometown. Its history is captivating; its memories are fond; its people are priceless. It is presented here with photographs classified into four chapters as a body of work for future generations yet unborn to build upon as they write their own chapters of history. Hopefully one hundred years hence they will consider us worthy stewards who have preserved local history and can use this book as a field guide to discover and explore the roads of home that for us will always pass through West Orange.

One

Discover Main Street

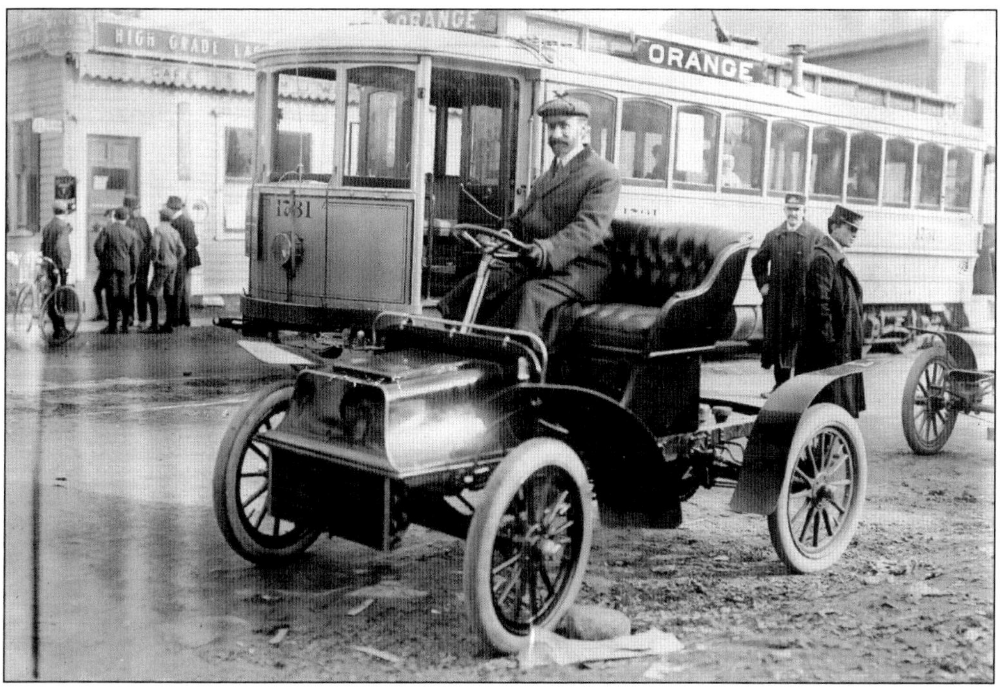

An unidentified driver poses in 1904 at the corner of Main Street and Eagle Rock Avenue. The building partially visible on the left was a café and restaurant with a hotel on the upper floors owned by William J. Woestendiek. At the time, this was the end of the trolley line on Main Street, as conductors can be seen waiting for a return trip back toward Orange. (DPL.)

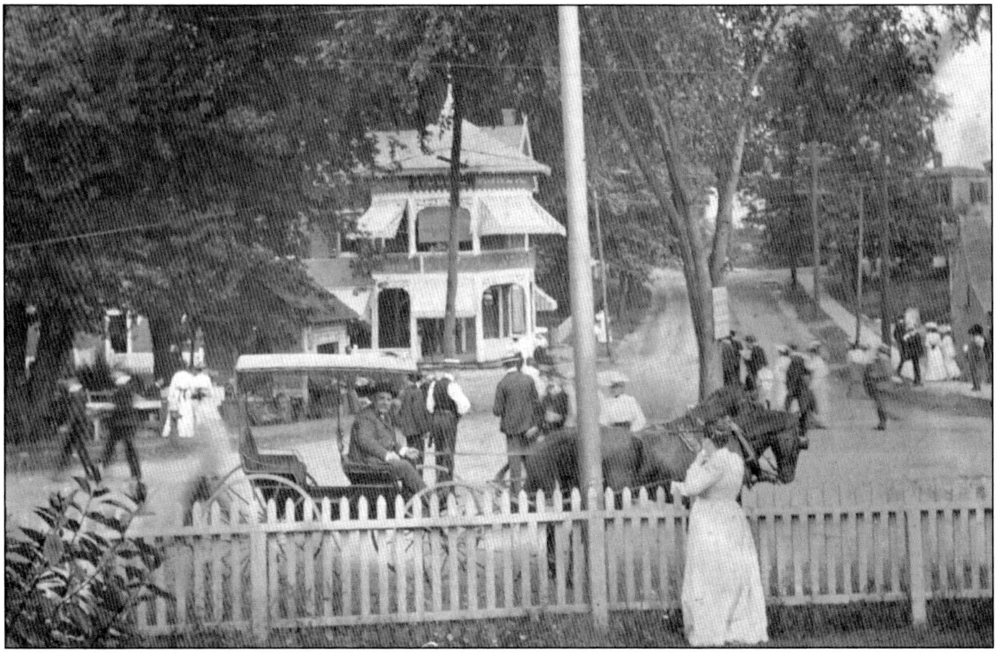

Looking directly up Harrison Avenue with Main Street to the right, this view of the bottom of Eagle Rock Avenue shows a busy intersection even in 1901. The picture was taken from the front lawn of the home of John Williams, whose former property is now a parking lot next to a building constructed in the 1920s on Main Street adjacent to this location.

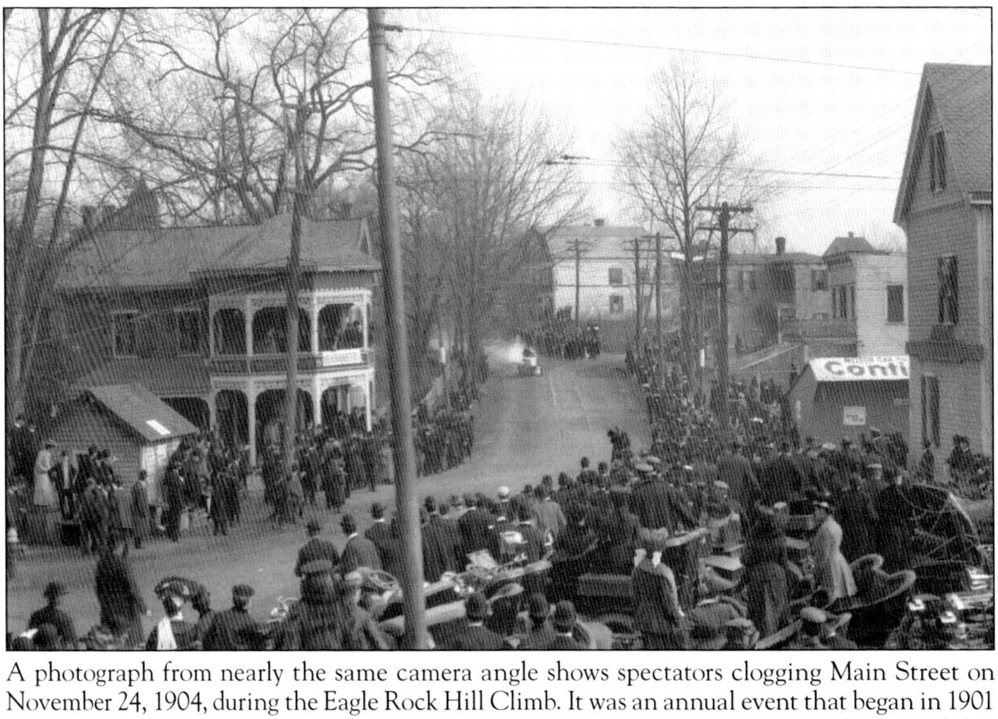

A photograph from nearly the same camera angle shows spectators clogging Main Street on November 24, 1904, during the Eagle Rock Hill Climb. It was an annual event that began in 1901 as drivers raced against the clock up Eagle Rock Avenue in endurance tests for early automobiles. This car is seen coming down Harrison Avenue, approaching the starting line.

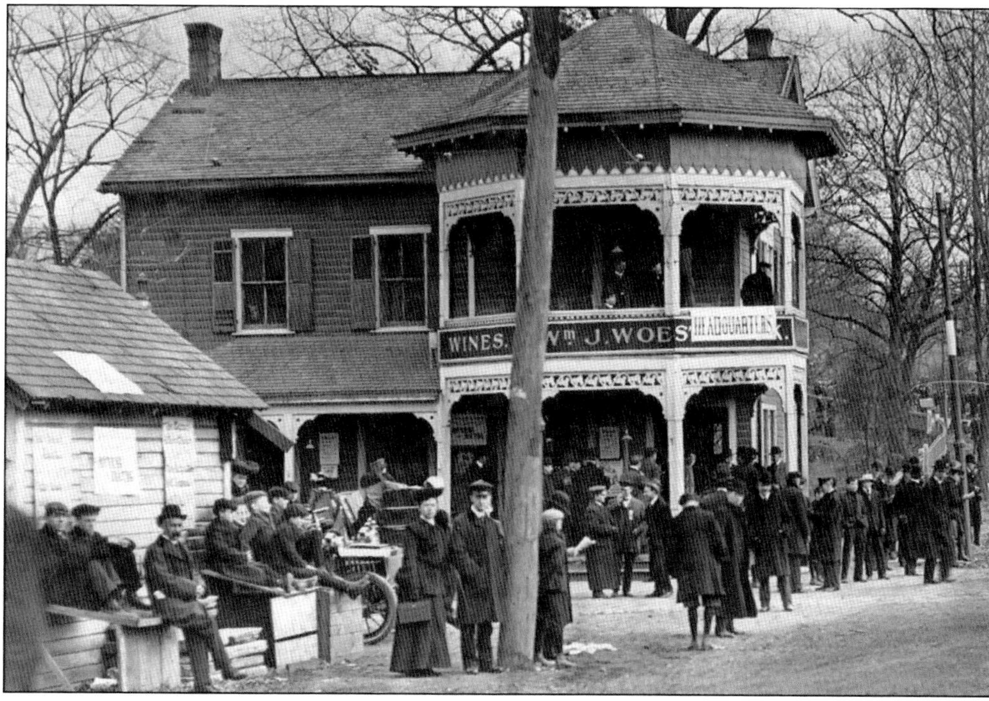

The liquor store of William J. Woestendiek on the corner of Mississippi and Harrison Avenues is pictured on November 24, 1904. The second floor offered an unobstructed bird's-eye view of the corner and served as headquarters for race officials during the Eagle Rock Hill Climb. This portion of the building was later removed and became Fink's Liquor and Confectionery Store in 1926. (DPL.)

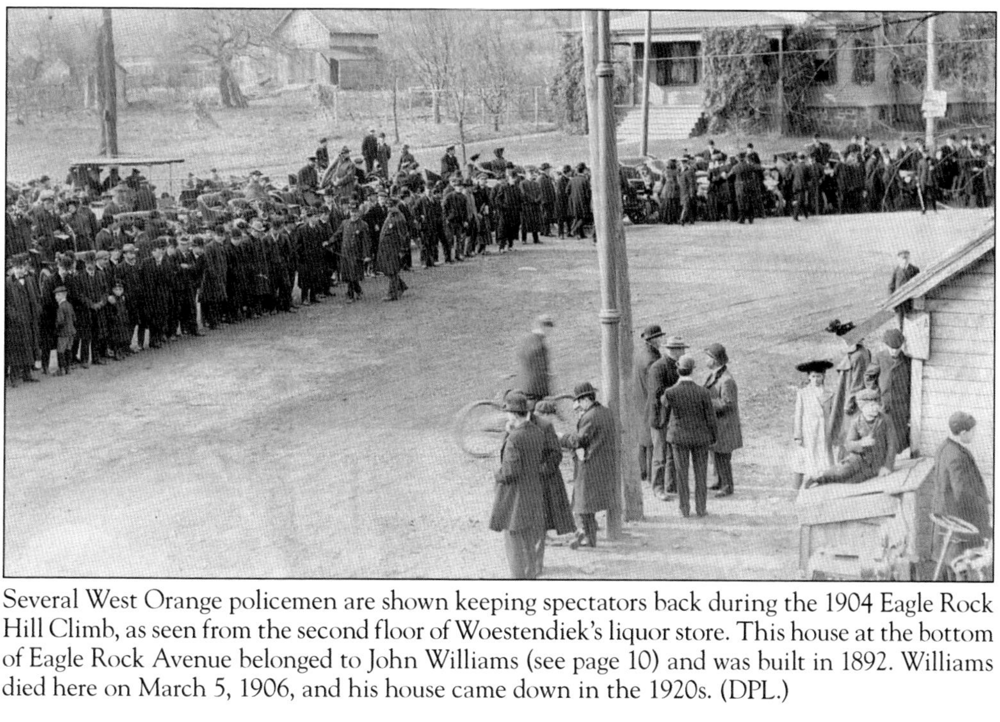

Several West Orange policemen are shown keeping spectators back during the 1904 Eagle Rock Hill Climb, as seen from the second floor of Woestendiek's liquor store. This house at the bottom of Eagle Rock Avenue belonged to John Williams (see page 10) and was built in 1892. Williams died here on March 5, 1906, and his house came down in the 1920s. (DPL.)

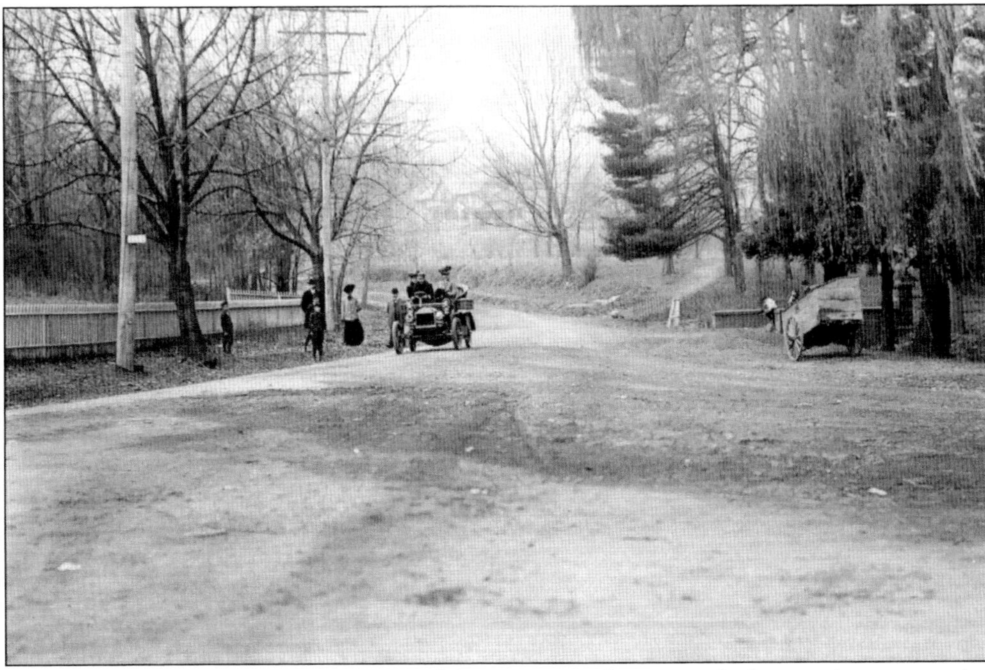

The sight of an automobile usually captured the attention of curious onlookers, as demonstrated in this view up Eagle Rock Avenue around 1902. The fence on the left is in front of John Williams's house and is the same fence seen in an opposite view at the top of page 10. Our Lady of Lourdes Church would later be built to the right. (DPL.)

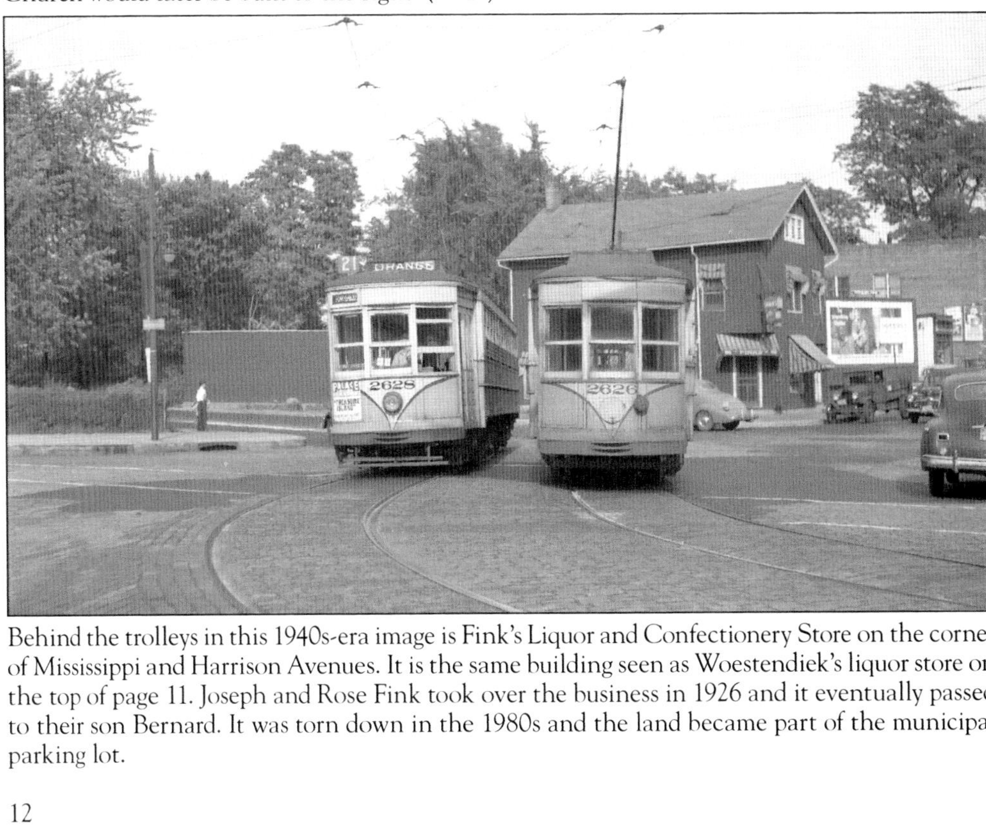

Behind the trolleys in this 1940s-era image is Fink's Liquor and Confectionery Store on the corner of Mississippi and Harrison Avenues. It is the same building seen as Woestendiek's liquor store on the top of page 11. Joseph and Rose Fink took over the business in 1926 and it eventually passed to their son Bernard. It was torn down in the 1980s and the land became part of the municipal parking lot.

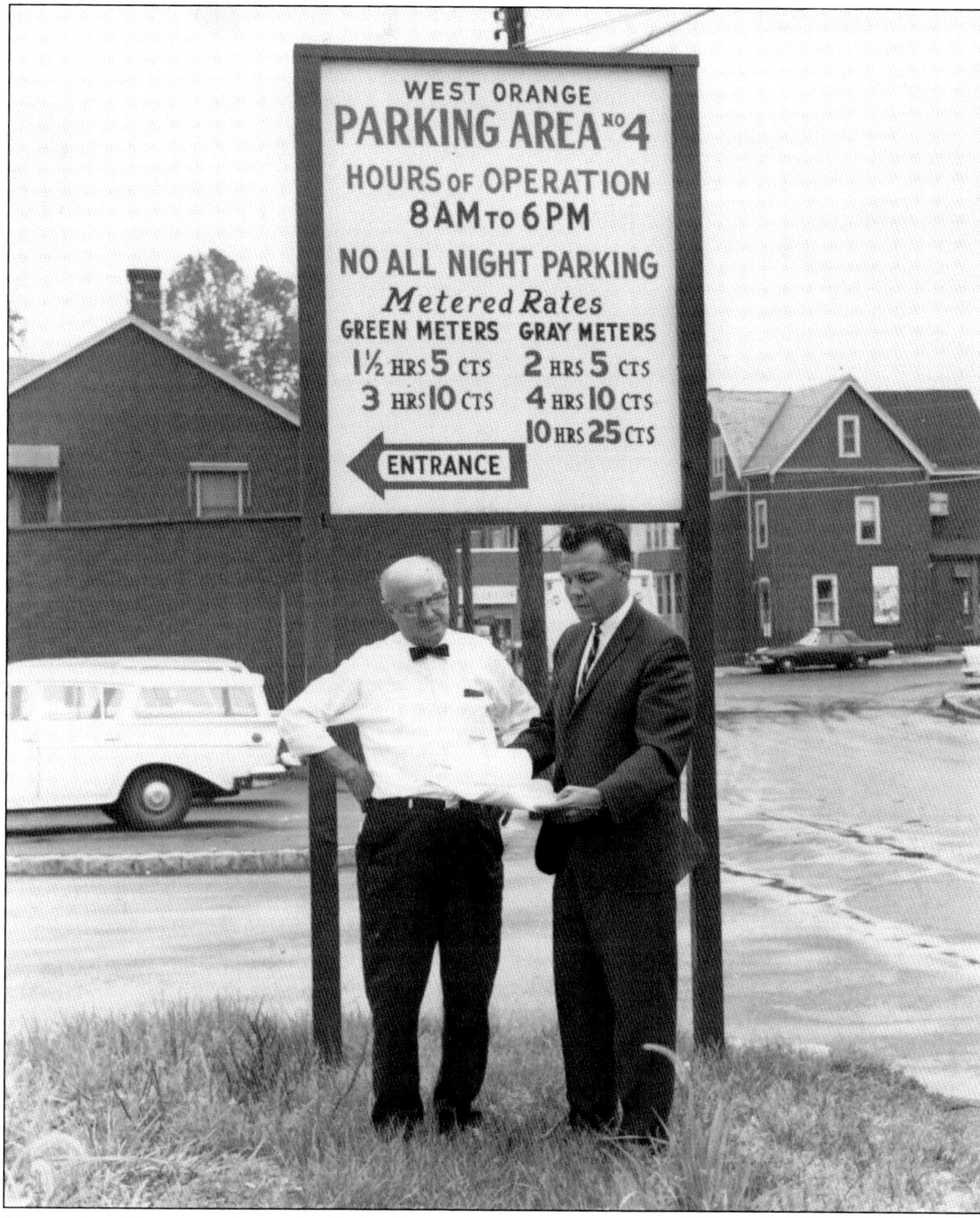

Recreation director Lefty Boland (left) is seen discussing plans with Mayor James Sheeran (right) at the municipal parking lot on Mississippi Avenue around 1965. Fink's is seen directly behind the sign. Sheeran graduated from West Orange High School in 1942 and was captured on June 6, 1944, during the Allied invasion of France while serving with the 101st Airborne Division. He escaped from the Germans by leaping from a speeding train heading to a prisoner-of-war (POW) camp. Sheeran subsequently fought with the French Underground and found refuge in the French town of Domrémy, which by a miraculous coincidence was the birthplace of his mother back in West Orange. He eventually rejoined his unit and was later wounded in combat in the small Belgian town of Bastogne during the Battle of the Bulge. Sheeran later served as West Orange mayor from 1958 to 1968 and insurance commissioner of New Jersey from 1974 to 1982; he passed away in 2007 at the age of 84. (FM.)

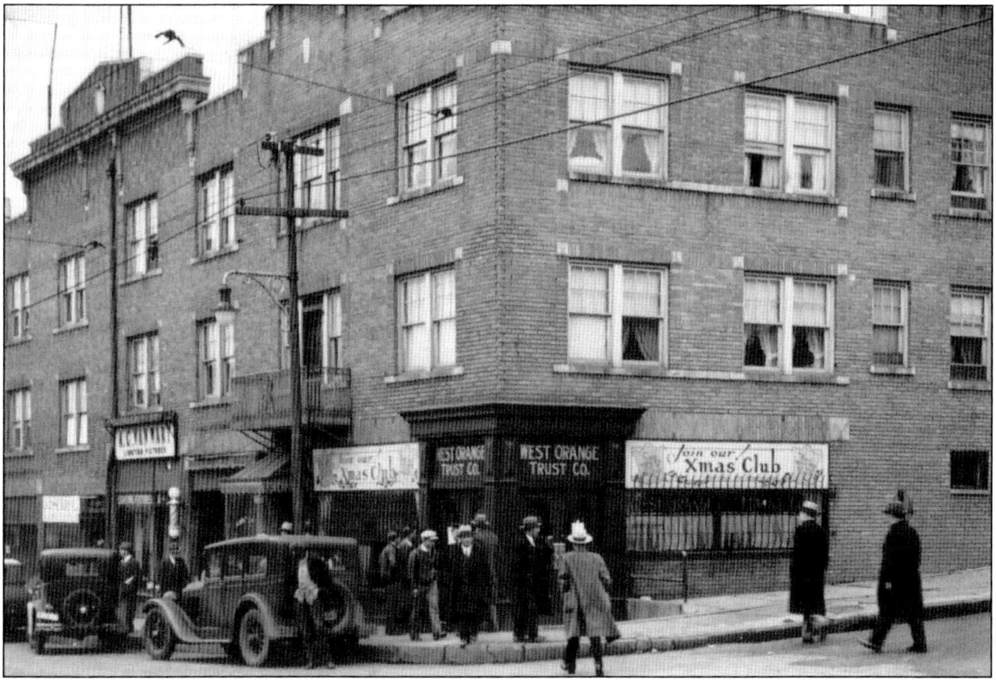

The West Orange Trust Company was located in this building constructed in 1927 on the corner of Main Street and Llewellyn Avenue. The bank closed in 1932—due to economic conditions and shortly after money disappeared from a trust fund. This building suffered a structural collapse in 1979 and a fire in 1981 but is still standing because the facade and interior were rebuilt in 1983.

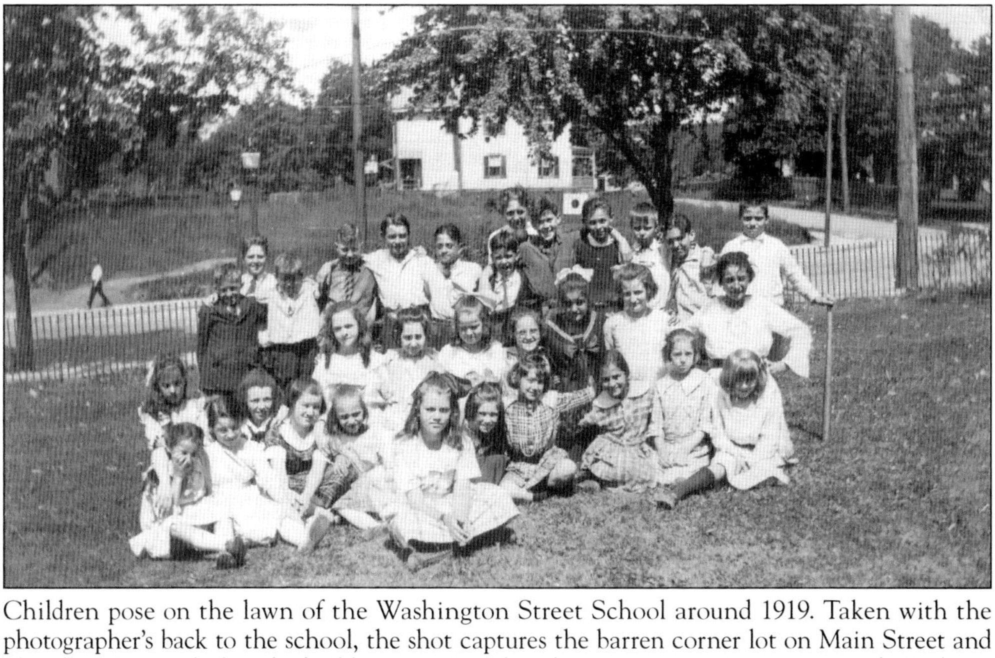

Children pose on the lawn of the Washington Street School around 1919. Taken with the photographer's back to the school, the shot captures the barren corner lot on Main Street and Llewellyn Avenue before the building mentioned in the previous caption was erected. Anthony Thompson was a former slave—the last surviving in Essex County—who passed away on September 16, 1884, at his small farm, which is partially seen at the left. (SF.)

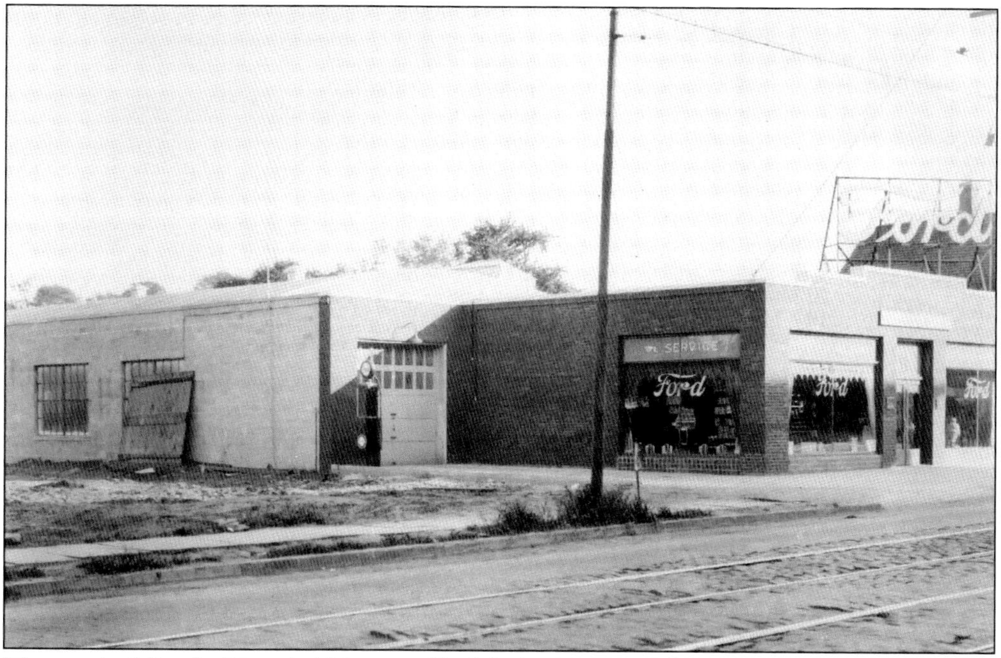

The new building for Henschel Motors, a Ford dealership, opened on Washington Street in 1927. In the 1950s, it became Washington Motors, owned by Rudy Collioud. The building has since undergone renovations but is still recognizable today. It is currently the home of Select Towing and Repair, which has been operated by West Orange native John McElroy for more then 30 years.

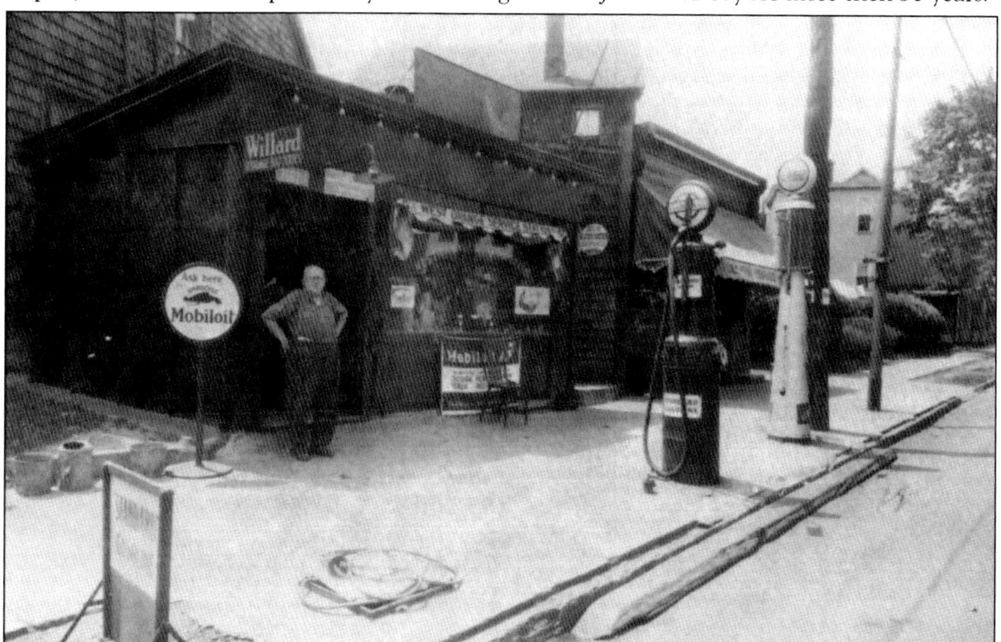

It is not known who opened the first filling station in West Orange, but Theodore Wendell's was one of the earliest. Wendell was born in Orange, New Jersey, on February 26, 1862—during the Civil War. He is pictured here in the 1930s at his West Orange Service Station at 10 Washington Street, and the house seen here behind him is still standing.

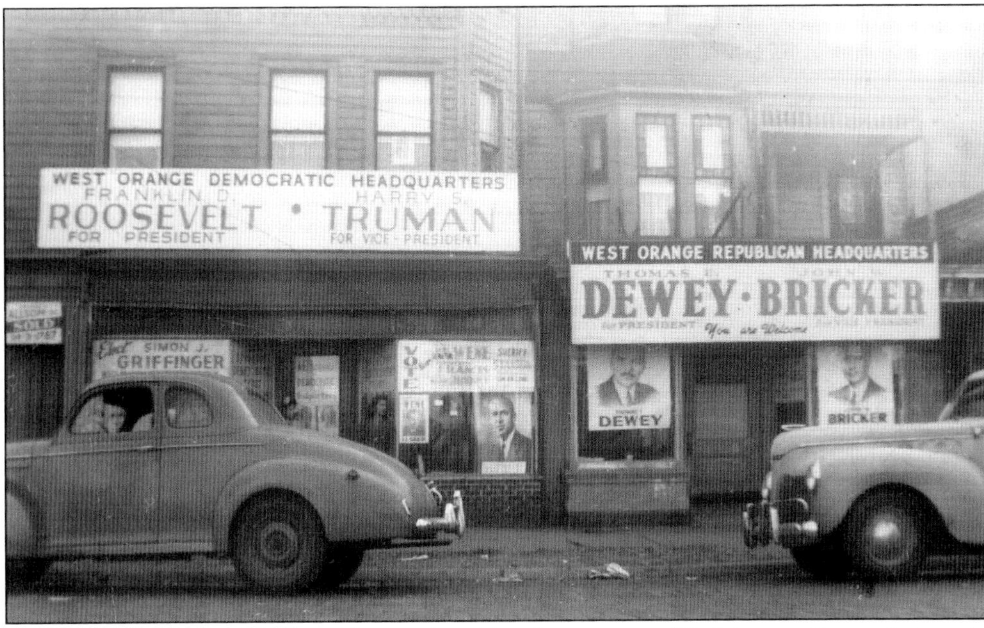

Major political parties had neighboring local headquarters on Washington Street during the presidential election of 1944. At the time, a promising outcome to World War II seemed imminent in both Europe and the South Pacific. President Roosevelt won his fourth term but passed away on April 12, 1945, only weeks before the defeat of Germany and less then five months before the surrender of Japan and never saw either victory.

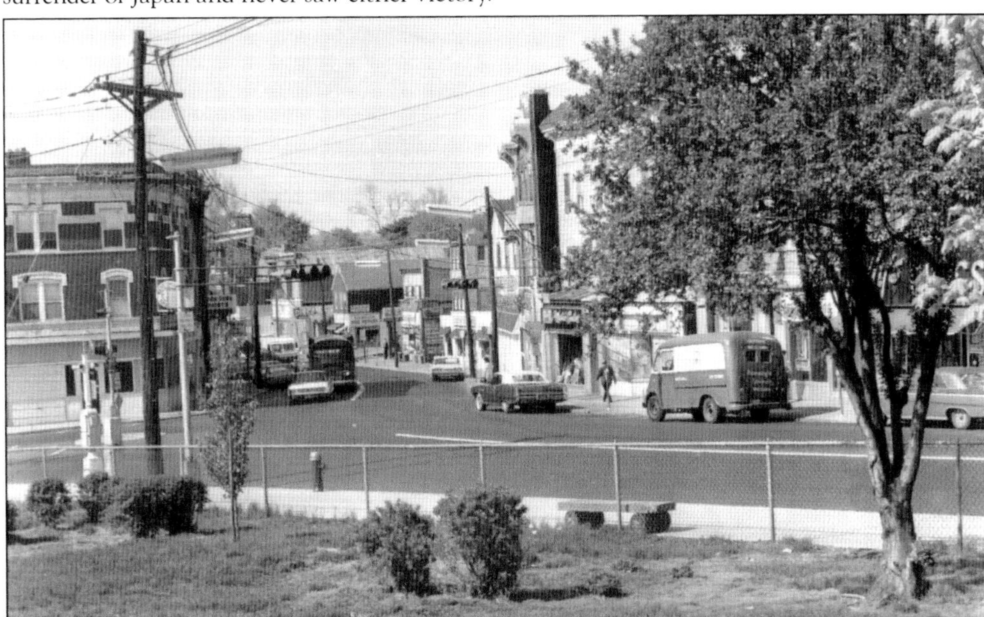

The section of town surrounding the intersection of Main and Washington Streets pictured here in the 1970s is still known as Tory Corner. It derived its name in the 1770s during the American Revolution when British sympathizers known as Tories gathered at this location. In the 1870s, an unsuccessful attempt was made to change the name to Northern Liberties.

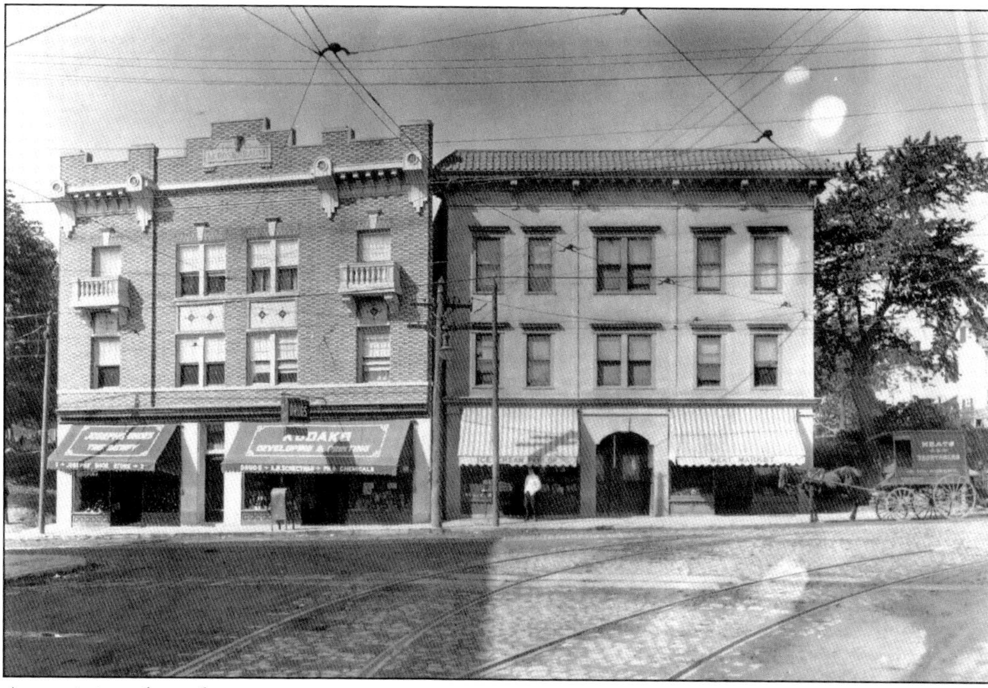

A surviving glass-plate negative provides a view looking up Washington Street at Tory Corner in 1915. This photograph was likely taken at that time of the opening of the new Rosenbaum Building on the left. Both structures are still standing today and are typical of several buildings along Main Street constructed in the last century.

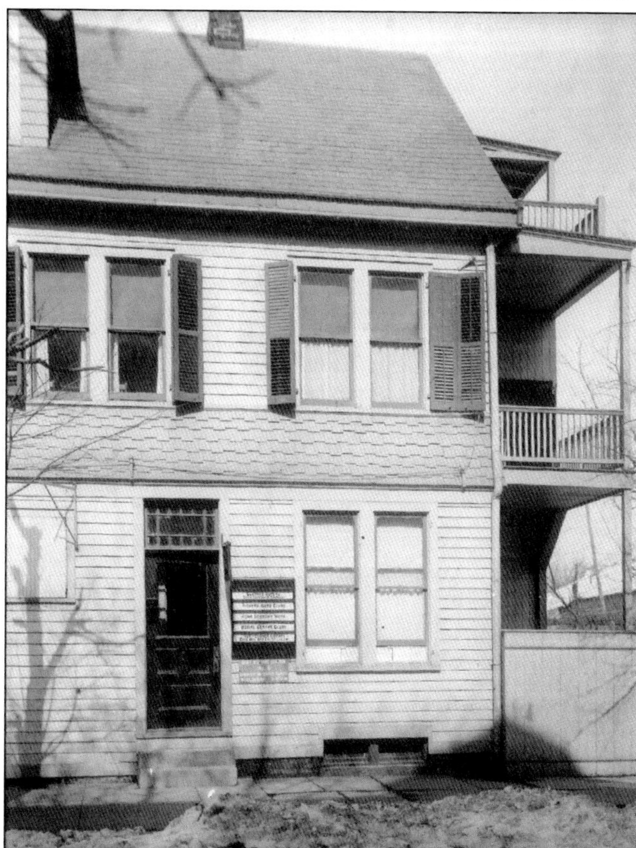

The West Orange Community League was an early organization in town providing social services and was the forerunner of the West Orange Community House. Its offices are seen here in 1916 at an unspecified address near Tory Corner. Beginning in 1901, four branches of the Orange Public Library opened around West Orange; by 1913, they had all closed—with the exception of one that remained open here.

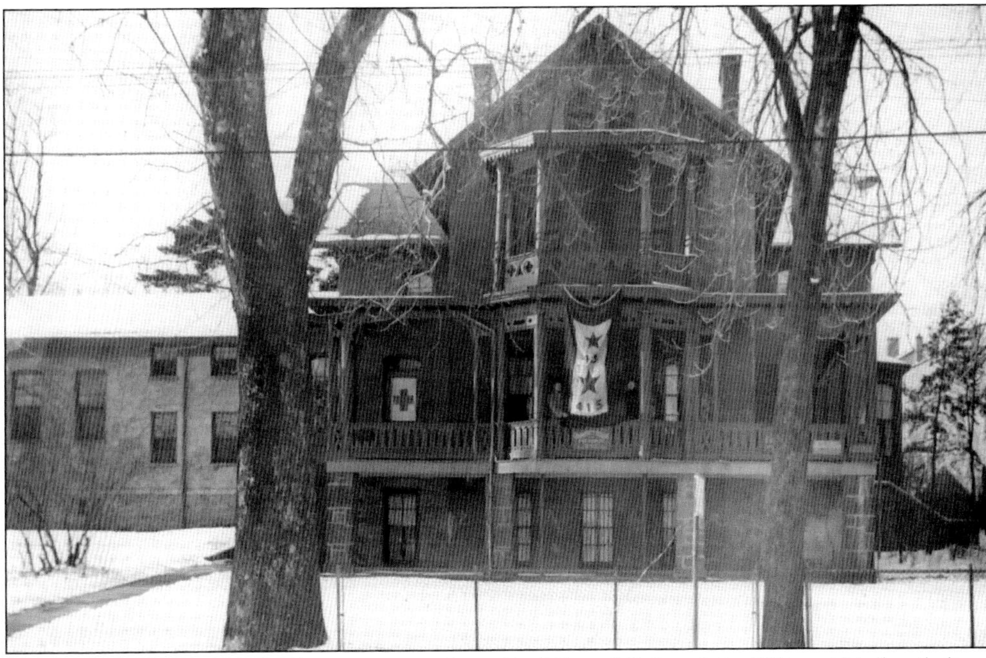

Originally built in 1846, this house was purchased by Edward Babcock in 1851 and his family lived there for 30 years. In 1918, Harriet, the wife of West Orange mayor Farnham Yardley, purchased the property and donated it to what became the West Orange Community House the following year. It has since been a center for town social activity and is pictured here in February 1945.

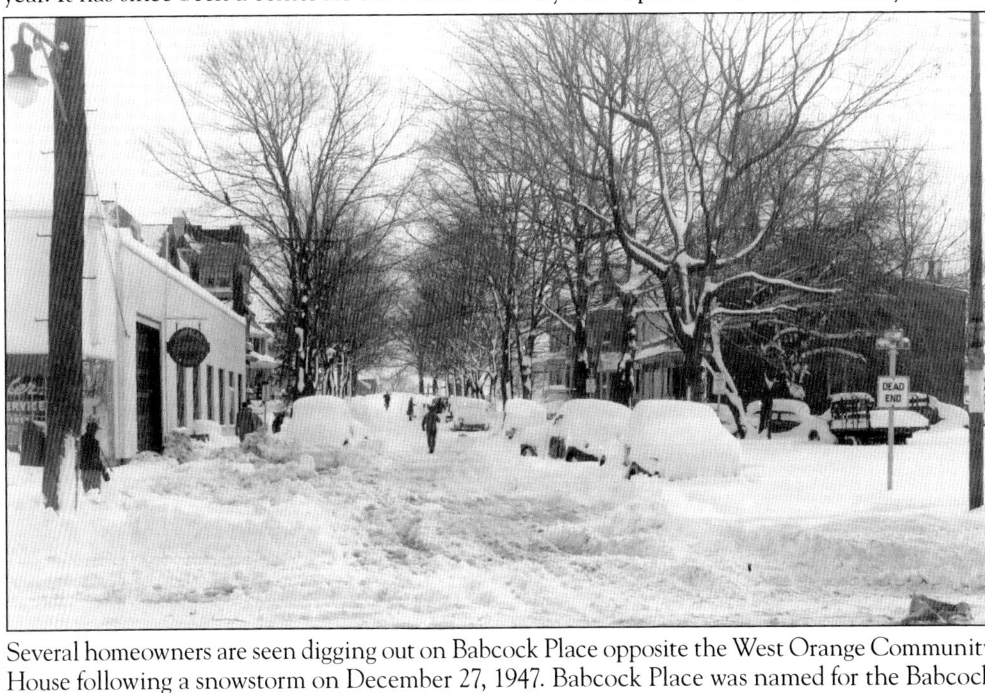

Several homeowners are seen digging out on Babcock Place opposite the West Orange Community House following a snowstorm on December 27, 1947. Babcock Place was named for the Babcock family who lived across from this location for 30 years. Shepard Terrace just to the south is named for Mrs. Babcock, who was a Shepard prior to marriage. Son Dwight Babcock served as township committee chairman, equivalent to mayor, from 1870 to 1872.

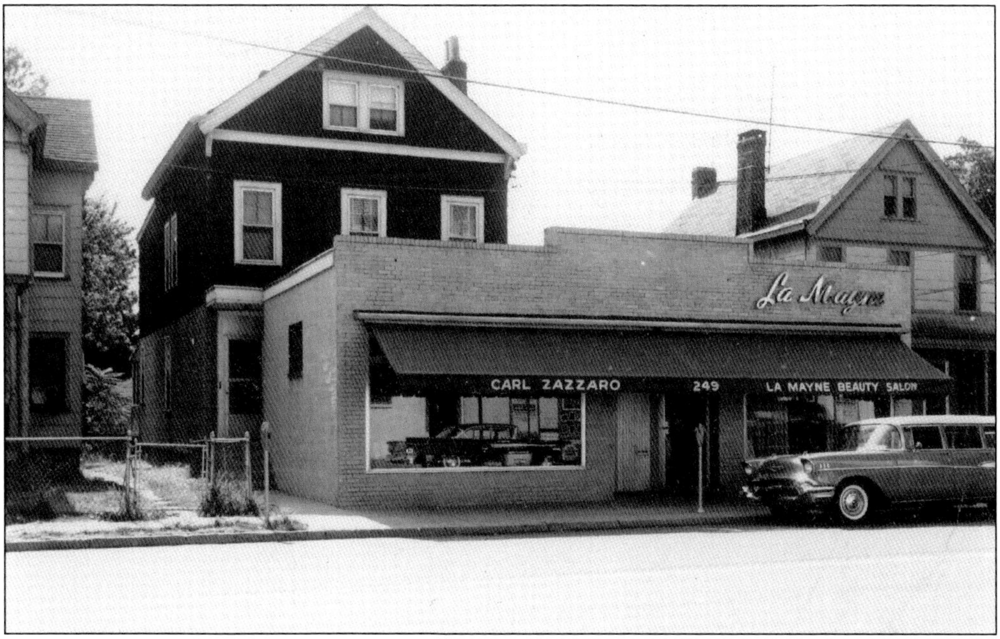

This building at 249 Main Street, seen here in 1958, is still standing and occupied by similar types of businesses. It is typical of several buildings along Main Street that were constructed directly in front of existing residences. Many of these homes date to the turn of the 20th century, before commercial development and when Main Street was known as Valley Road.

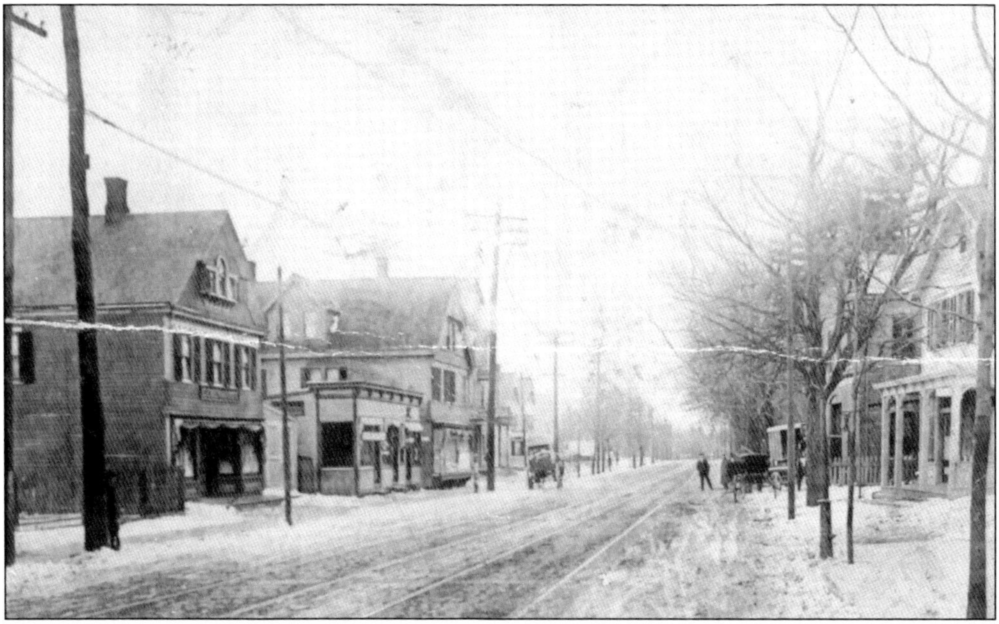

The house at 249 Main Street is barely distinguishable to the left in this real-photo postcard. It offers a rare view of Main Street around 1900 when it still had appeal as a residential neighborhood. Trolleys on the Orange line from Newark first reached this location on February 1, 1892.

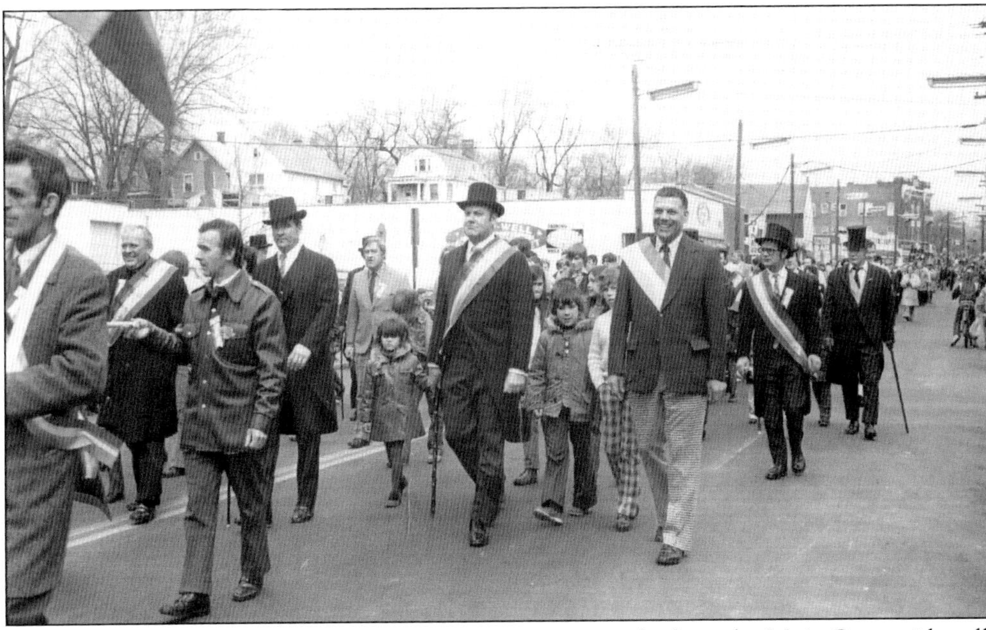

Beginning in 1951, two Irish American organizations marched on the Main Street sidewalk before boarding buses to attend an annual St. Patrick's Day parade in Newark. By 1974, crowds increased, making it necessary to march down Main Street. Seen here in 1975, the march became an official parade in West Orange the following year and is still held annually. Sam Spina (in the checkered pants) would go on to serve as town mayor from 1978 to 1998.

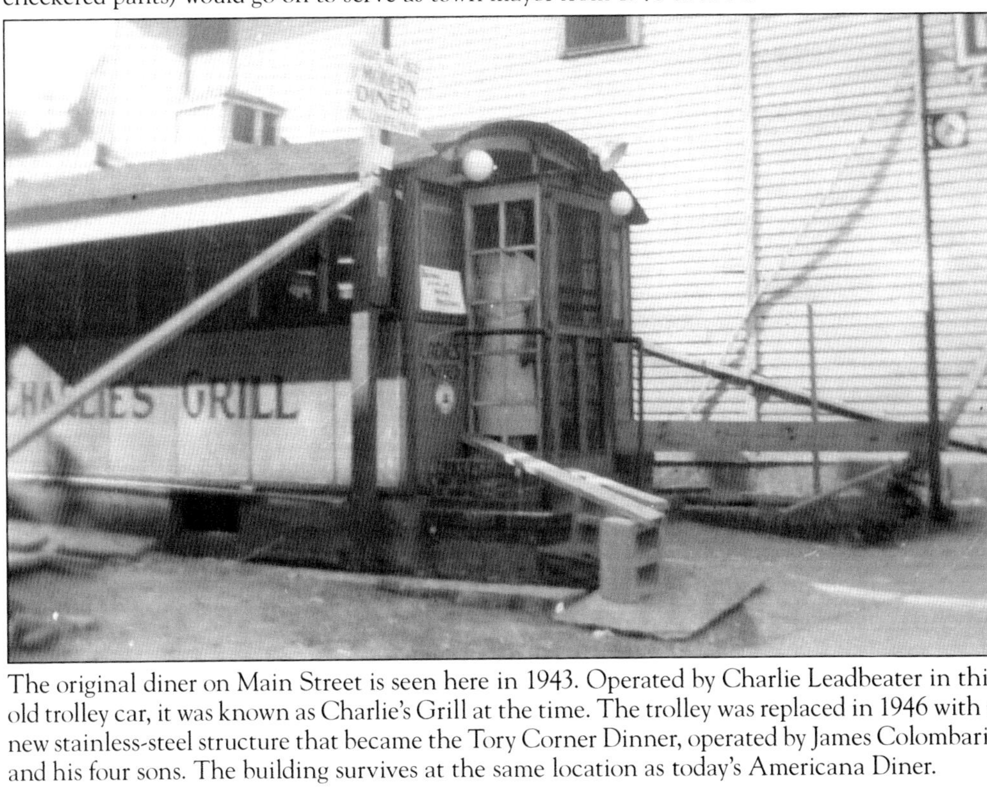

The original diner on Main Street is seen here in 1943. Operated by Charlie Leadbeater in this old trolley car, it was known as Charlie's Grill at the time. The trolley was replaced in 1946 with a new stainless-steel structure that became the Tory Corner Dinner, operated by James Colombaris and his four sons. The building survives at the same location as today's Americana Diner.

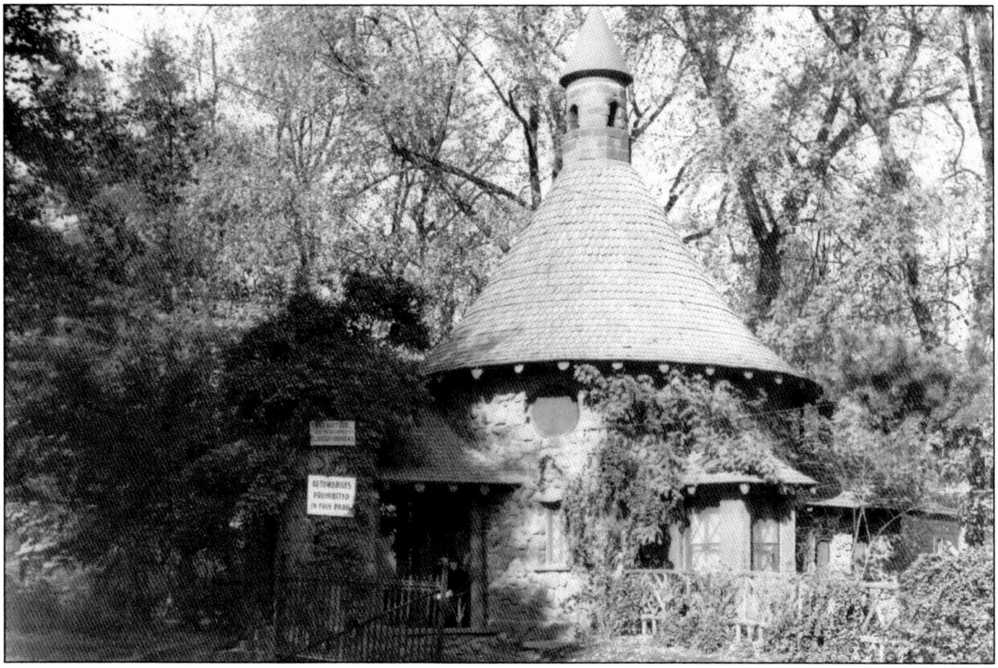

The gatehouse at the Main Street entrance to Llewellyn Park was built around 1857 and still looks the same today. This photograph displaying a sign prohibiting automobiles in the park is likely prior to 1899. It was in September of that year when Llewellyn Park resident Arthur Moulton was reported to own the first automobile in West Orange, which would have apparently conflicted with park regulations.

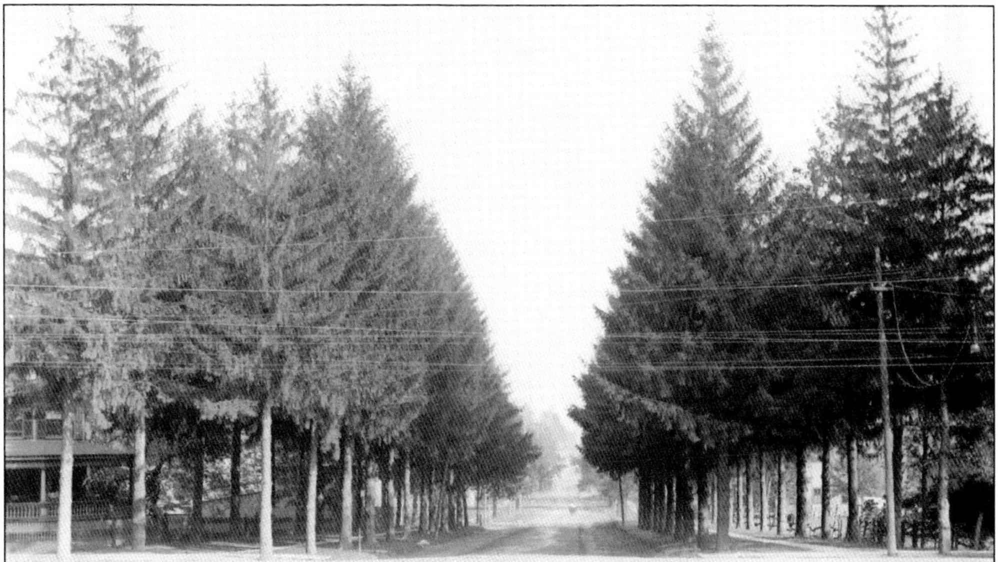

This c. 1896 view looks down Park Avenue opposite the Llewellyn Park entrance on Main Street. Essex County officials had intended Park Avenue to become a parkway connecting all county parks. The proposed route passed directly through picturesque Llewellyn Park to the Eagle Rock Reservation owned by the county. Acquiring the necessary land and gaining public support proved to be an insurmountable obstacle, and the parkway idea was abandoned.

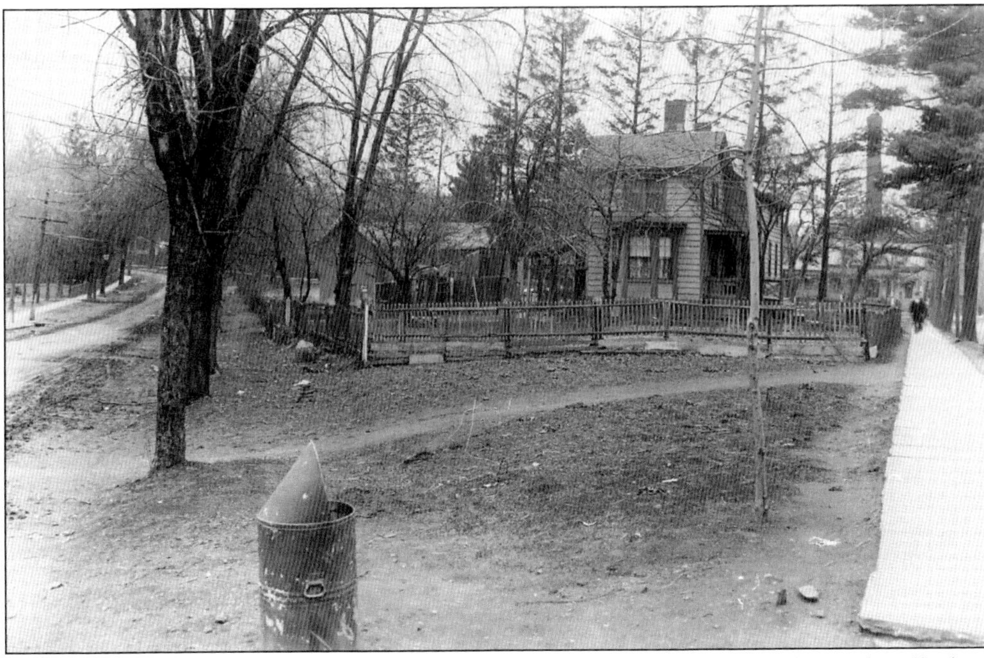

The Hardenburg house is seen in 1913 with Fairmount Avenue to the left and the sidewalk along Main Street to the right. Following World War I, the home was razed to make way for Memorial Park, with a bronze tablet honoring West Orange boys killed during the war. Today, West Orange Town Hall, the police and justice building, and Veterans Memorial Park all sit on the former Hardenburg estate.

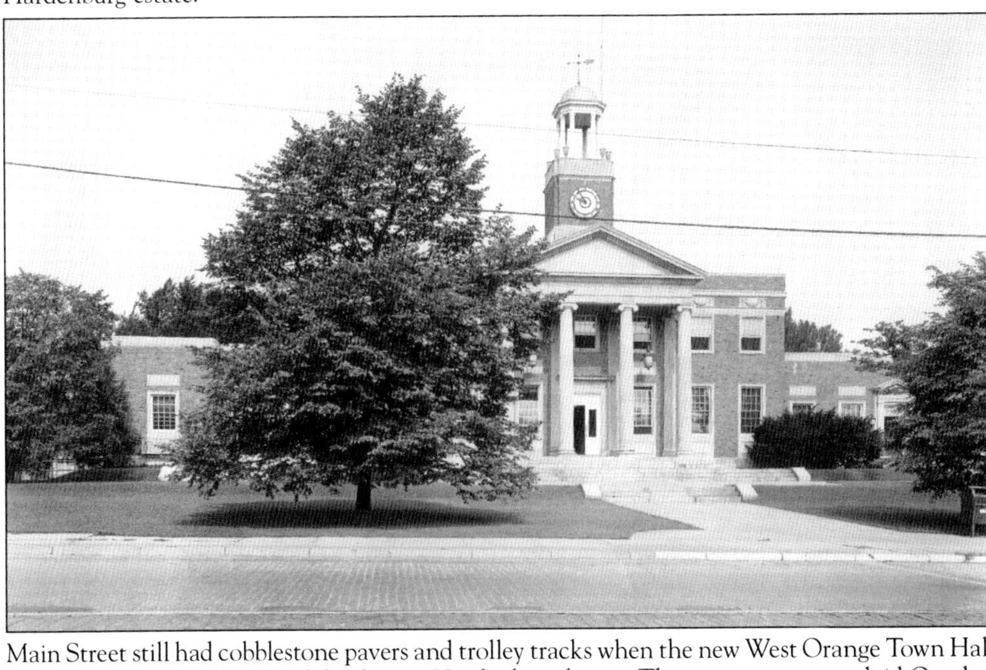

Main Street still had cobblestone pavers and trolley tracks when the new West Orange Town Hall opened in 1937 on the site of the former Hardenburg home. The cornerstone was laid October 31, 1936, and additions have since been made to the second floor. The building is still entirely recognizable today and has been in continuous service since it opened on March 11, 1937.

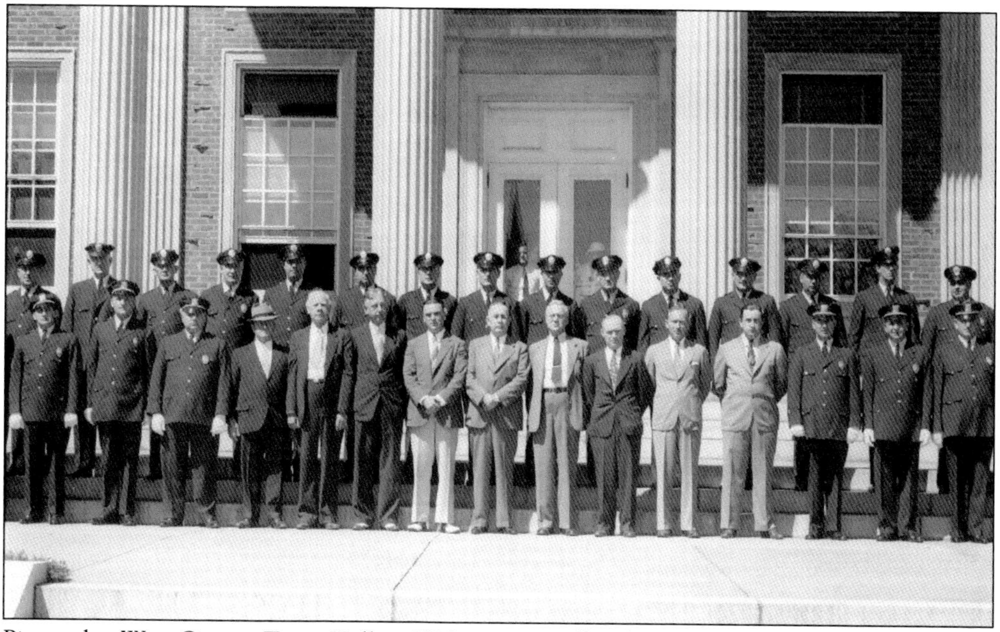

Pictured at West Orange Town Hall in 1938 are town officials and members of the West Orange Police Department. The fourth man from the left in the first row is Bernard Heslin. He was the town's first bicycle patrolman, in 1907, and the first motorcycle cop, in 1910. Heslin subsequently became the department's first police detective, in 1914, and retired in 1947 after 41 years of service. He passed away on March 20, 1955.

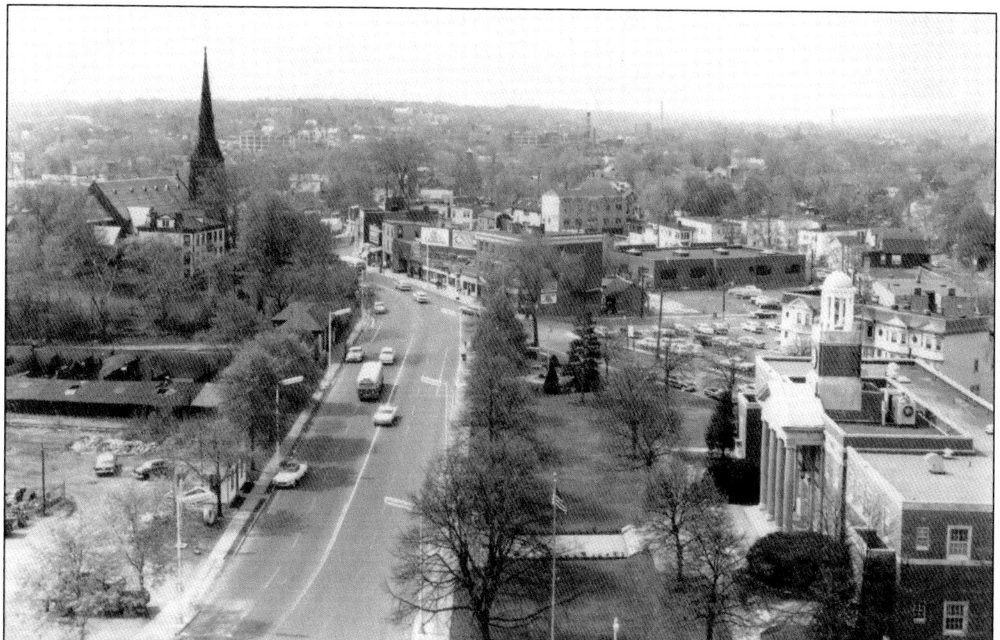

A 1960s aerial view shows the area across from West Orange Town Hall to the left, where the Erie Railroad freight yard once existed. Office buildings constructed in 1966 as part of urban renewal now occupy this site. The row houses, seen behind town hall, were also demolished as part of the same project, and this area is now a parking lot.

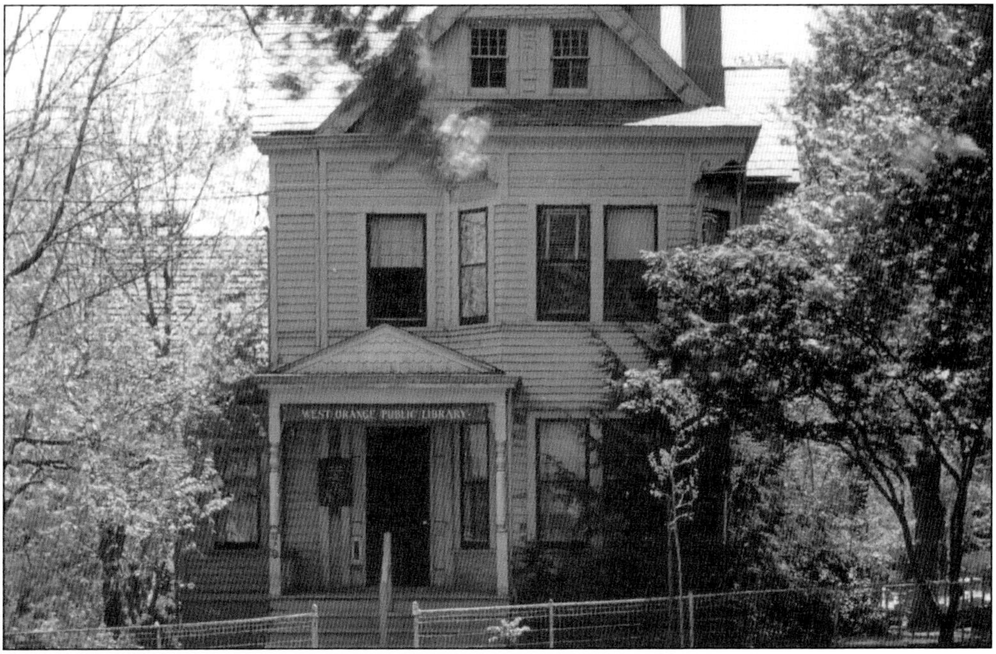

Library facilities for town residents remained in Orange until 1943, when the West Orange Community Council established the West Orange Library Association. The association acquired this house in 1947 on the corner of Mount Pleasant Avenue and Gaston Street for the town's first library independent from Orange. The West Orange Public Library was established in 1950 and housed here until 1959, when a new building was constructed.

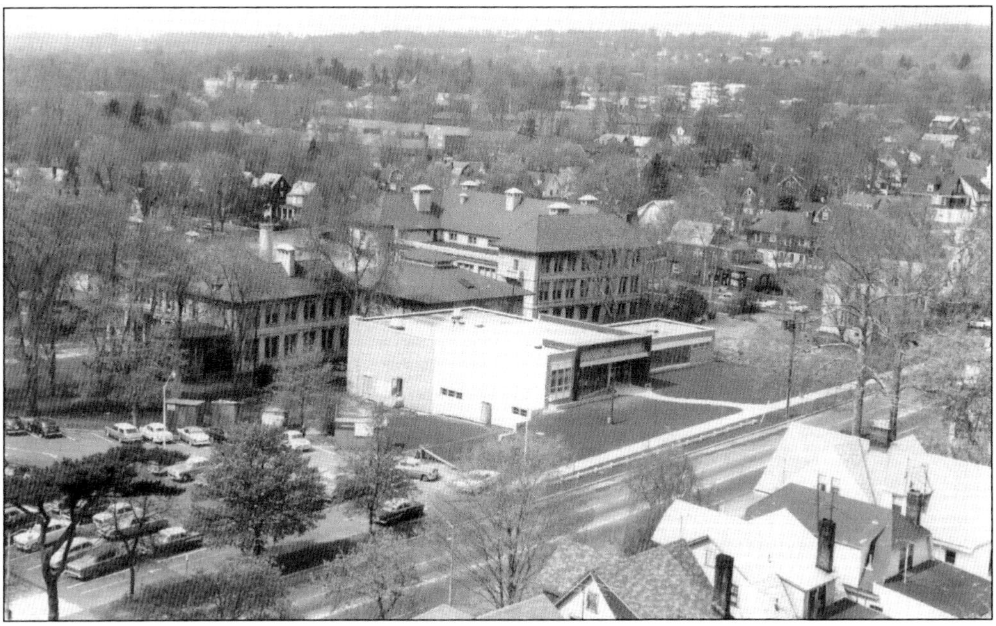

The newly constructed West Orange Public Library Building on Mount Pleasant Avenue is seen in the center of the photograph around the time it opened in 1960. A glimpse of the former library on the corner of Gaston Street is visible behind the trees. It was torn down shortly after the new library opened to make room for a parking lot.

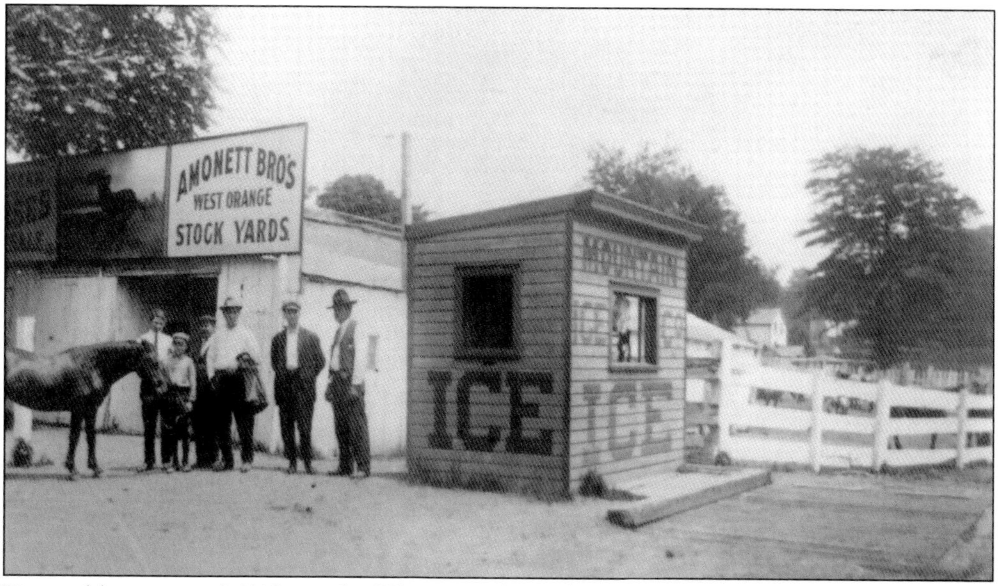

Pictured here around 1910 are the Western-style stockyards once on Main Street across from current-day town hall site; they were operated by the Amonett Brothers from the 1880s to about the mid-1910s. The stockyards employed real cowboys to handle horses, and in later years the cowboy was adopted by West Orange High School as its mascot. The man with the cowboy hat is likely Joe Amonett.

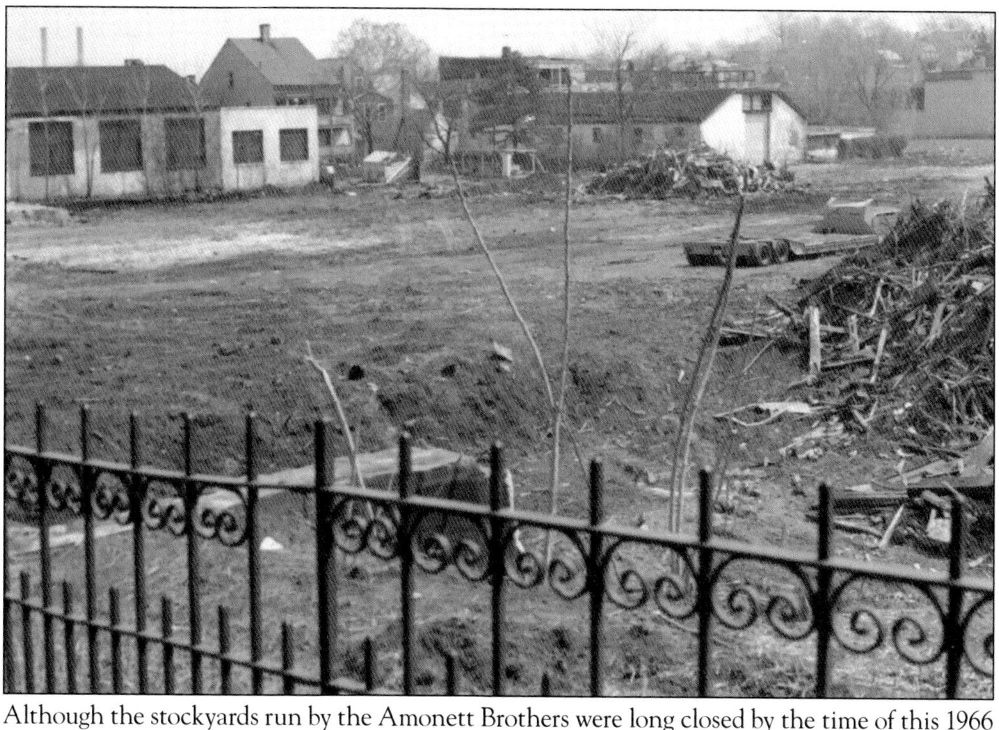
Although the stockyards run by the Amonett Brothers were long closed by the time of this 1966 picture, a pile of rubble is seen occupying their former site. The Erie Railroad freight yard, also located here, provided shipments of horses, which arrived from out west and were offered for sale to the residents of West Orange and surrounding towns.

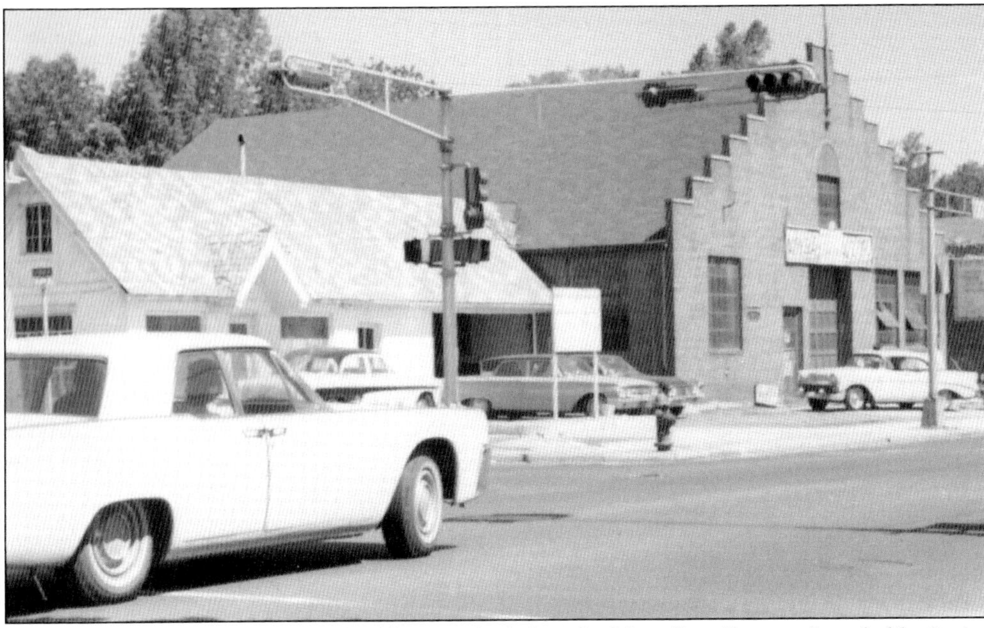

Pictured in the 1960s, the white building to the left is the Llewellyn Garage, founded by Irving Loveless. It was a filling station and automotive repair shop located on the corner of Main Street and Mount Pleasant Avenue. Loveless worked for Thomas Edison from 1896 until 1926, and went into the service station business at two previous West Orange locations before this small building was constructed about 1931.

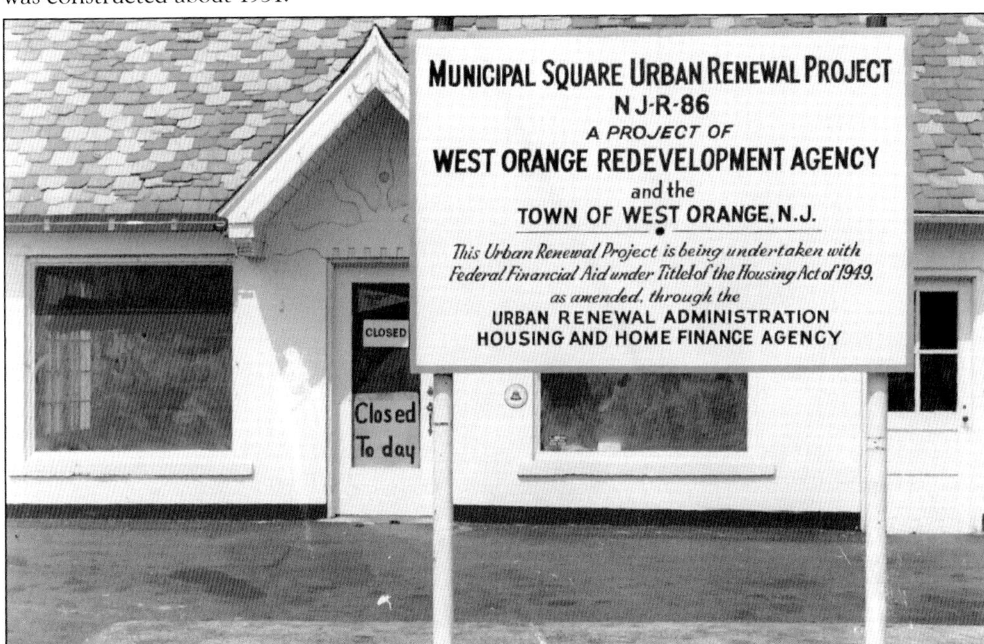

The sign on the door reads "Closed Today," but the Llewellyn Garage was actually closed forever. Seen here in 1966, it was soon to be demolished as part of urban renewal in downtown West Orange. This was the last gas station in New Jersey that carried more than one brand of gasoline at the same time—until 1952, when it started selling only the Amoco brand.

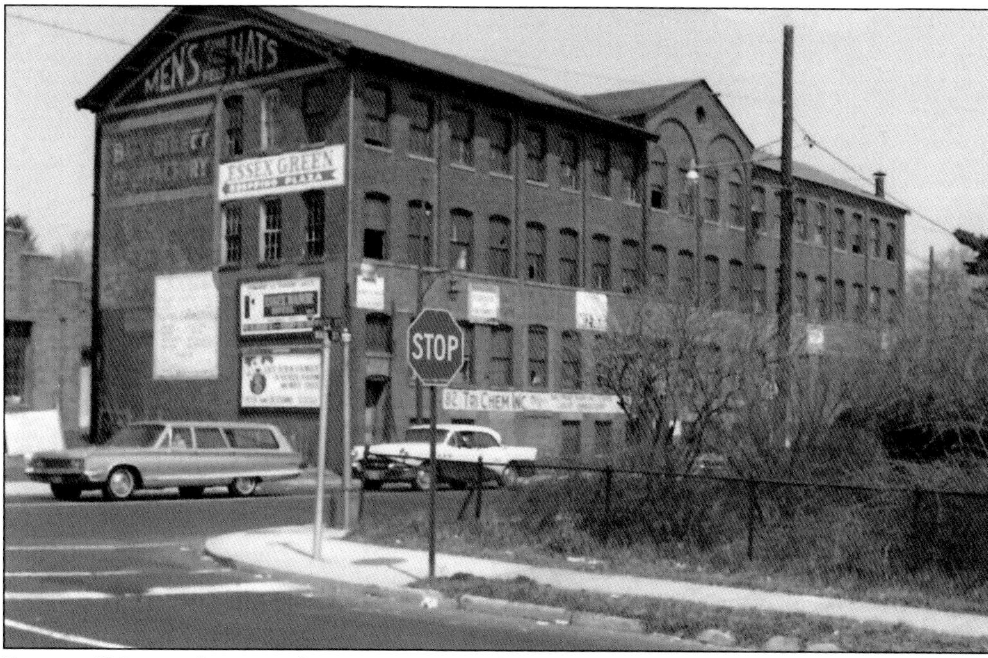

For over 100 years, hat manufacturing was one of the principle industries of the Oranges. It began about 1790, and within decades, hat factories dotted the landscape in and around the Orange Valley, including two in West Orange. This one on Main Street, near the corner of Mount Pleasant Avenue, was built in the late 1880s and was originally known as the C.B. Rutan Company.

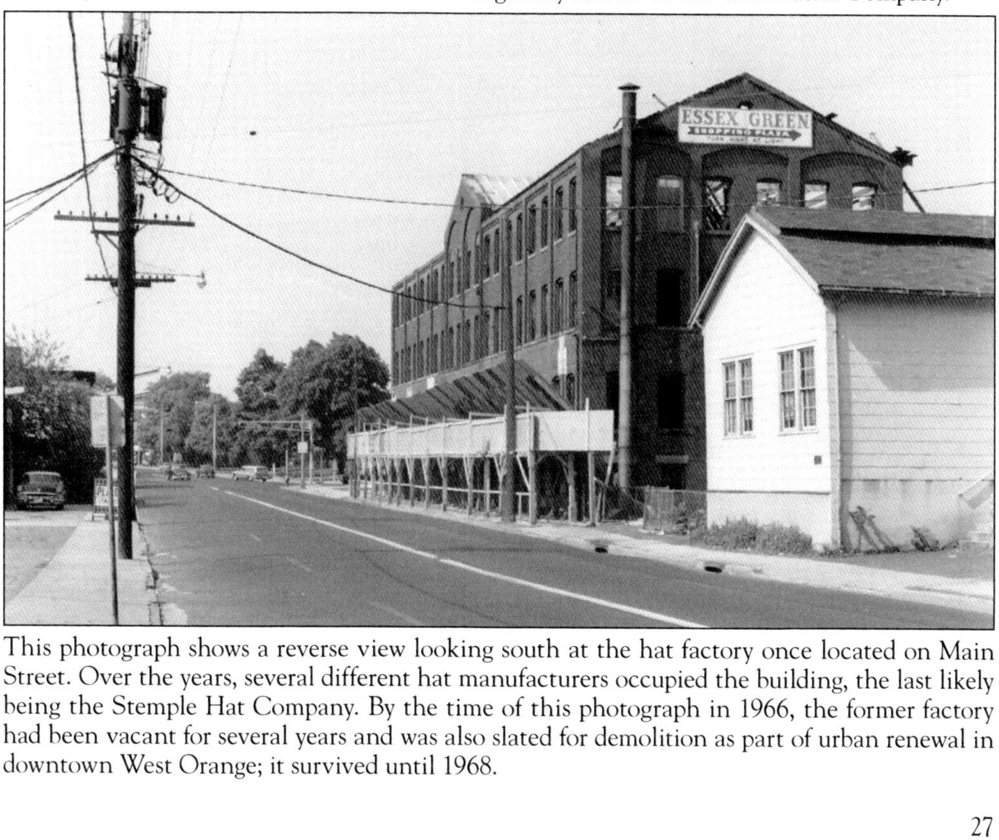

This photograph shows a reverse view looking south at the hat factory once located on Main Street. Over the years, several different hat manufacturers occupied the building, the last likely being the Stemple Hat Company. By the time of this photograph in 1966, the former factory had been vacant for several years and was also slated for demolition as part of urban renewal in downtown West Orange; it survived until 1968.

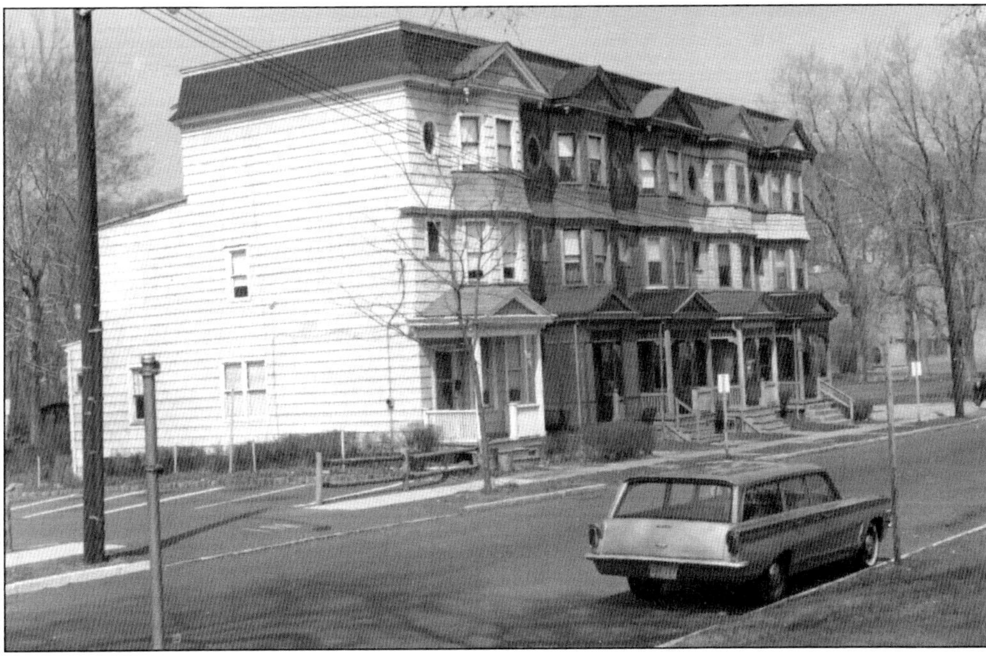

These row houses, pictured here in the 1960s, were located off Mount Pleasant Avenue on Fairmount Avenue, which once ran behind current-day town hall. They were constructed sometime between 1890 and 1904 when they first appeared on maps. A parking lot behind town hall now occupies this site.

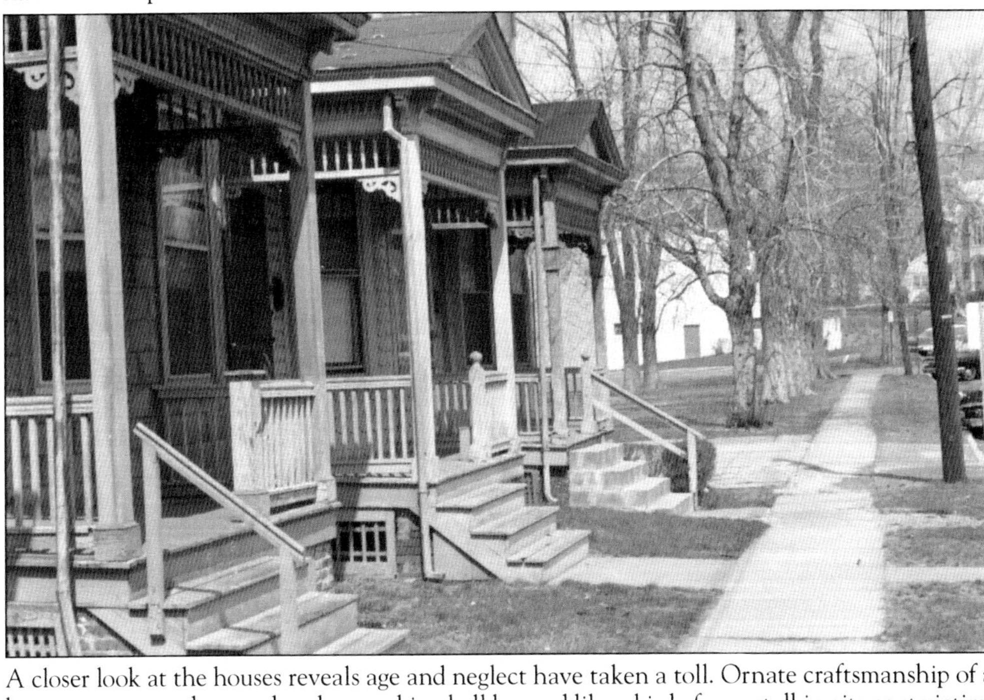

A closer look at the houses reveals age and neglect have taken a toll. Ornate craftsmanship of a bygone era was endangered as the wrecking ball loomed like a bird of prey stalking its next victim. No one seemed to notice or care as these structures vanished from the landscape in June 1966. The rear of the West Orange Public Library can be seen in the distance.

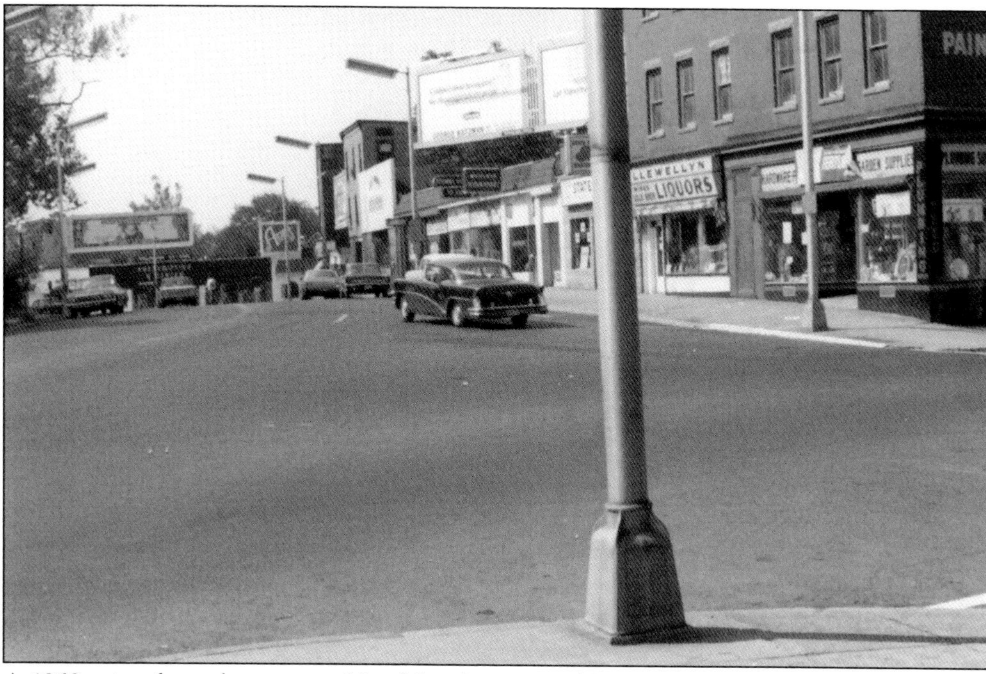

A 1960s view from the corner of Lindsley Avenue and Main Street would be nearly identical today, with only the names of some of the businesses changed. Llewellyn Liquors, seen in the corner building on the right, is still there. In 1978, writing dating to the 1890s was discovered on a rear stairwell; it was done by prisoners when this building, known as Hedges Block, housed the town's first jail.

Here, the back of the building seen in the previous image is shown in a view that looks along Lindsley Avenue toward Main Street. The original building that sat here was constructed in 1873 and was operated as a grain and flour business; it was destroyed in a 1892 fire. This structure was built shortly after the fire; it is still there today and since the 1930s has been home to a hardware store with several owners.

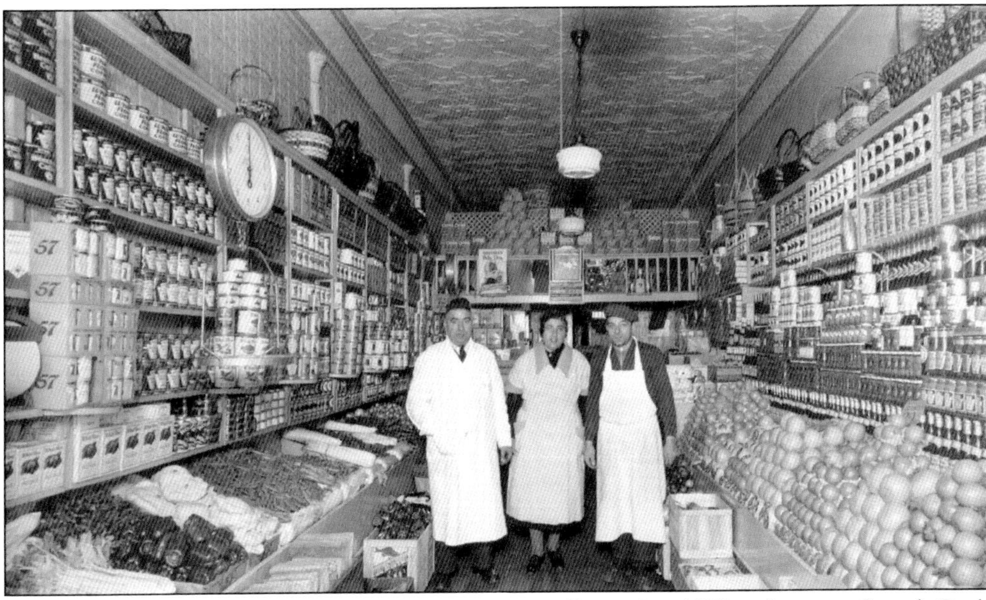

The interior of the Popular Fruit Company is seen in December 1937 with owner Joseph Scala on the left. Although located in nearby Orange, it was typical of the countless mom-and-pop businesses that once lined Main Street throughout all the Oranges. In the days before national chain stores and supermarkets, most neighborhoods relied on a small grocery store in walking distance, such as this.

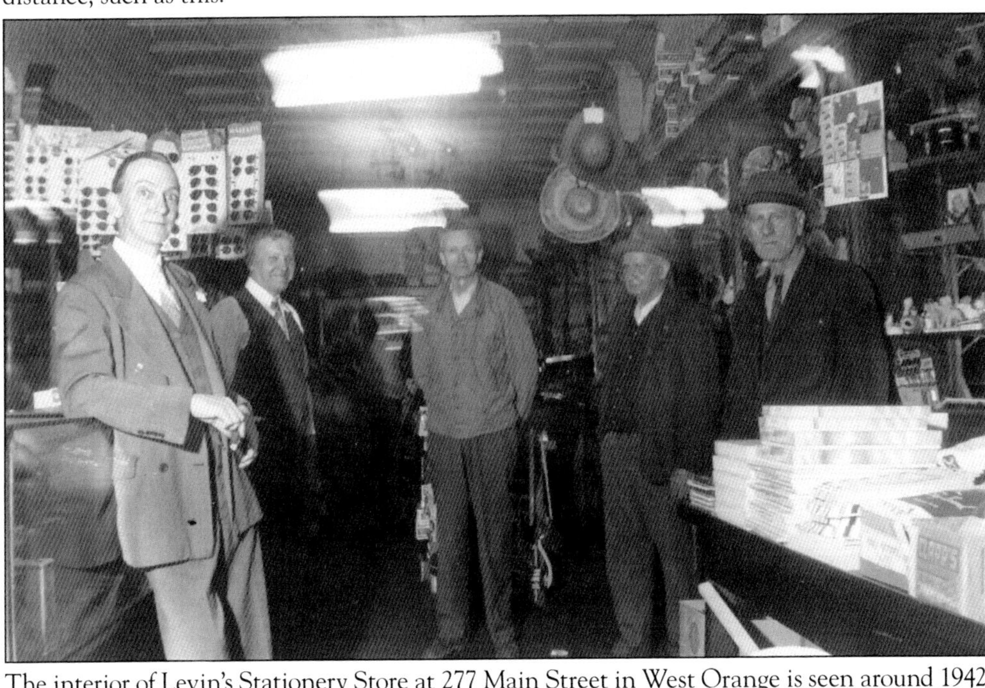

The interior of Levin's Stationery Store at 277 Main Street in West Orange is seen around 1942. This location is now home to a restaurant. Many local businesses at this time also served as small unofficial neighborhood social centers. Isadore Levin is second from the left, and Fred Ward, on the extreme left, is a grandfather of David Cassidy, the 1970s pop star who grew up in town during the 1950s.

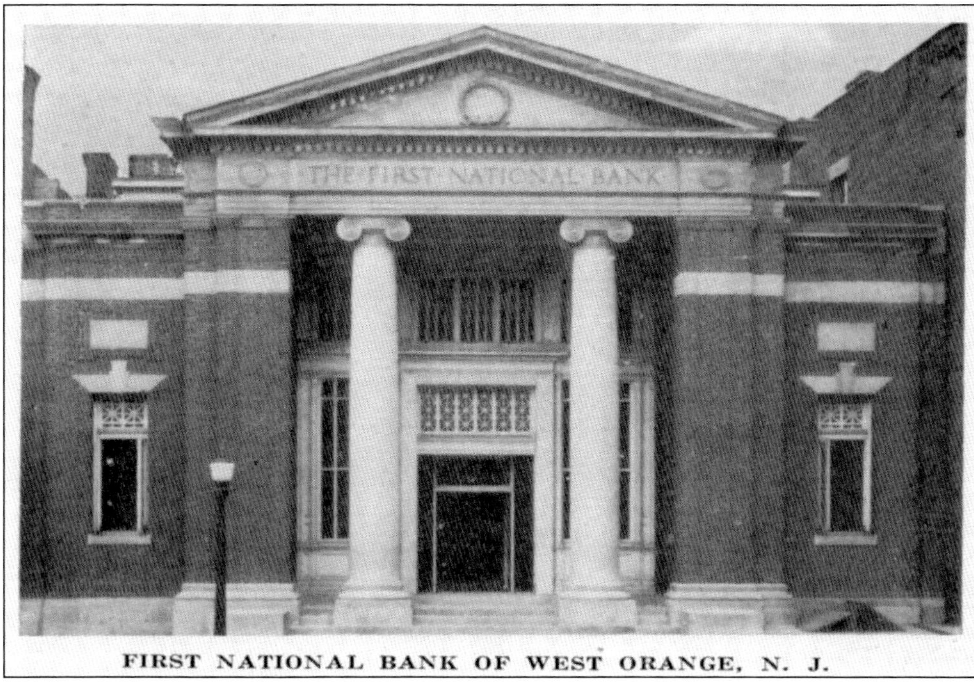

The First National Bank of West Orange became the first bank in town when it opened for business on September 20, 1909, in a rented storefront on Main Street. In 1913, it moved only a short distance into this new building, which still stands at the town center. West Orange resident T.H. Powers Farr was the bank's first president and served in that capacity until his death in 1938.

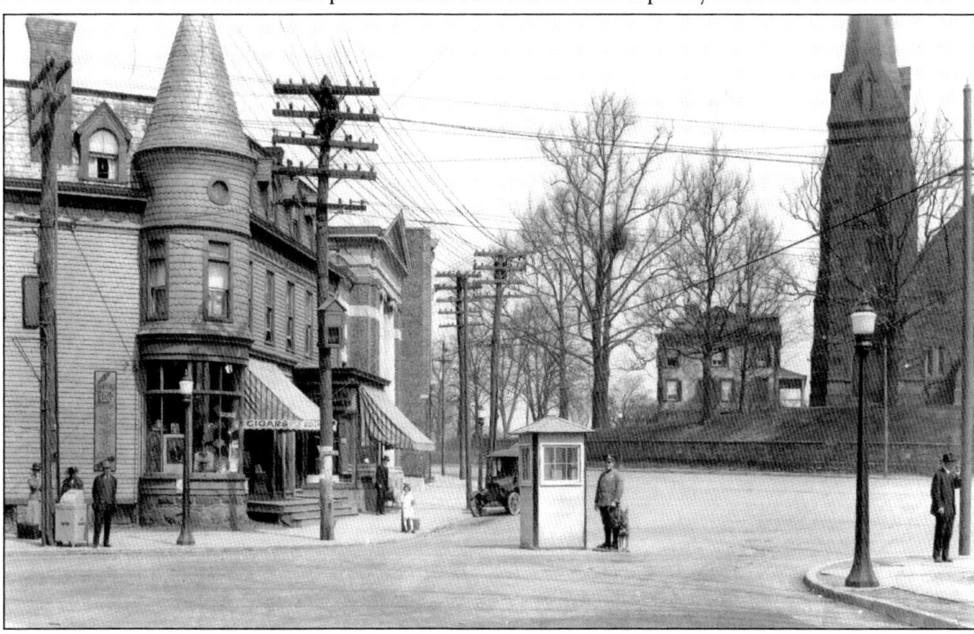

The front of the First National Bank can partially be seen from the side on February 2, 1921. Patrolman Ben Dangler is seen posing in front of his post at the new traffic house put into operation at this time. Its purpose was to help control increased automobile traffic and provide protection for the officer at this busy intersection of Main Street and Northfield Avenue.

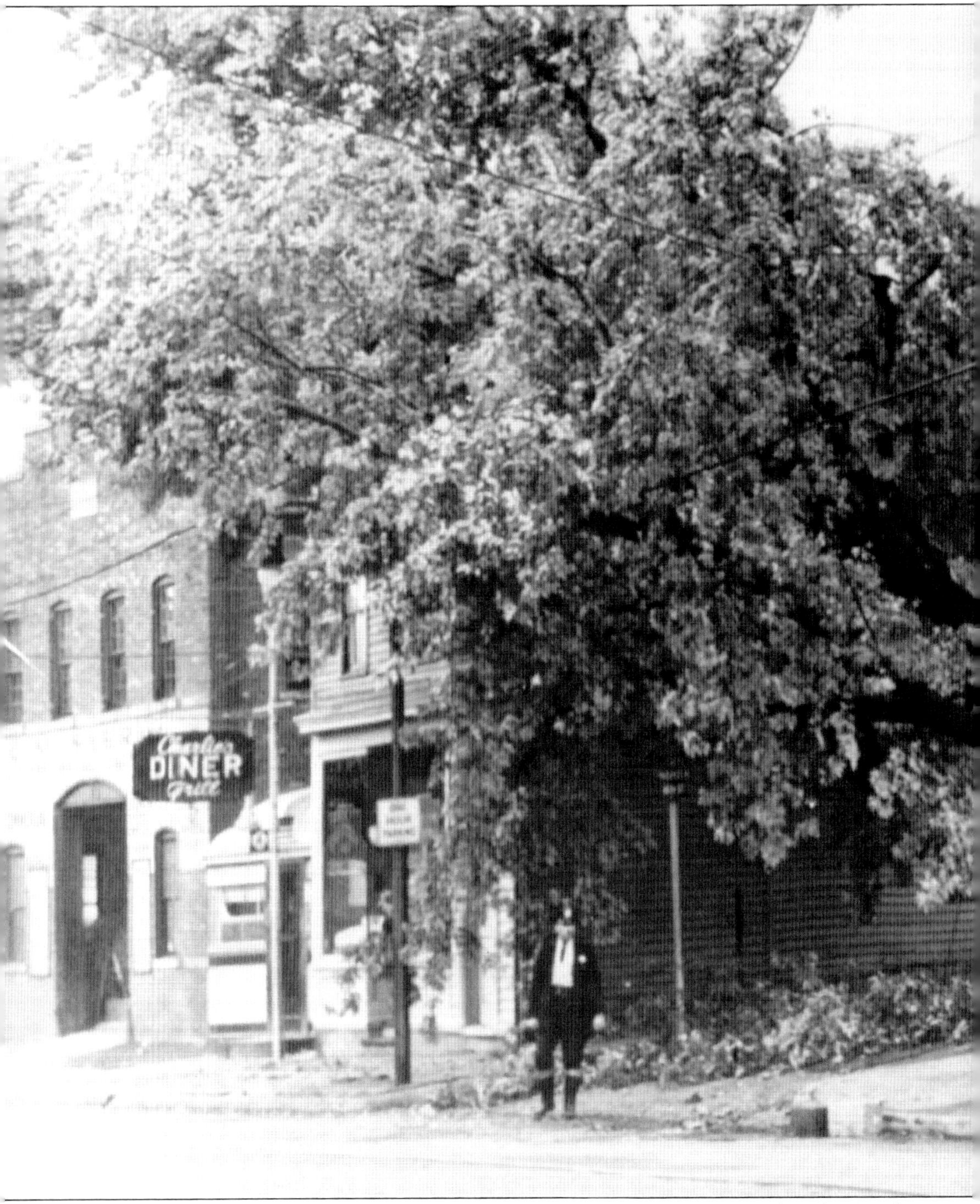

This view of Main Street from the late 1930s blends the past with the present. Schneider's Hardware on the right was founded in 1923 by Isadore and Beckie Schneider just a few doors down from this location. It moved here in 1936 and is West Orange's oldest business, now operated by Roger and Gerald Schneider, third-generation owners, in this same building. Both the Tory Corner Tavern and the house with the tree on its roof are still standing and entirely recognizable today but are

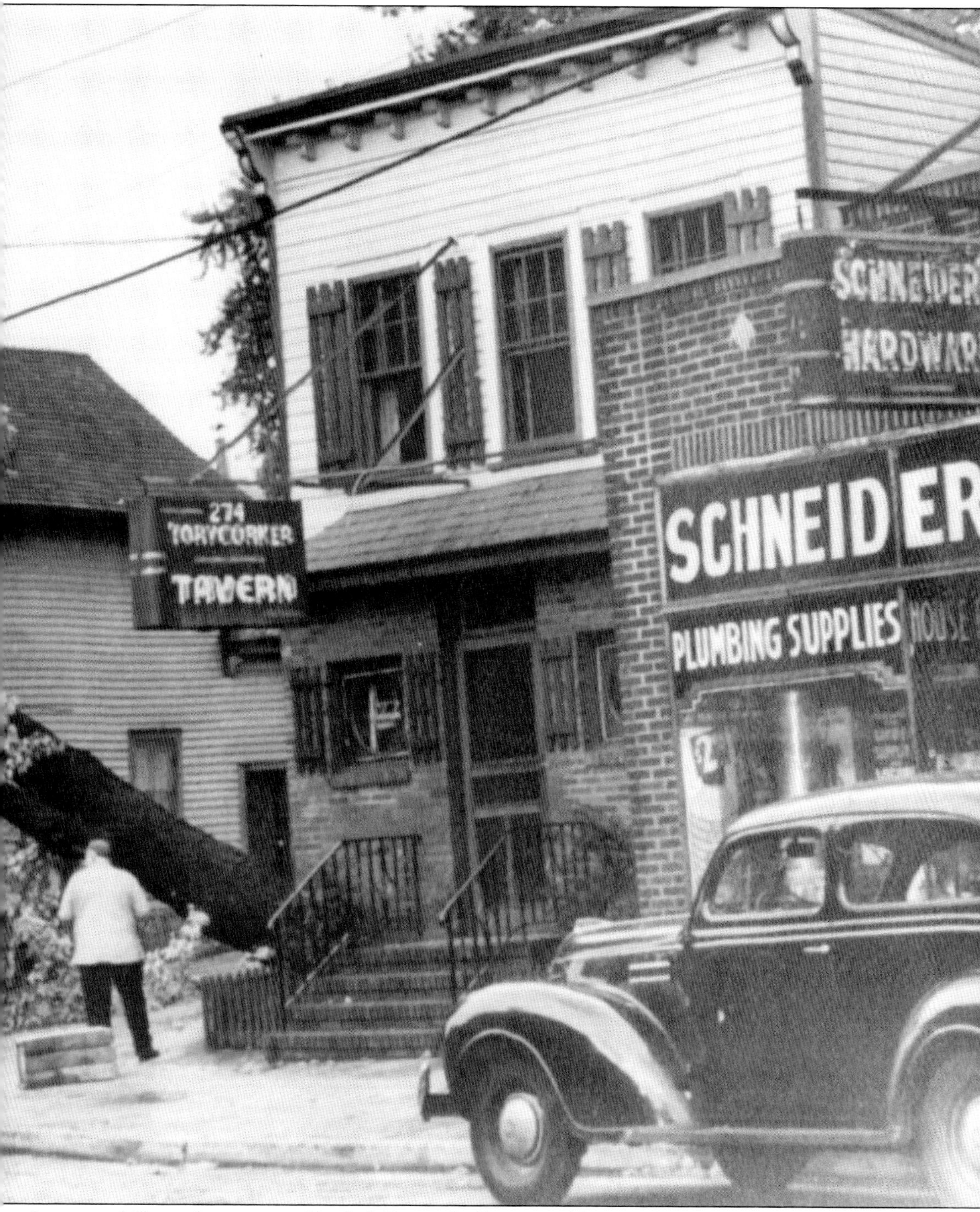

home to different businesses. Charlie's Diner Grill operated by Charlie Leadbeater was a small diner housed in a converted trolley car. In 1946, Leadbeater replaced it with a new stainless-steel diner, which is today's Americana Diner. Musler's blacksmith shop to the extreme left was torn down in 1959 to make room for the diner parking lot.

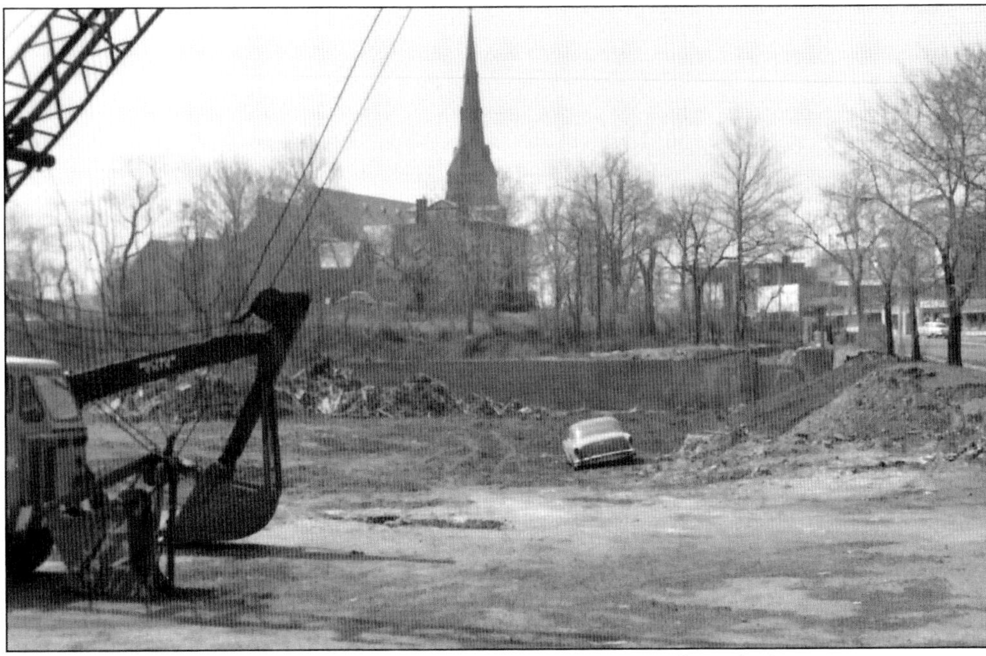

A symbolic clash of the titans is seen as the wrecking crane casts a long shadow over its conquered terrain near town hall in 1966. The century-old St. Mark's Church steeple was not threatened by urban renewal but looms tall as if standing in silent defiance. It towers over the scattered rubble as if paying homage to a departed friend, before a new office building was erected that still occupies this site.

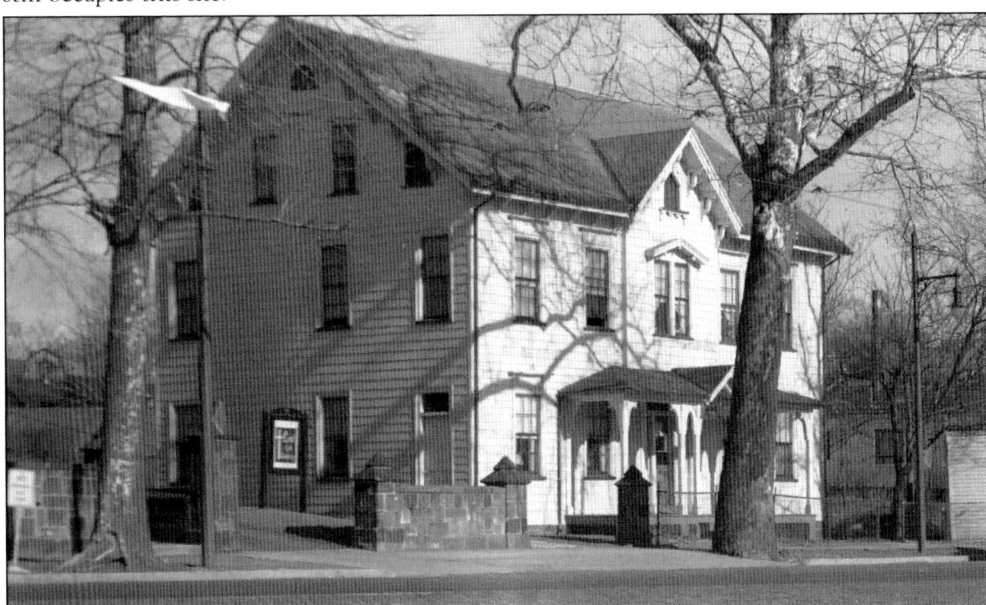

The Condit House on Main Street opposite Northfield Avenue is seen here on February 27, 1951, and was considered the last Federal-style building in Essex County. It was built in 1812 and stood here for 177 years until it was torn down on September 14, 1989. It joined those dwellings that vanished 20 years earlier during urban renewal.

Two

EXPLORE AROUND TOWN

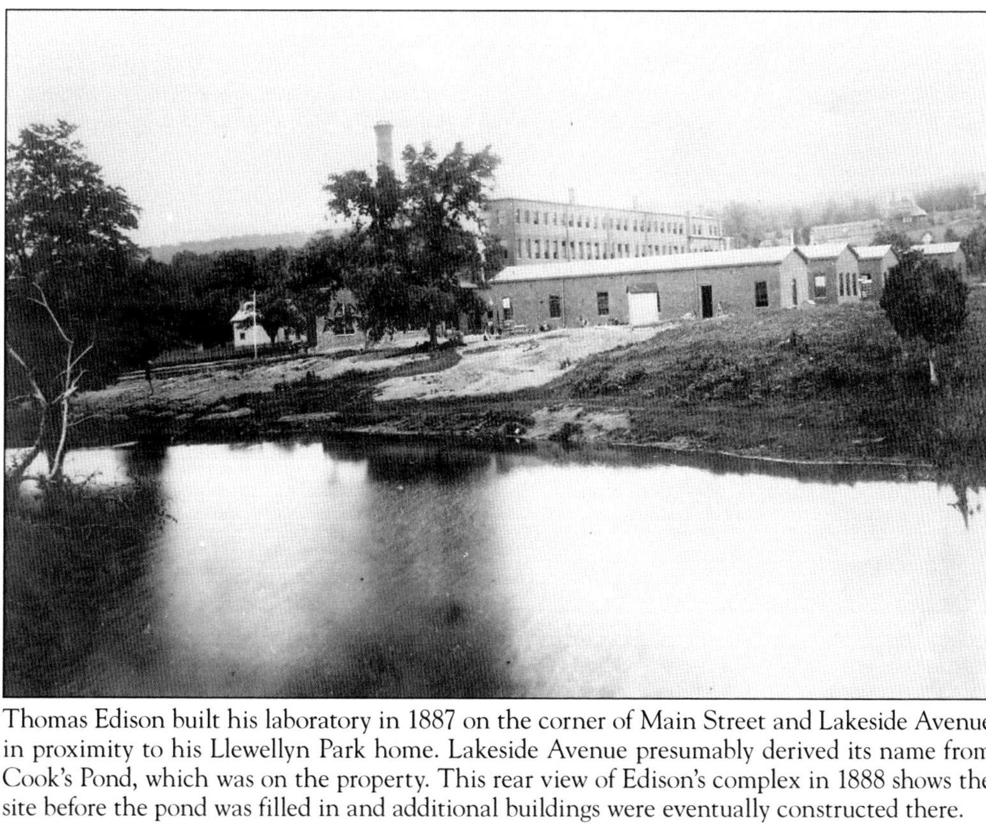

Thomas Edison built his laboratory in 1887 on the corner of Main Street and Lakeside Avenue in proximity to his Llewellyn Park home. Lakeside Avenue presumably derived its name from Cook's Pond, which was on the property. This rear view of Edison's complex in 1888 shows the site before the pond was filled in and additional buildings were eventually constructed there.

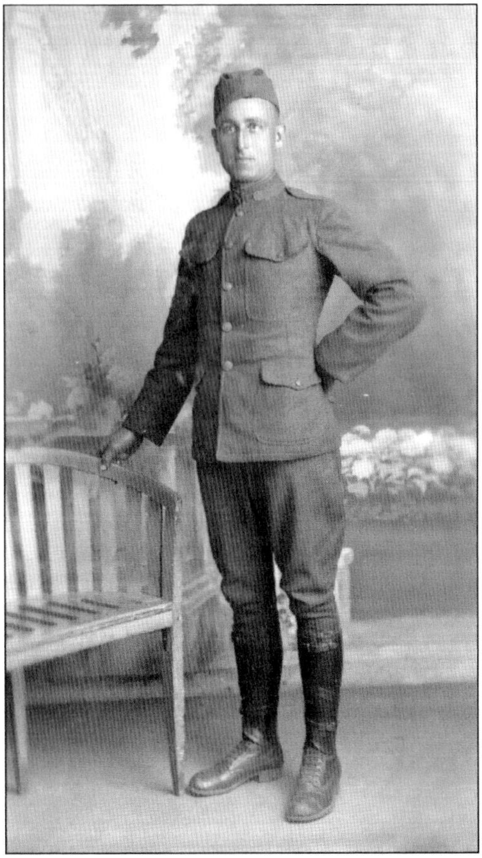

Seen here is John Egan, who lived at 41 South Valley Road. In 1918, he was one of 151 young men from West Orange who left to fight in World War I. During the war, 28 of these men were killed in action, and 17 of them have West Orange streets named in their honor. Egan survived the war and moved to Montclair in 1923.

Pictured here in 1921 in front of the Washington Street School is the original group of West Orange World War I veterans who founded Veterans of Foreign Wars Post 376. The Glennon-Sayers Post, as it is known, was named after John Glennon and James Sayers from West Orange. They were childhood friends who enlisted together and were both killed in action, almost simultaneously, on October 12, 1918.

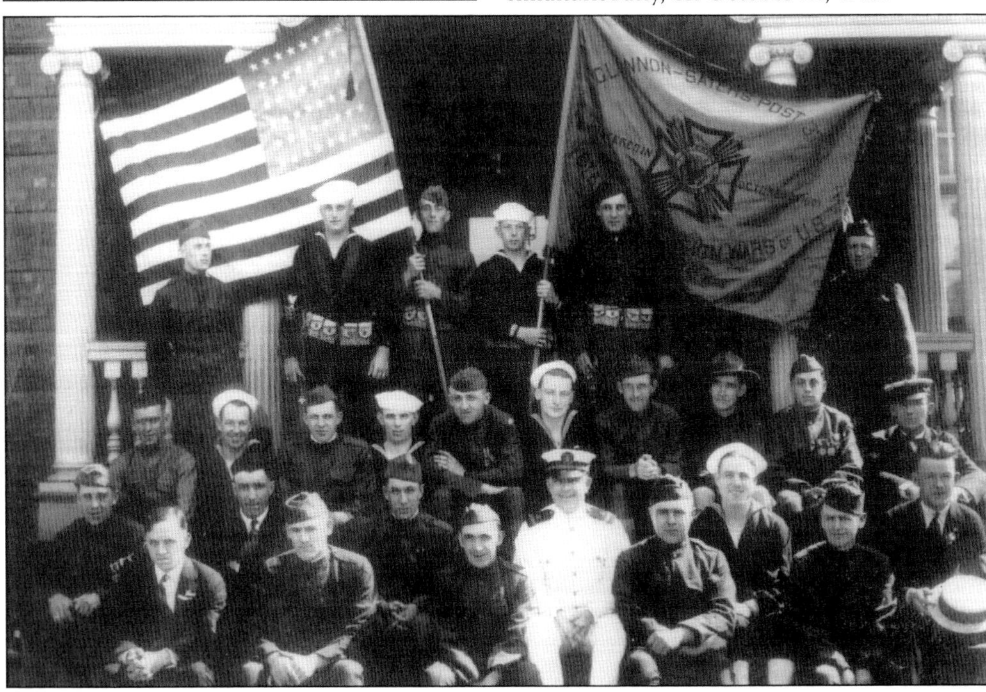

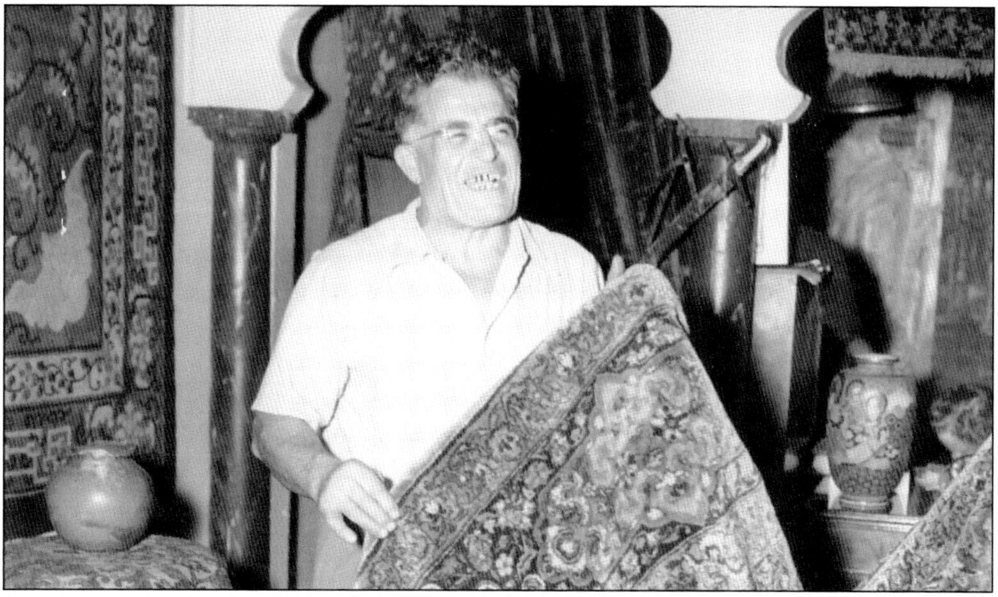

Seen here in 1946 at his Oriental rug store in Montclair is C. Melkon Arslanian. He so loved the outdoors that he lived in a tree house with a telephone 65 feet above the ground on Prospect Avenue near Crystal Lake in West Orange. He moved there in 1930 and stayed for 16 years and was know as Tarzan by local residents for his unusual lifestyle.

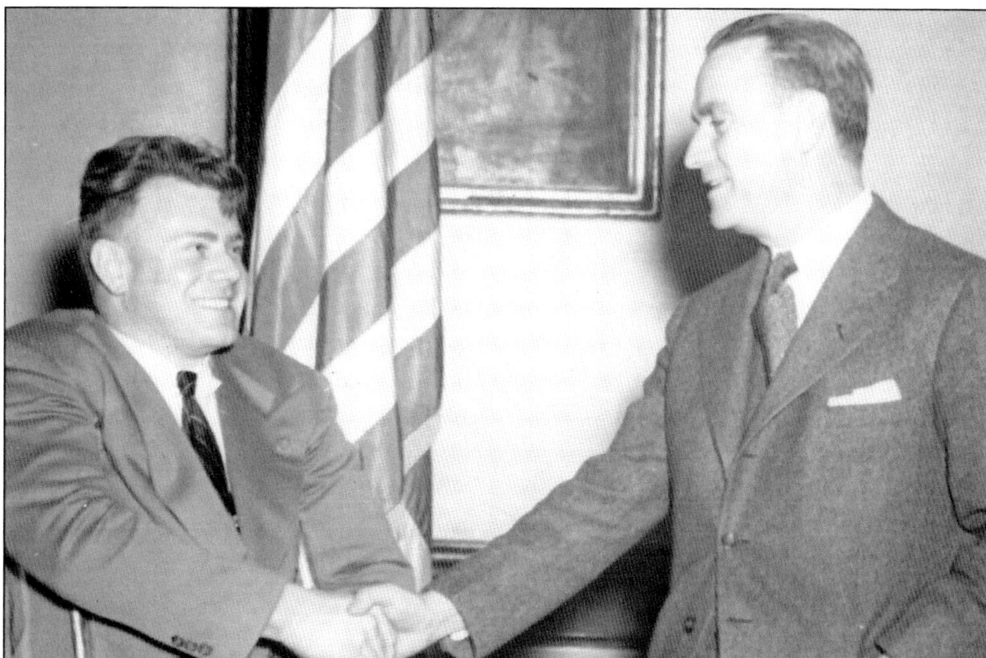

West Orange mayor Bernard Degnan (right) is seen greeting Stanley Ditzel at West Orange Town Hall around 1938. Ditzel would be appointed the town's first official historian on November 24, 1970. He started writing newspaper articles about West Orange history in 1945 and continued throughout his life. He grew up in town, worked the switchboard at town hall for 38 years, and passed away on December 31, 1977.

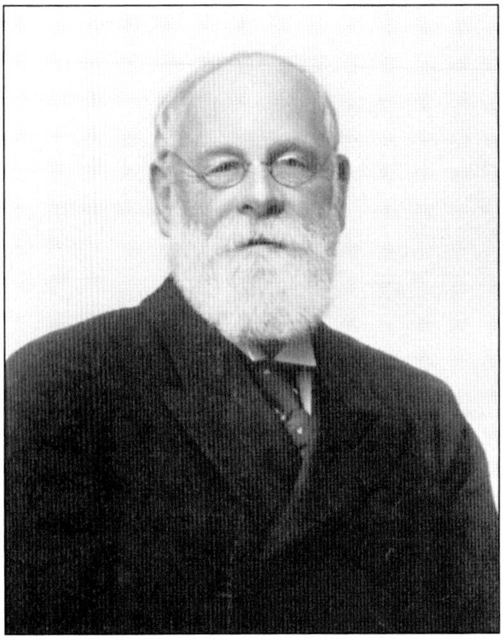

Seen here around 1890 is John Crosby Brown, one of West Orange's most generous and prominent residents and a New York banker. Brown Brothers Harriman & Co. was founded by his grandfather and still survives today. He acquired a 40-acre wooded tract along the ridge near Prospect Avenue in West Orange in the mid-1870s where he built this home named Brighthurst as part of a sprawling estate. Brighthurst is pictured in 1900. It was here that John Crosby Brown passed away on June 24, 1909. In 1925, a fire destroyed several buildings on the estate grounds, but Brighthurst was spared. In 1928, the property was sold and Brighthurst was torn down. Brown's carriage house became the West Orange Women's Club in 1950 and is today the Shillelagh Club; it is the only surviving building from the Brighthurst grounds.

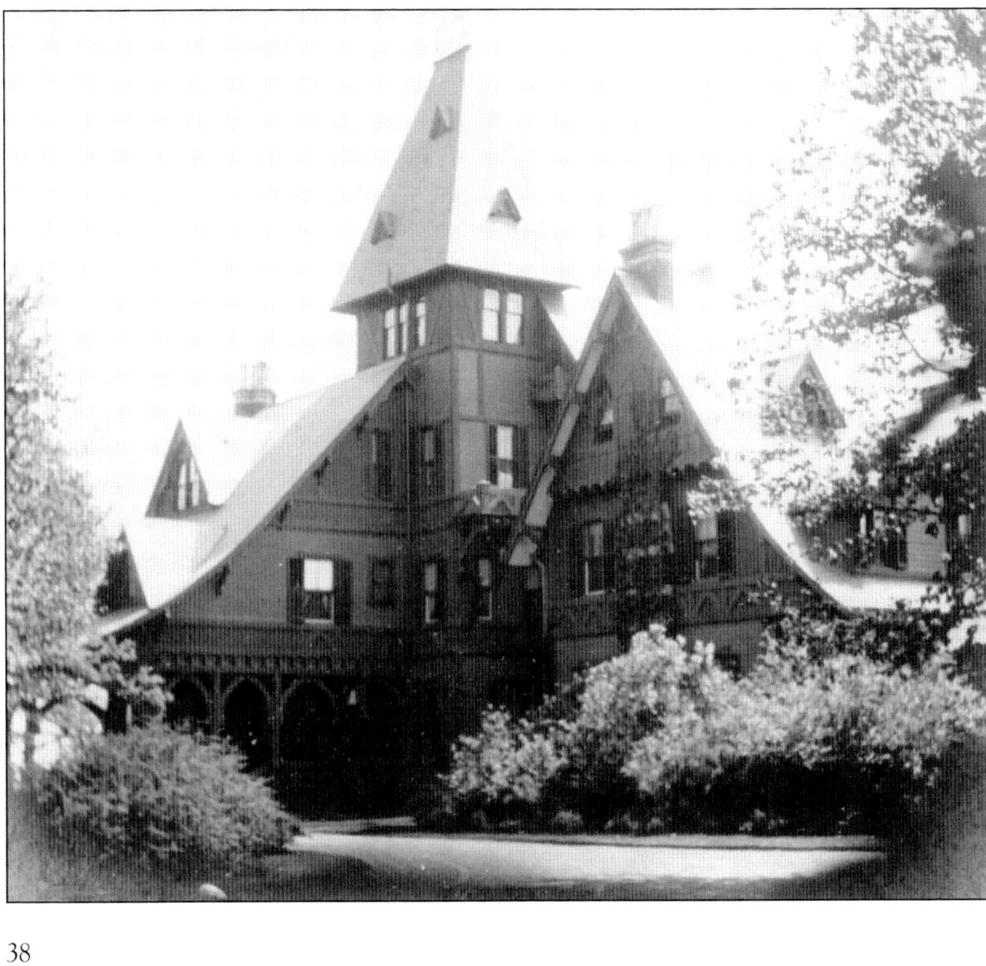

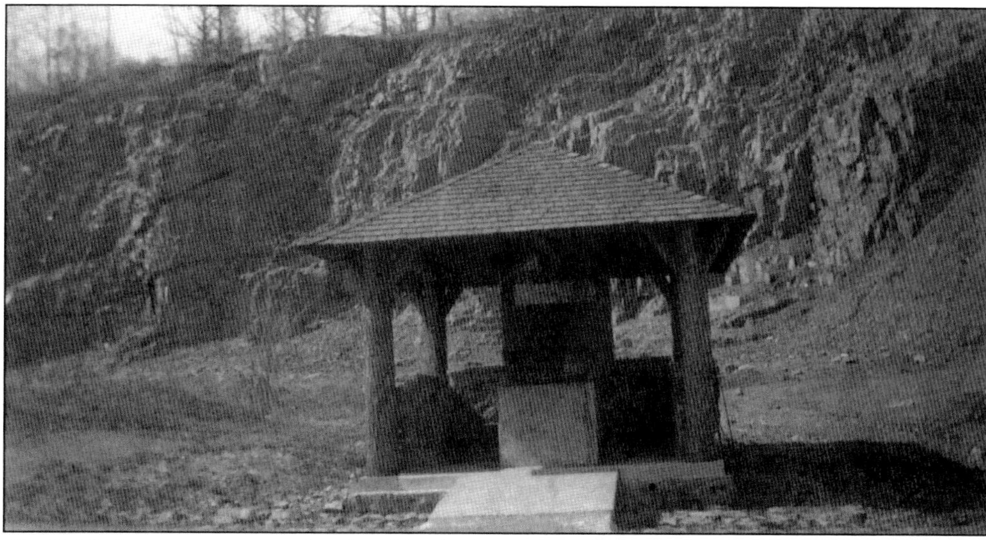

The Brighthurst property was bordered by the Spottiswoode Quarry on Northfield Avenue. In the 1890s, John Crosby Brown purchased the quarry to stop further encroachment on the mountain. In 1900, Brown constructed a springhouse in the former quarry, seen here on March 19, 1903, for weary travelers. The springhouse is gone, but Brown's plaque inviting guests to rest awhile is still there, sandwiched between contemporary homes.

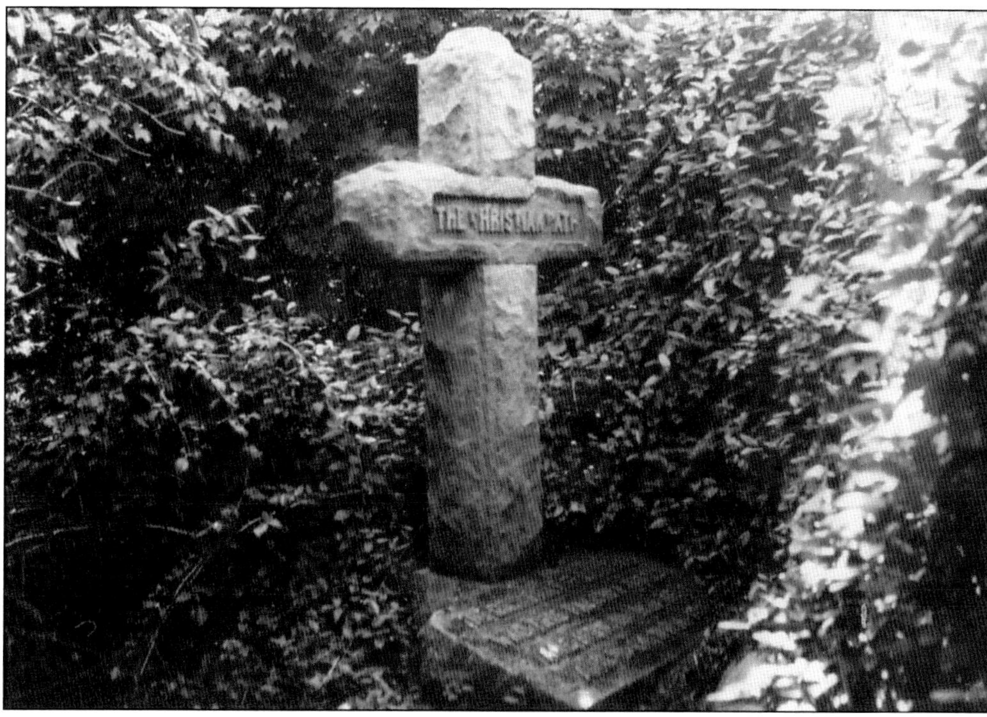

An Indian trail used by early settlers traveling from outlying districts throughout western Essex County to attend worship services in Orange took on the name Christian's Path. When John Crosby Brown realized this path crossed through his property, he constructed the Pilgrim's Cross in 1878 to honor the settlers' memory. The cross seen here in the 1930s still survives today on the grounds of the former St. Cloud Presbyterian Church.

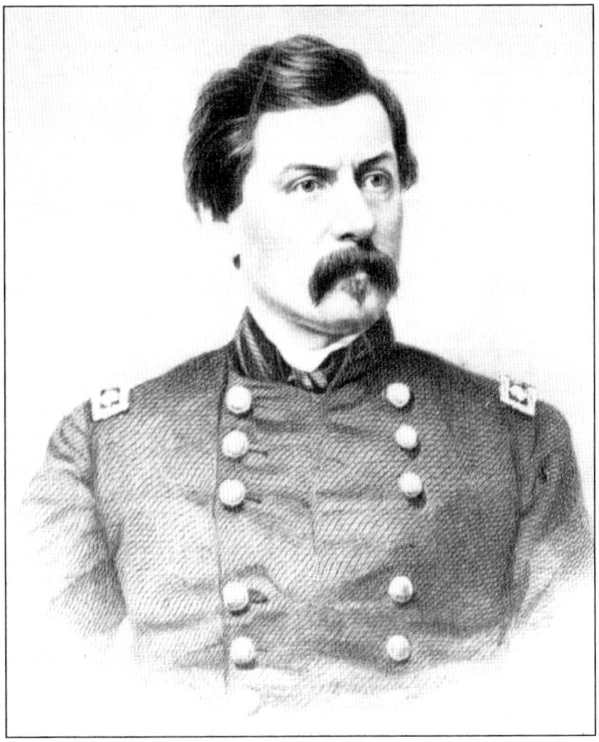

Seen here in an undated Civil War photograph is Gen. George B. McClellan. He had been relieved of his command by President Lincoln following the Battle of Antietam in 1862. McClellan came to West Orange in 1863 to take up residence at the home of his wife's uncle while still on active duty but was never called back to a battlefield command during the war.

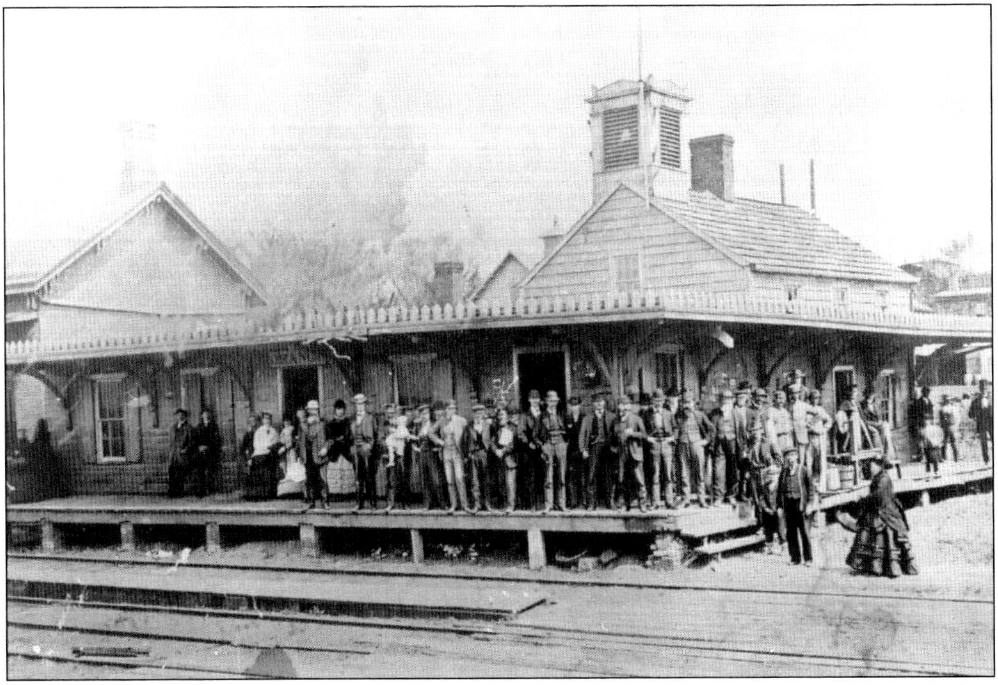

The Orange train station is seen here in the 1870s much as it looked when McClellan arrived on Saturday, June 27, 1863. McClellan emerged onto the platform wearing nothing to disclose his rank among resounding cheers from an estimated crowd of 1,000 well-wishers. A cannon fired a salute as McClellan gave his nod of approval while being driven away in a carriage to West Orange.

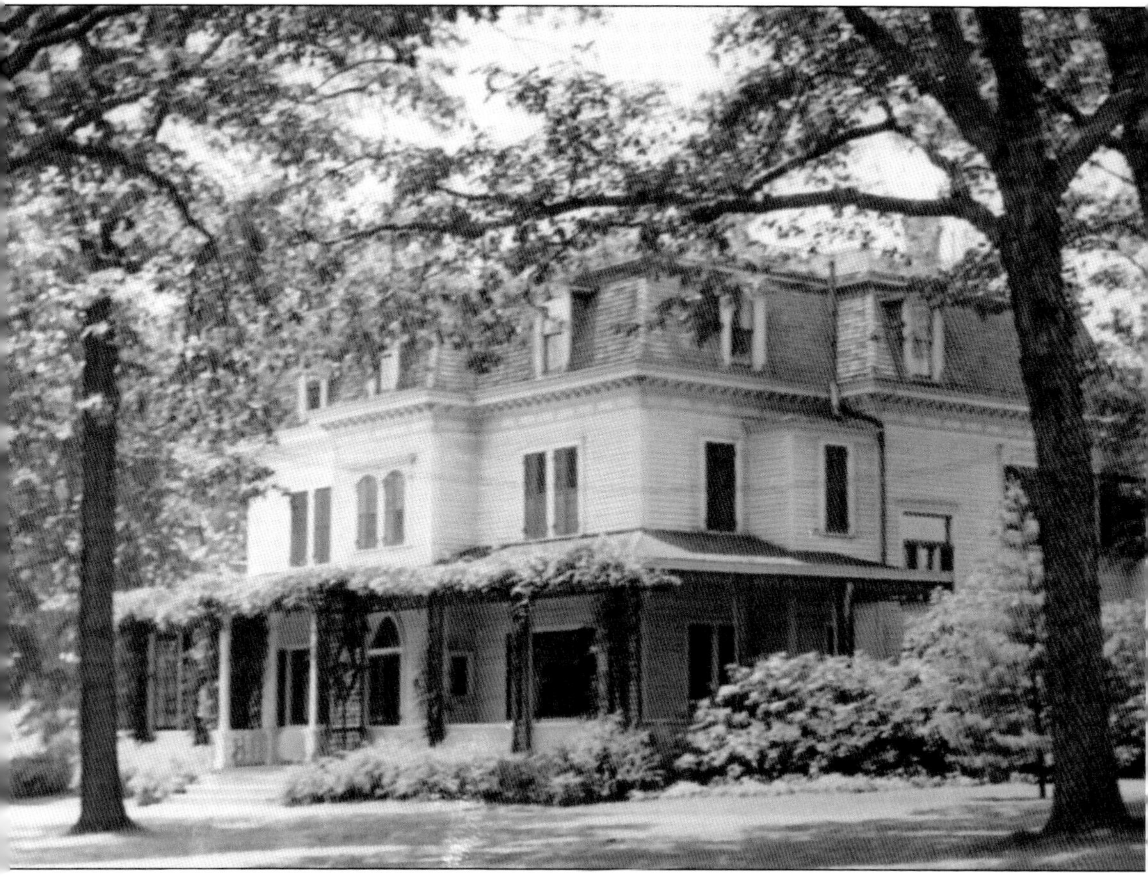

McClellan quickly appreciated the peaceful surroundings of West Orange. In 1871, he expanded a small summer cottage into this larger home, named Maywood for his daughter. Although he would maintain an apartment in New York City and at times live abroad, McClellan lived in West Orange until his death at home on October 29, 1885. Most newspapers failed to realize his home was actually in West Orange and reported his death in Orange. This inaccuracy is still propagated today. McClellan was living in West Orange when he received word on August 31, 1864, that he had received the nomination of the Democratic Party to oppose Abraham Lincoln in the presidential election of 1864. A big reception was held in West Orange that night to celebrate. He ultimately lost to Lincoln and remained mostly in West Orange during the campaign. McClellan later served as New Jersey governor from 1878 to 1881; he was one of four governors from West Orange. McClellan's former home Maywood was sold following his death and was torn down in 1938.

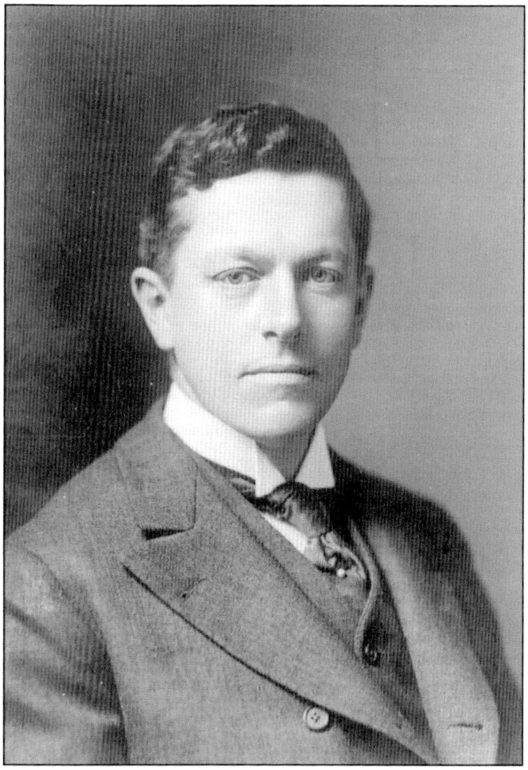

Following McClellan's death, his wife and daughter moved to France, but his son George McClellan Jr., seen here in 1905, relocated to New York City. He states in his autobiography that he was never fond of briefly living in West Orange. He served as New York City mayor from 1903 to 1909 and was the first motorman in 1904 on the first subway train in the history of the city.

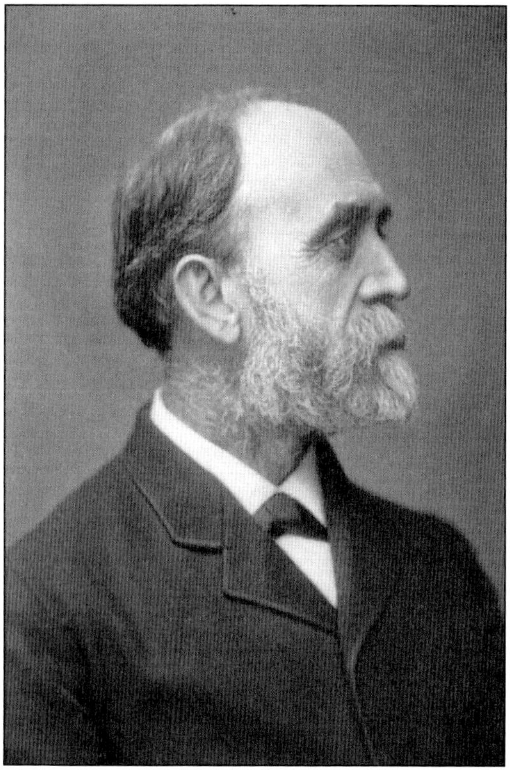

Seen here in 1894 is Wendell P. Garrison, son of nationally known abolitionist William Lloyd Garrison. He married Lucy McKim and, from 1866 to the end of his life, lived in West Orange. He was literary editor for a New York City magazine called *The Nation*, which was devoted to the Reconstruction effort. He served for more than 17 years on the West Orange Board of Education and passed away in 1907.

An undated photograph shows Frederick Stott, who emigrated to the United States in 1911 while his wife, Laura, and five children remained in England. They joined him in 1919 in West Orange and first lived on Franklin Avenue and later on Maple Street, where a sixth child was born. Frederick worked as a carpenter during the construction of Thomas A. Edison Junior High School in 1929. (SF.)

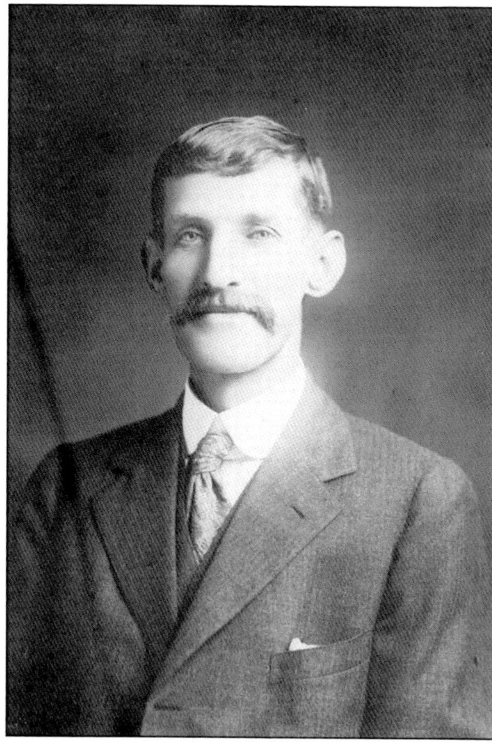

Seen here in 1968, fire headquarters was housed in this brick building erected in 1907. It stood in the path of a proposed east-west freeway through West Orange and was eventually torn down in 1970 for the construction of Interstate 280. A new fire headquarters was built just south of this location on Valley Road and still serves the community today.

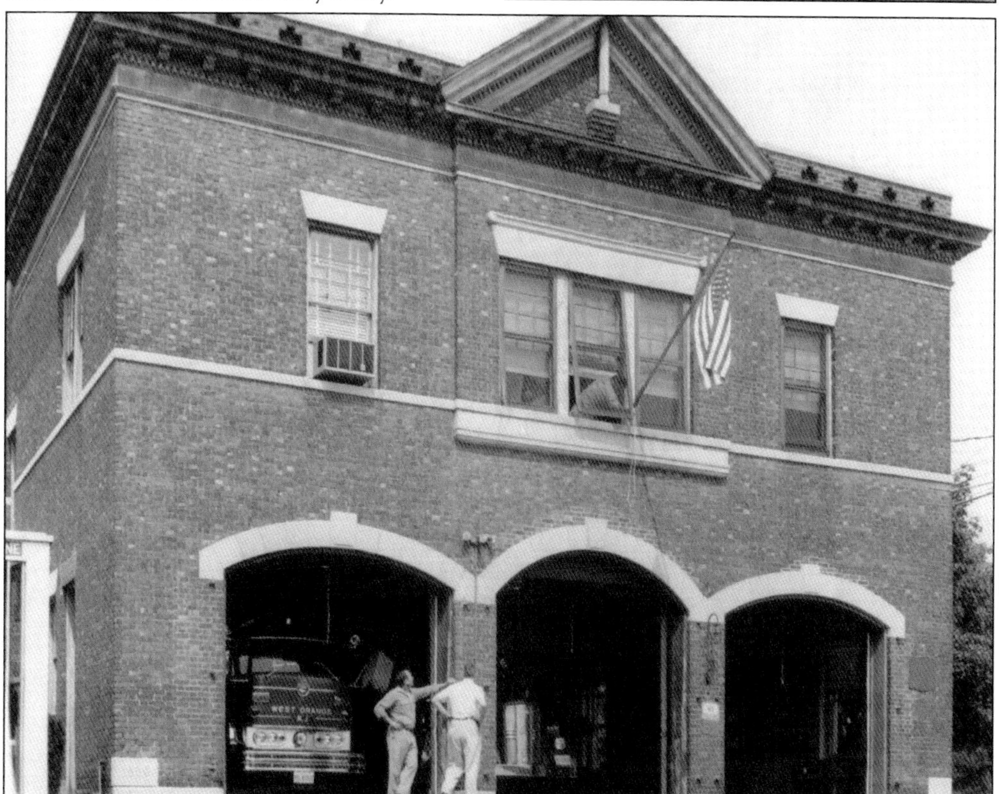

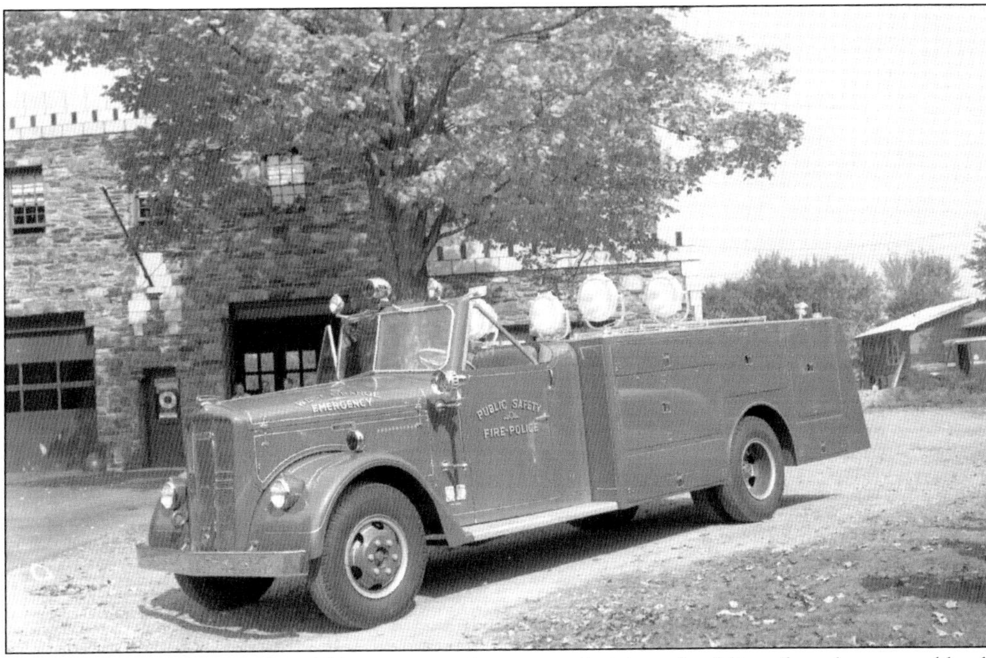

The vehicle seen here in the 1950s was part of a service division of public safety that served both the fire and police departments. It is parked in front of Fire Station No. 3 on Mount Pleasant Place; the station was in service from 1929 to 1957. The building was the home of the West Orange First Aid Squad from 1965 to 2015 and is still standing today.

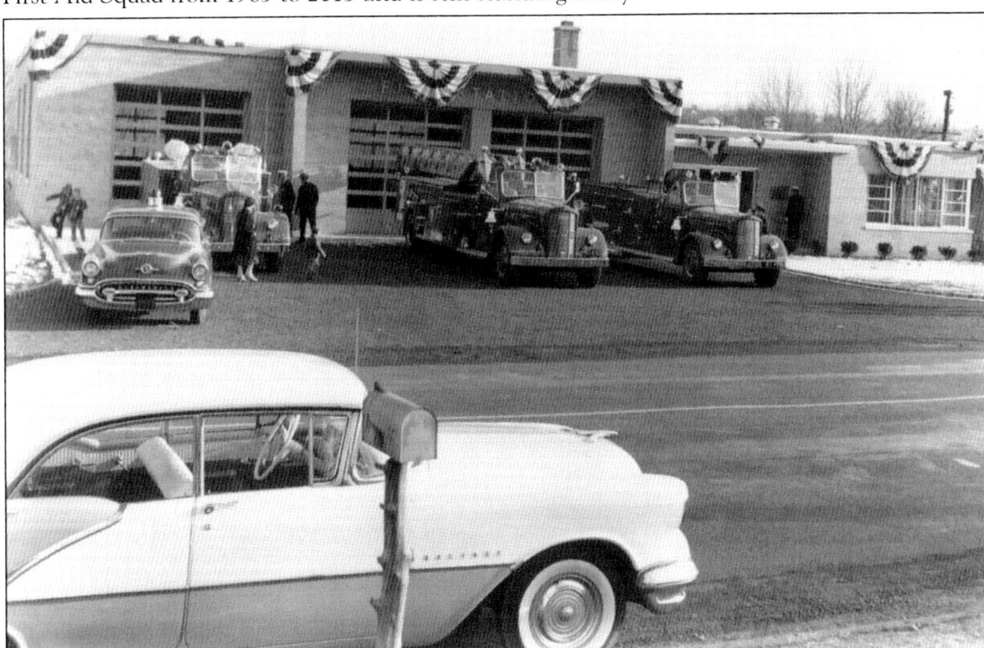
A new firehouse given the designation Fire Station No. 4, located on Pleasant Valley Way, is seen shortly following dedication ceremonies on January 26, 1957. It opened the same day as the new Fire Station No. 3, located across town on Ridgeway Avenue. Both fire stations are still in operation today. (FM.)

Seen here in 1945 on Harrison Avenue is West Orange police officer Daniel Laird. On October 28, 1946, he and his partner, patrolman Albert Hooper, were traveling east down Northfield Avenue. A speeding car came towards them in a dense fog and Laird swerved to avoid the vehicle and struck a utility pole near the intersection of Koewing Place. Hooper survived the crash but Laird was killed instantly.

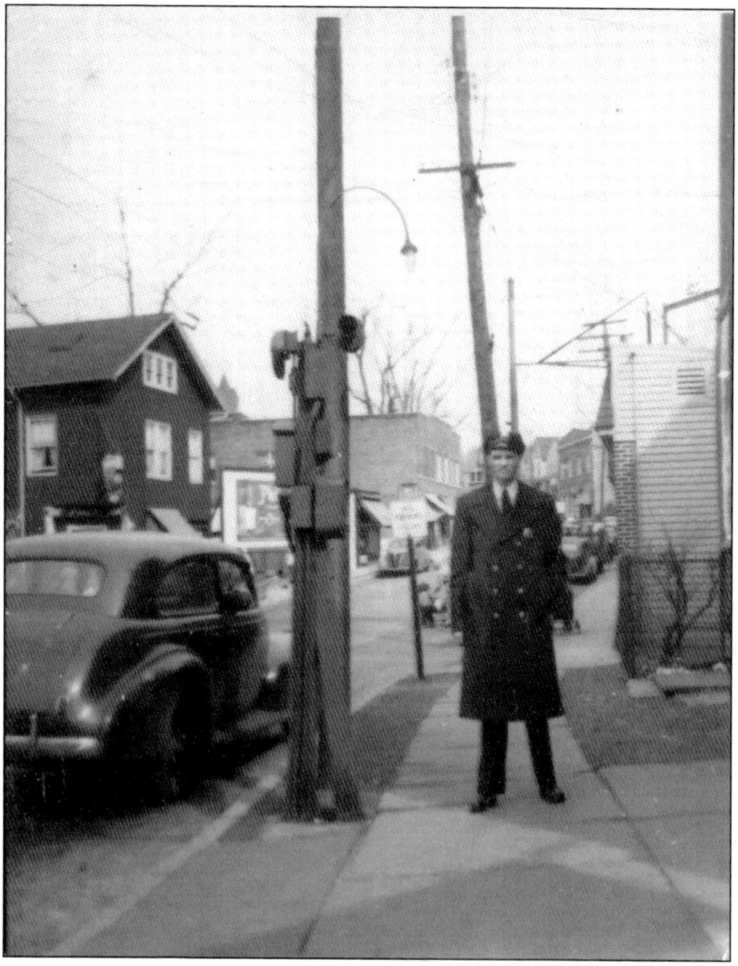

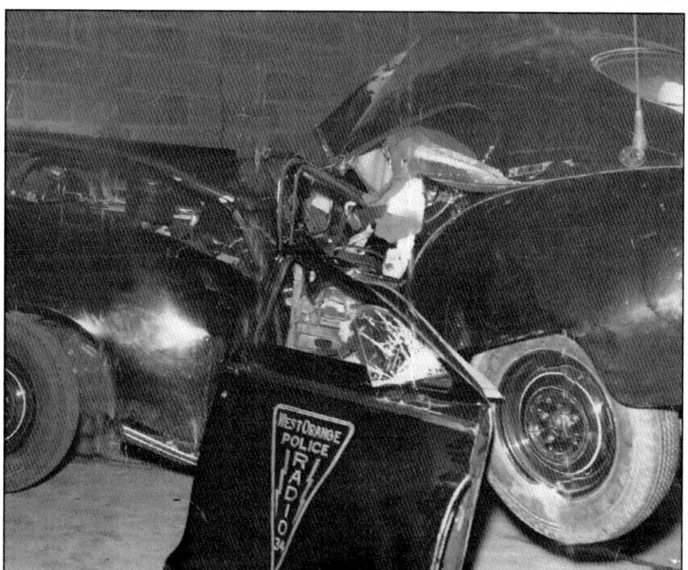

The West Orange police car from the accident that claimed the life of patrolman Daniel Laird and critically injured patrolman Albert Hooper is seen shortly after being removed from the accident scene. The East Orange Fire Department rescue squad and crews from the utility company responded to the accident, and it took more than a hour to remove the victims. Laird Drive in West Orange is named for Patrolman Laird.

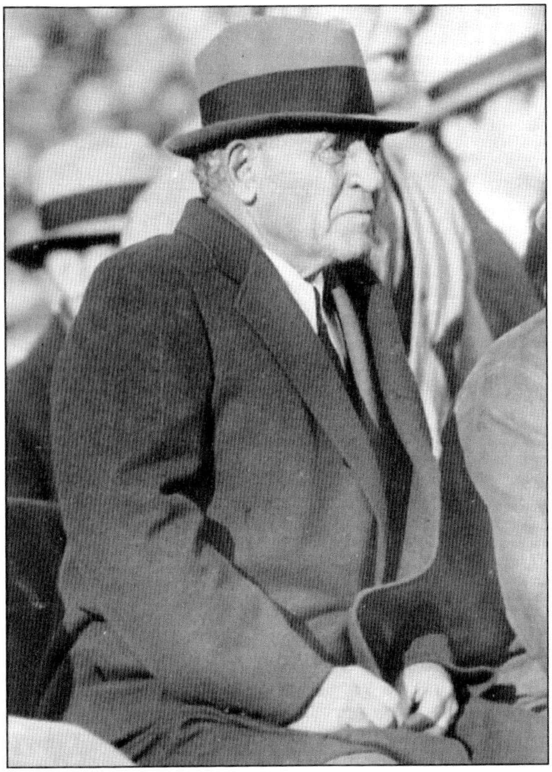

Known as the Grand Old Man of Football, Amos Alonzo Stagg, seen here in the 1930s, was born in August 1862 in what would, the following year, become West Orange. He grew up in town, and his legendary college football career spanned 71 years. Stagg developed many early innovations of the game still used today and is a member of the College Football Hall of Fame as both a player and coach.

Stagg was the fifth of eight children all born at this house built in 1848. When Stagg was born, the town was still part of neighboring Orange. It became West Orange in 1863, and years later, he had to pay tuition to attend Orange High School because West Orange had none. Pictured around 1875, the house is still standing today on Valley Road in West Orange. (RS.)

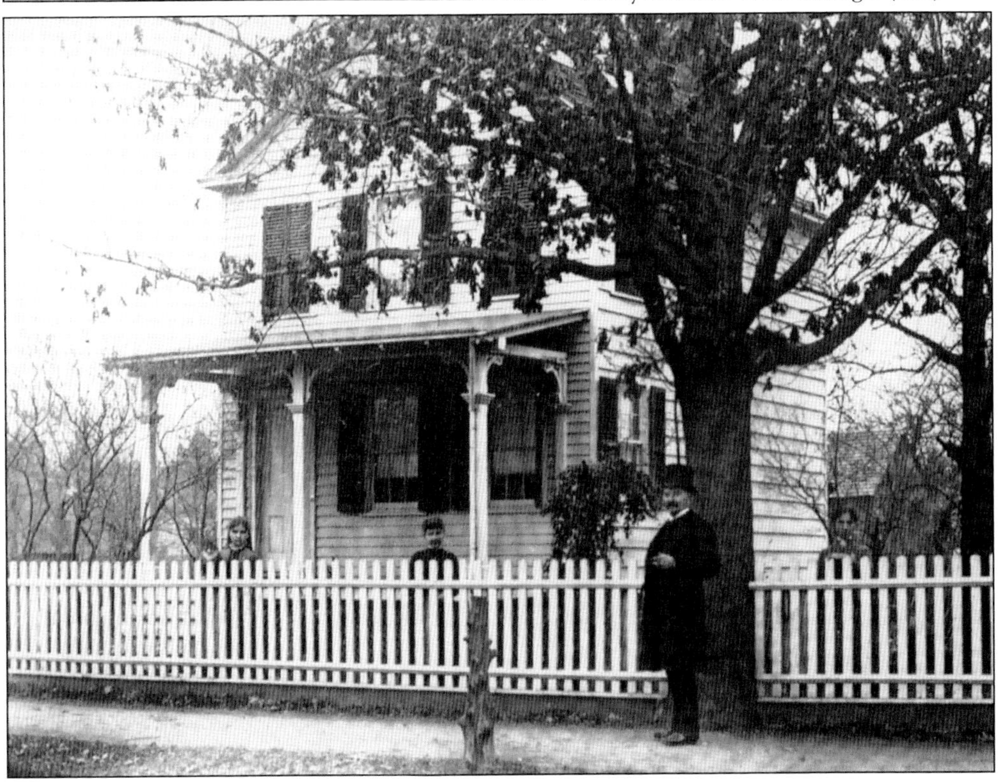

Pictured in 1898 is Amos's elder brother George R. Stagg. He too was born and grew up in West Orange. In 1892, New Jersey enacted a new law requiring all townships to establish a local board of education. George Stagg had been previously committed to public education for 15 years and served as the first president of the West Orange Board of Education from 1892 to 1897.

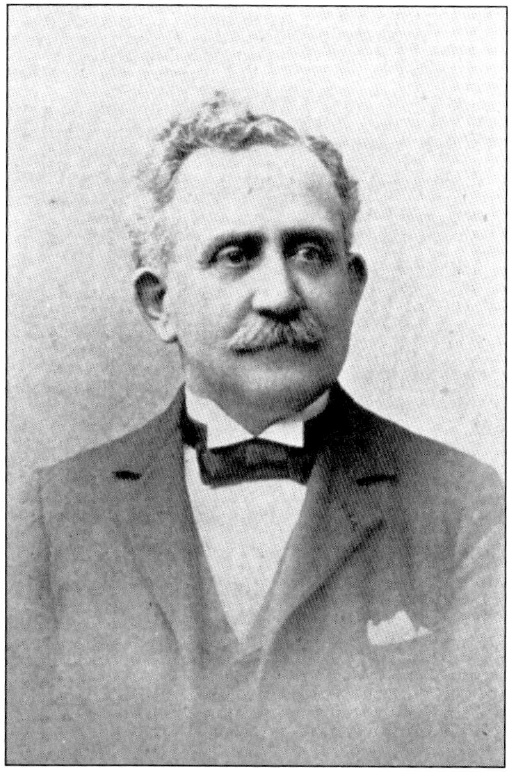

In 1940, the Carteret Academy relocated from Orange and opened in West Orange as the Carteret School and instituted awards named for Thomas Edison and Theodore Roosevelt. Pictured at the school presentation of the awards named for their respective late husbands on May 9, 1940, are, from left to right, Edith K. Roosevelt and Mina M. Edison Hughes along with recipients Lawrence Norton III and Bradford Palmer.

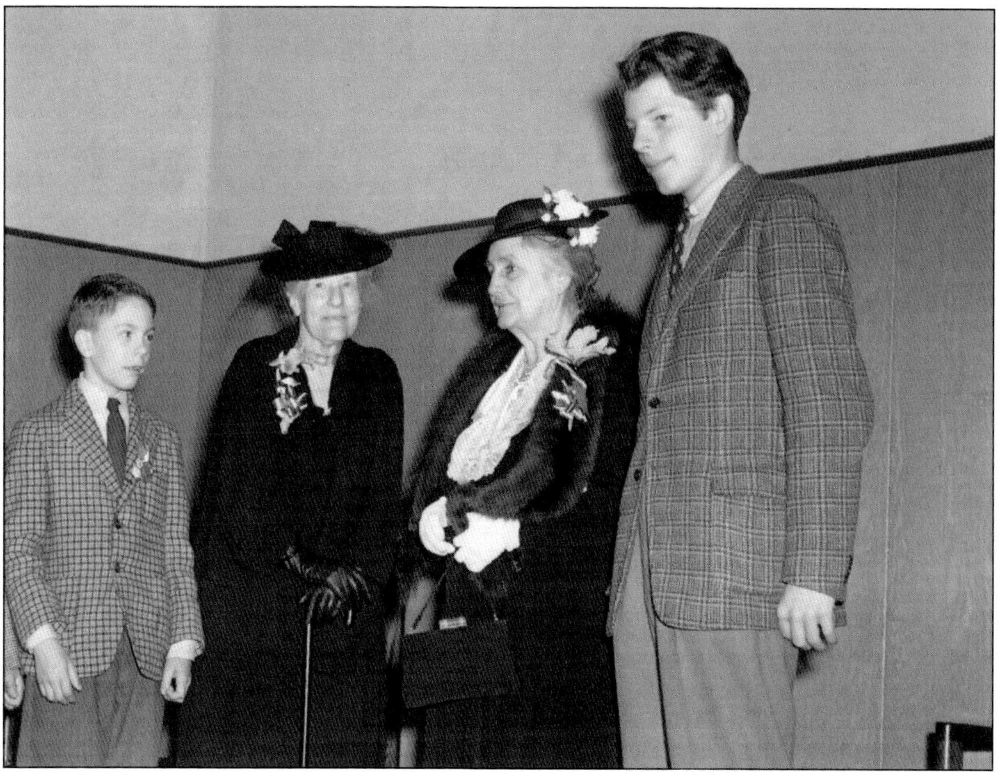

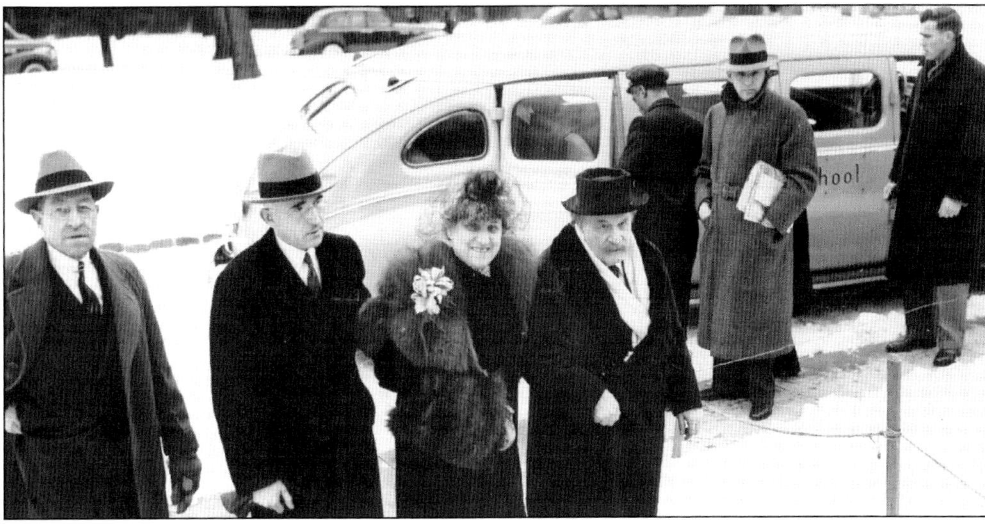

A concert by local child prodigy pianist Kenneth Amada was held at the Carteret School on January 26, 1941. Amada's instructor was world-renowned Hungarian pianist Hedwig Kanner Rosenthal. Walking in the foreground to attend the concert are, from left to right, unidentified, school president George Hofe, Hedwig Kanner Rosenthal, and her husband, Moriz Rosenthal, also a world-renowned pianist. Traffic on Prospect Avenue is seen in the background.

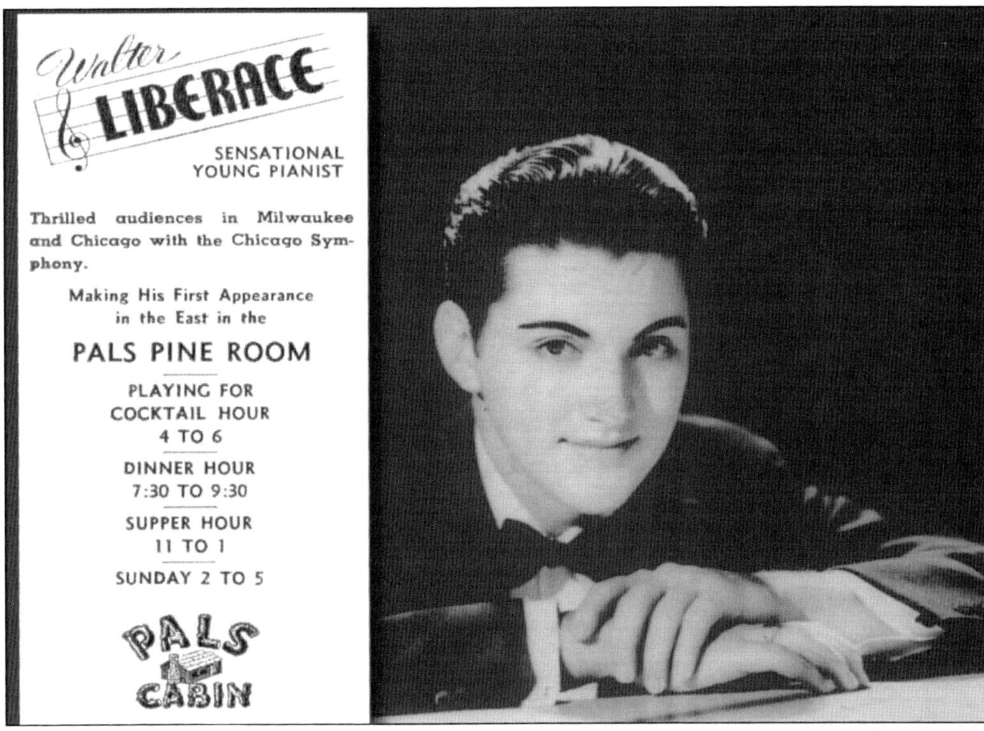

Pal's Cabin Restaurant was on Prospect Avenue only a short distance away from the Carteret School. By coincidence, as the Amada concert was taking place with two world-renowned pianists in attendance, a relatively unknown Liberace was performing at Pal's Cabin. He was just a young kid from Milwaukee who got his East Coast start with a one-year engagement at the West Orange restaurant beginning in January 1941.

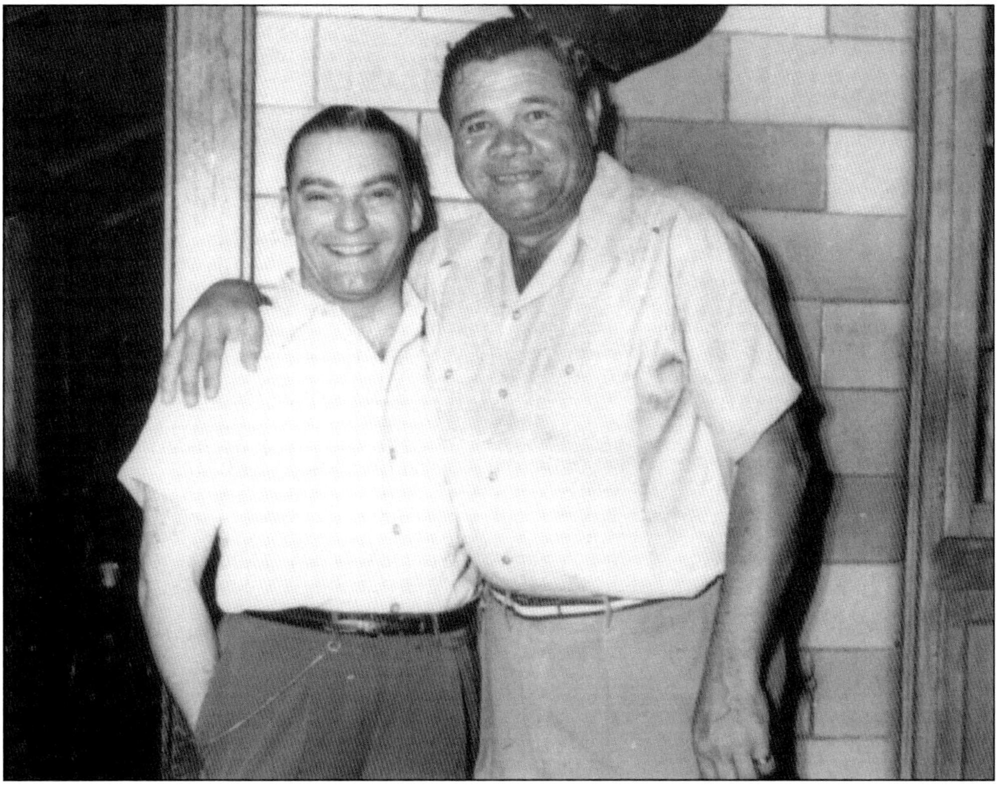

Marty Horn Sr. (left), owner of Pal's Cabin Restaurant, is seen with former New York Yankees slugger Babe Ruth on September 1, 1942. Ruth's legendary baseball playing career had ended in 1935, but he remained a popular celebrity, making many personal appearances. He is seen here with Horn at the New Jersey State Hotel Association's golf tournament held that year at the Crestmont Country Club in West Orange.

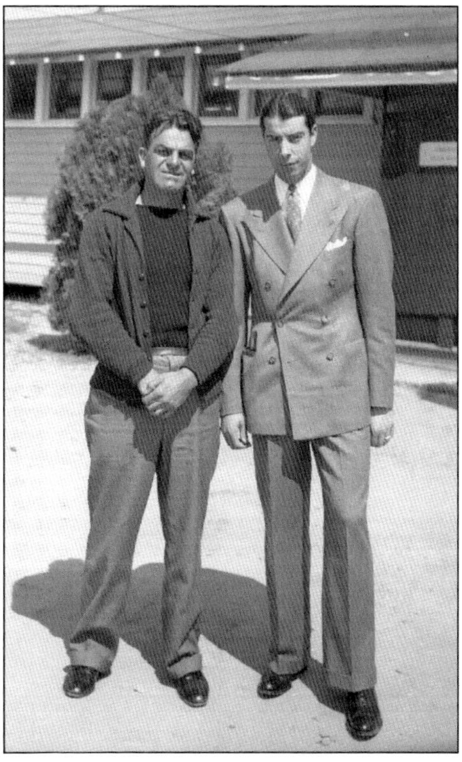

Charles "Larry" Franco (left) is pictured with New York Yankees star Joe DiMaggio at an unidentified location in the 1940s. Franco served during World War I and then became the first director at Lafayette Playground in 1921. He celebrated 40 years there in 1961; the only interruption to his work was with his service in Europe with the Army Air Forces during World War II. During the war, Franco may have briefly crossed paths with DiMaggio at Fort Dix.

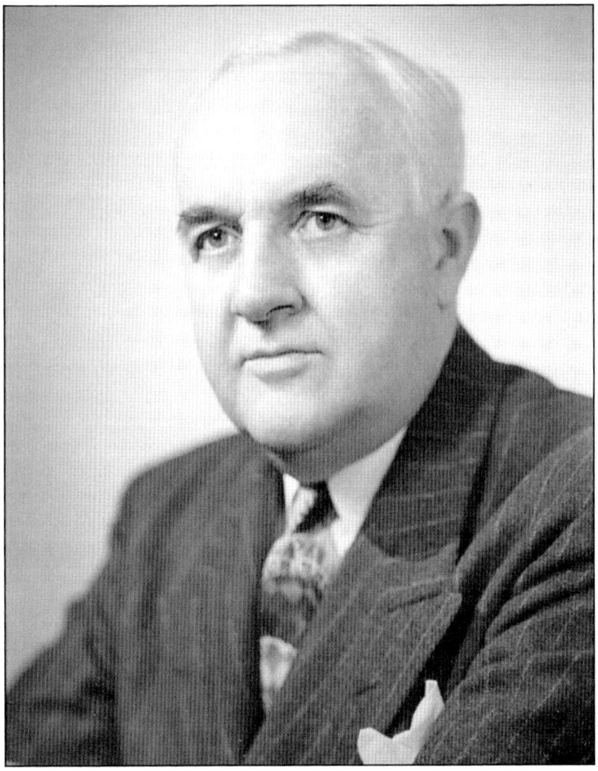

Charles Neill was typical of countless successful West Orange businessmen who served the community over the decades. He was a former commissioner of the West Orange Public Welfare Department and was elected to four-year terms in 1942, 1946, and 1950. He was a Navy veteran of World War I, a member of the Glennon-Sayers Veterans of Foreign Wars Post in West Orange, and passed away May 28, 1954.

In 1941, the town dump was an unsightly place strewn with mounds of garbage. Town commissioner Charles Neill was instrumental in purchasing this bulldozer to level off the garbage mounds in an attempt to make the dump less unattractive. The operator is seen here in 1942 moving piles of debris with a glimpse of rural Mount Pleasant Avenue in the background.

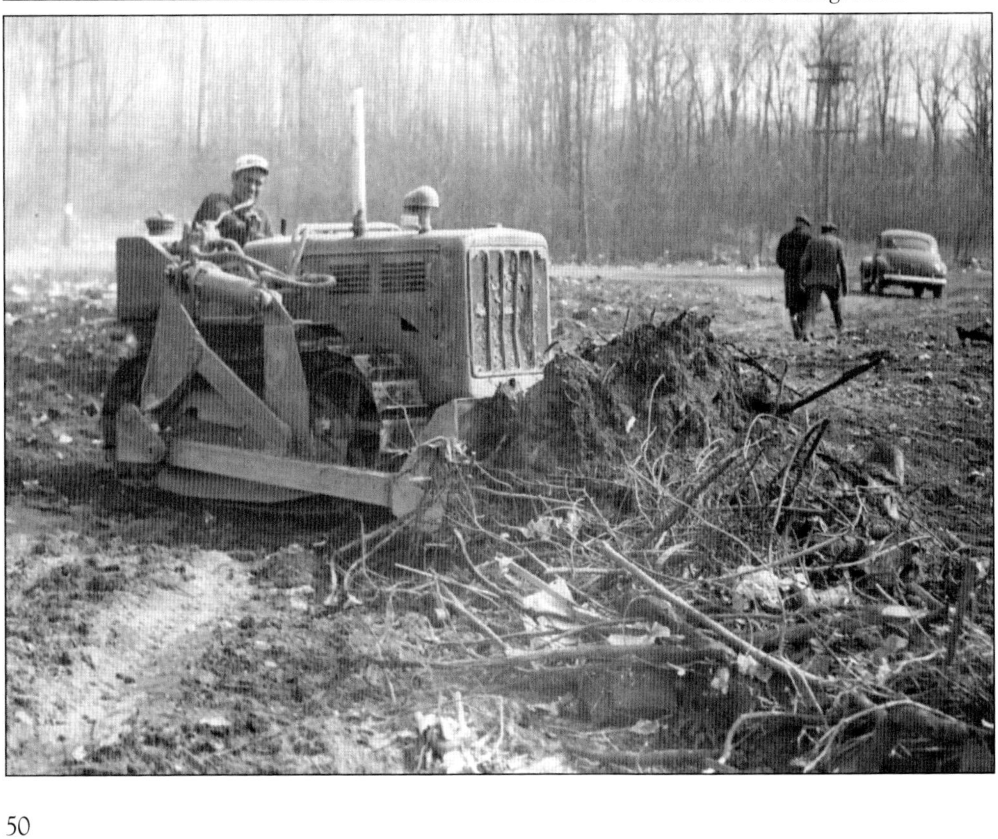

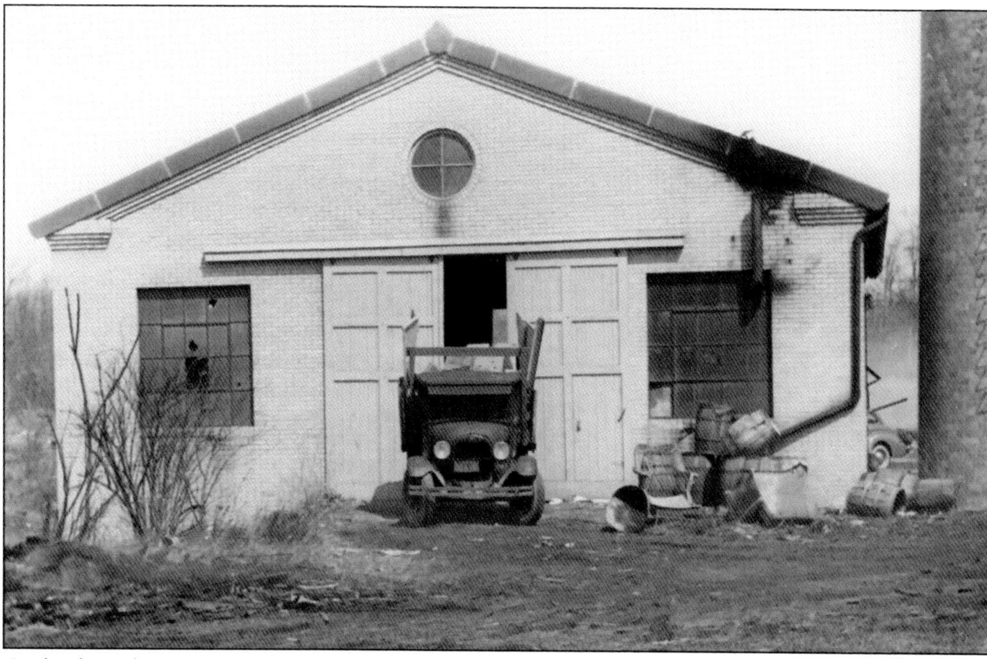

Curbside garbage pickup began for West Orange residents in 1903. It was taken to the town dump located on Mount Pleasant Avenue on top of the second mountain when it was still sparsely populated. The town incinerator, seen here during the 1930s, was built in 1926. Garbage is no longer burned, and the former dump is now the town recycling center, where this building still stands.

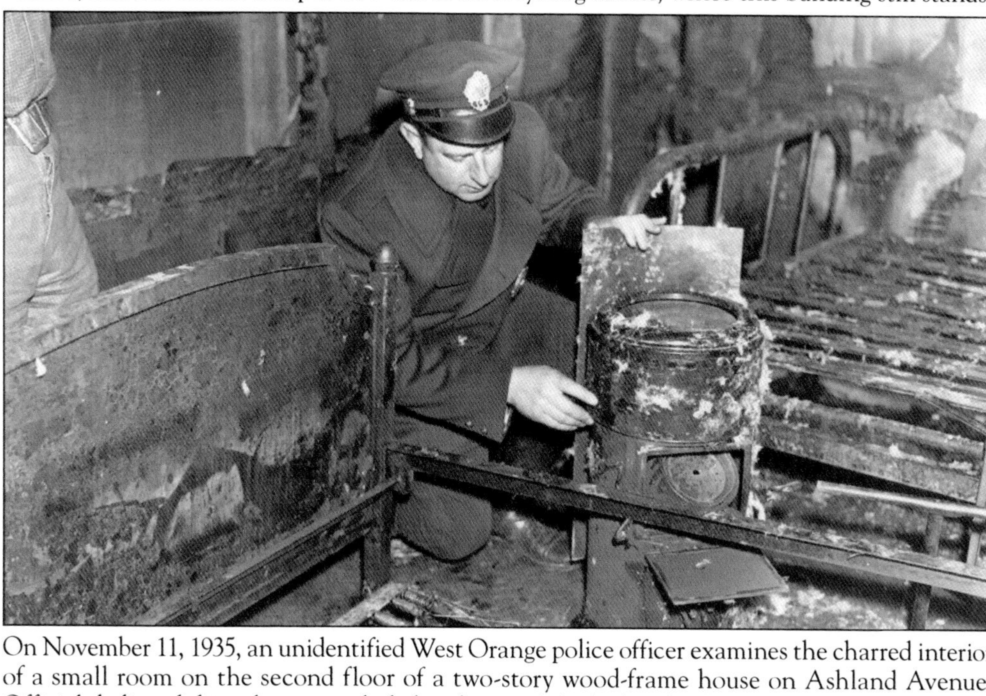

On November 11, 1935, an unidentified West Orange police officer examines the charred interior of a small room on the second floor of a two-story wood-frame house on Ashland Avenue. Officials believed this oil stove exploded and ignited the beds. The flames spread so quickly that the four sons of Joseph Ciampi, ranging in age from five to thirteen, stood no chance to escape and perished.

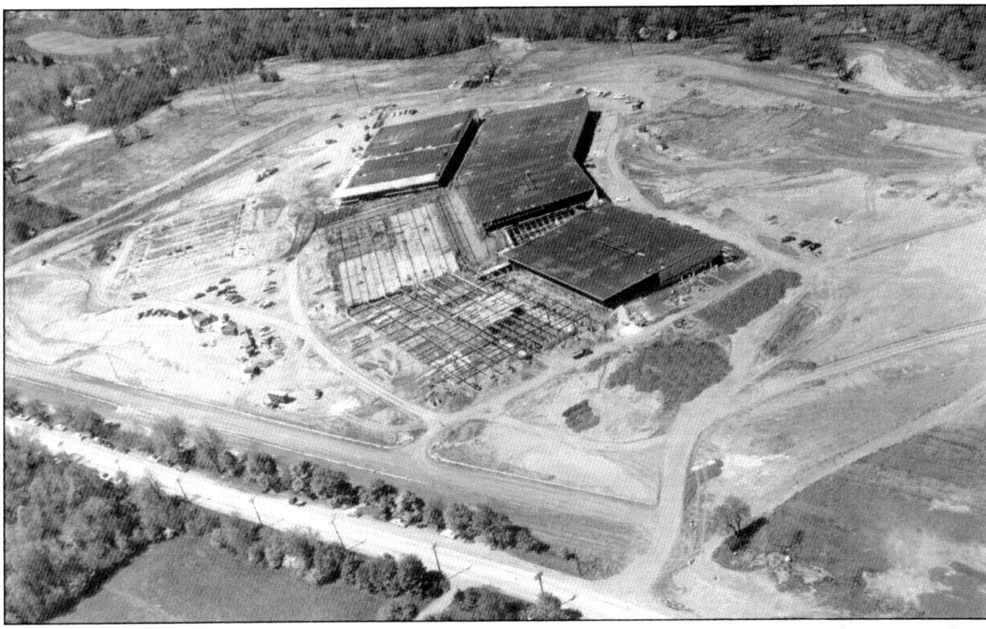

As early as 1955, a commercial shopping center was conceived for West Orange by Long Island developer Sol G. Atlas. Construction is seen taking form for the Essex Green Shopping Center in an aerial view from June 1957. It was constructed on the former golf course of the Mountain Ridge Country Club on Prospect Avenue, which is the road seen running from left to right in the foreground.

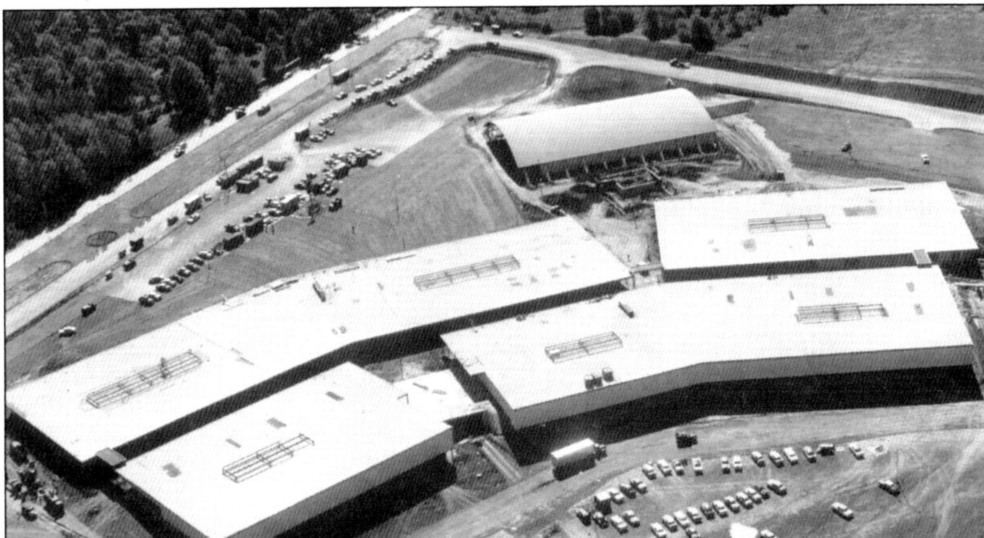

By October 1957, the estimated $15 million shopping center was nearing completion and on target to open before year's end. Prospect Avenue is to the left, and the road around Essex Green named Rooney Circle is seen at the top of the photograph. It was named after William Rooney, who was a former West Orange police officer killed in the South Pacific in 1944 during World War II.

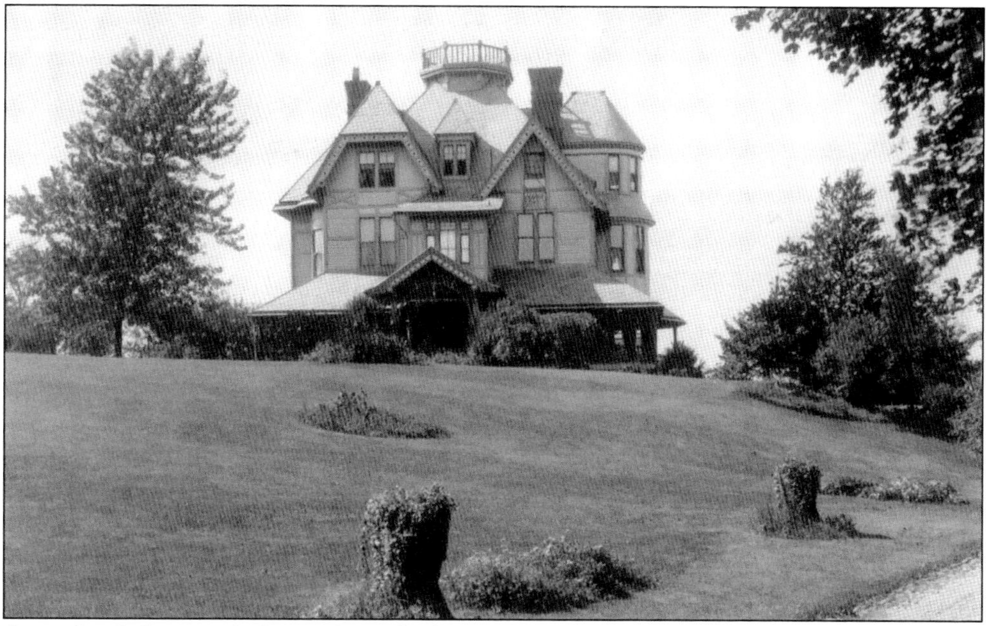

An undated photograph shows a house built in 1875 that became the clubhouse for the Mountain Ridge Country Club on Prospect Avenue. It opened in 1912, but playing golf on a hilly terrain proved difficult. The club moved to West Caldwell in 1929 and celebrated its 100th anniversary in 2012. This house was destroyed by fire in 1956, and the land is now part of the Essex Green Shopping Center.

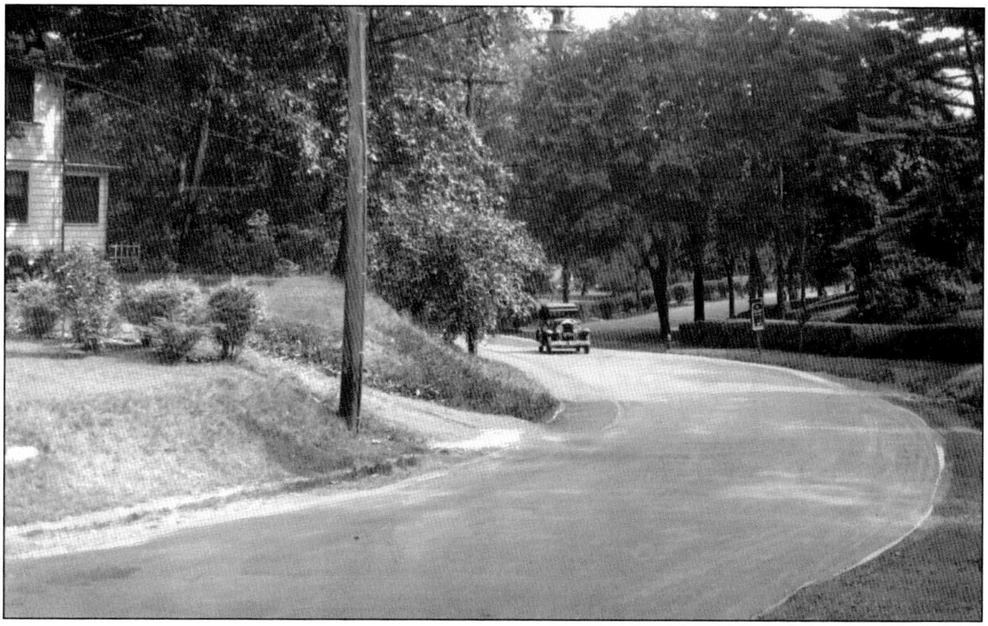

A driver can be seen navigating the dangerous narrow curve on Gregory Avenue in July 1931. At that time, West Orange Town commissioners had adopted a resolution calling on Essex County officials to widen the road for safety purposes. The county road extends south from Mount Pleasant Avenue to South Orange, where it takes on the name Wyoming Avenue and continues through to Millburn.

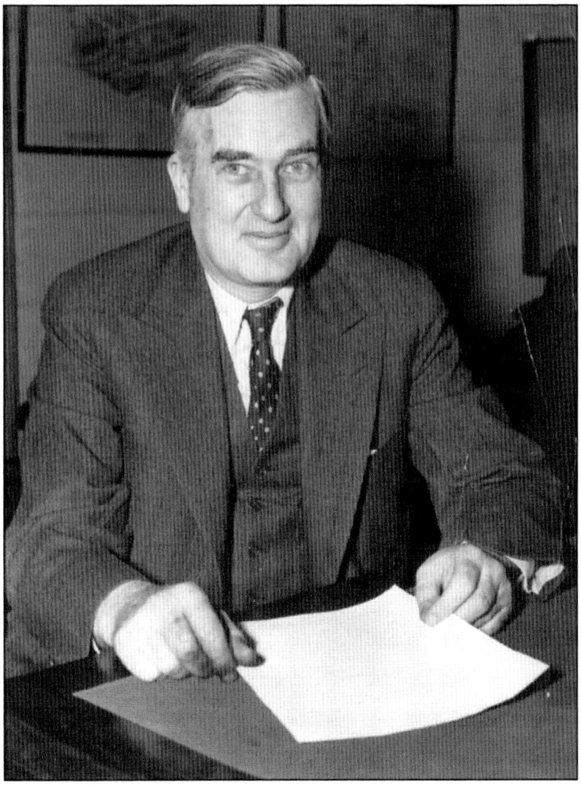

Charles Edison, son of Thomas Edison, was elected governor of New Jersey in 1940. He is seen here in his West Orange home shortly before voting for himself in the gubernatorial election at the Gaston Street School on May 21, 1940. He joined George McClellan, Brendan Byrne, and Richard Codey as former town residents who became New Jersey governors but was the only one actually born in West Orange.

The construction of the power station by Public Service Electric and Gas Company on the corner of Mount Pleasant and Prospect Avenue is seen nearing completion in September 1928. It eventually opened in 1931 and still serves the community today. The unique architectural design and the symmetrical layout of the electrical equipment were considered to be eye-pleasing for an industrial building in a mostly residential neighborhood.

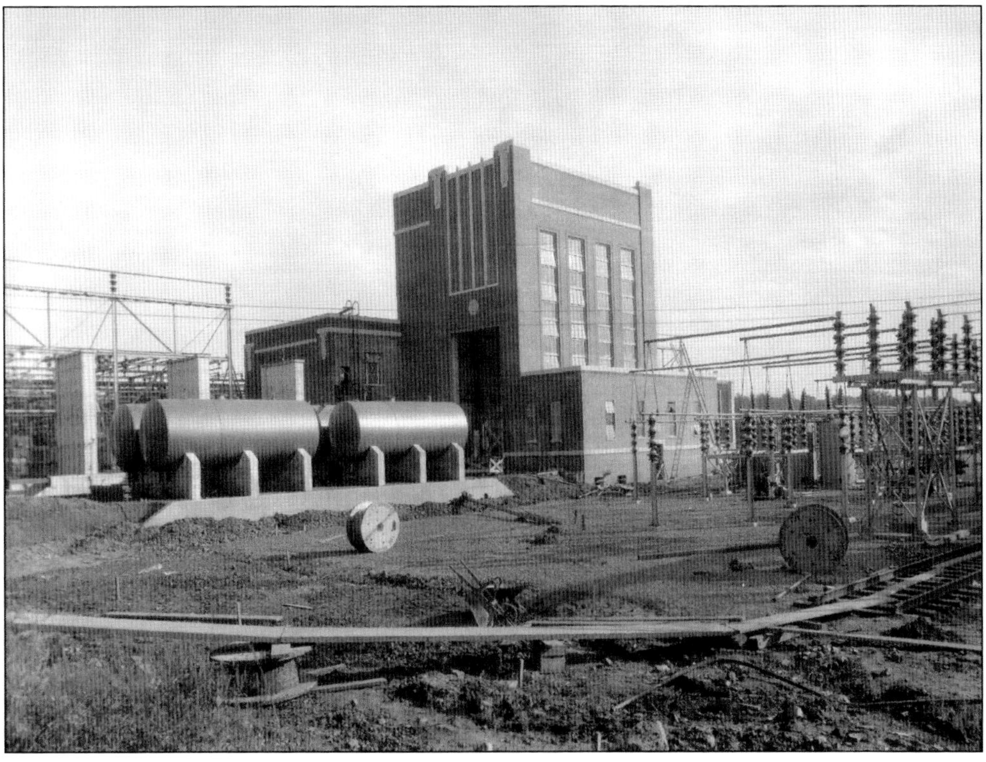

Seen here on May 1, 1953, is Gilbert Dixon hard at work performing an experiment inside the Edison laboratories in West Orange. Dixon was an above-average high school student who was accepted into the Embryo Edisons program. The program granted Dixon a scholarship to attend Newark College of Engineering at night and allowed him to work side by side with Edison research scientists by day.

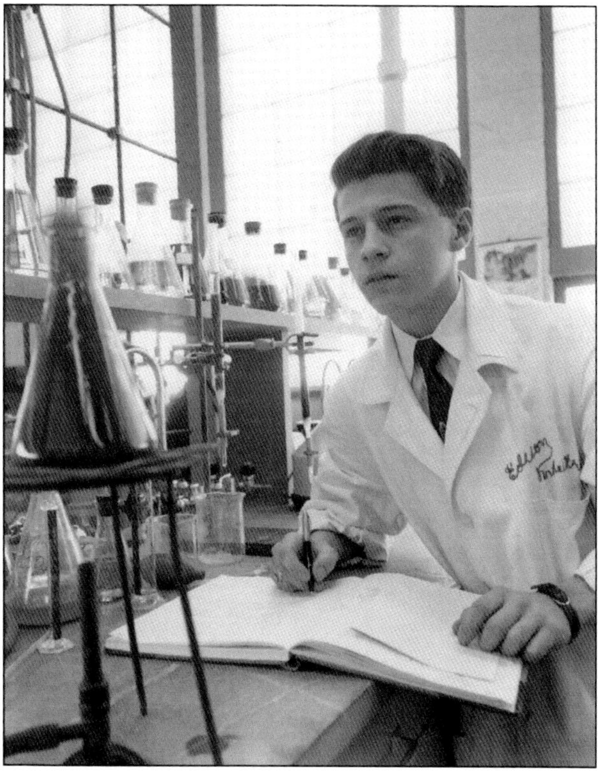

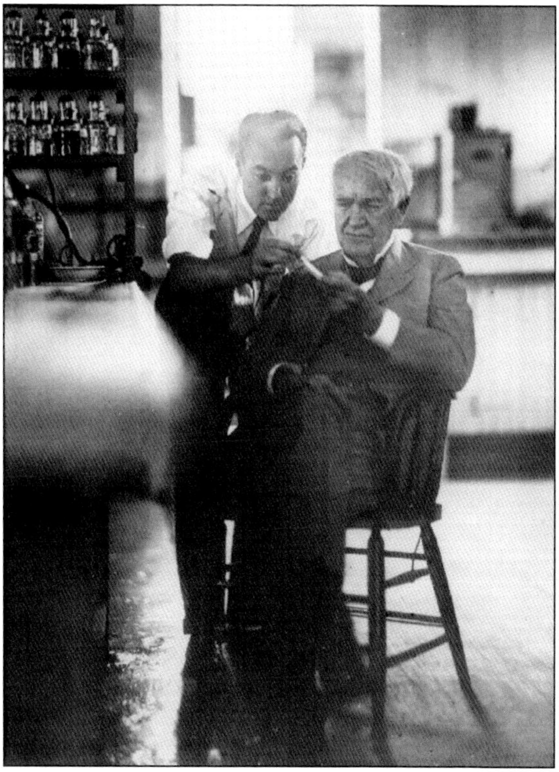

Thomas Edison (right) is seen conferring with assistant George Hart in his West Orange laboratory on July 11, 1930. They are working on one of Edison's many rubber experiments and seem oblivious to the presence of the photographer. This photograph was considered one of the best candid shots of an aging Edison, who passed away the following year.

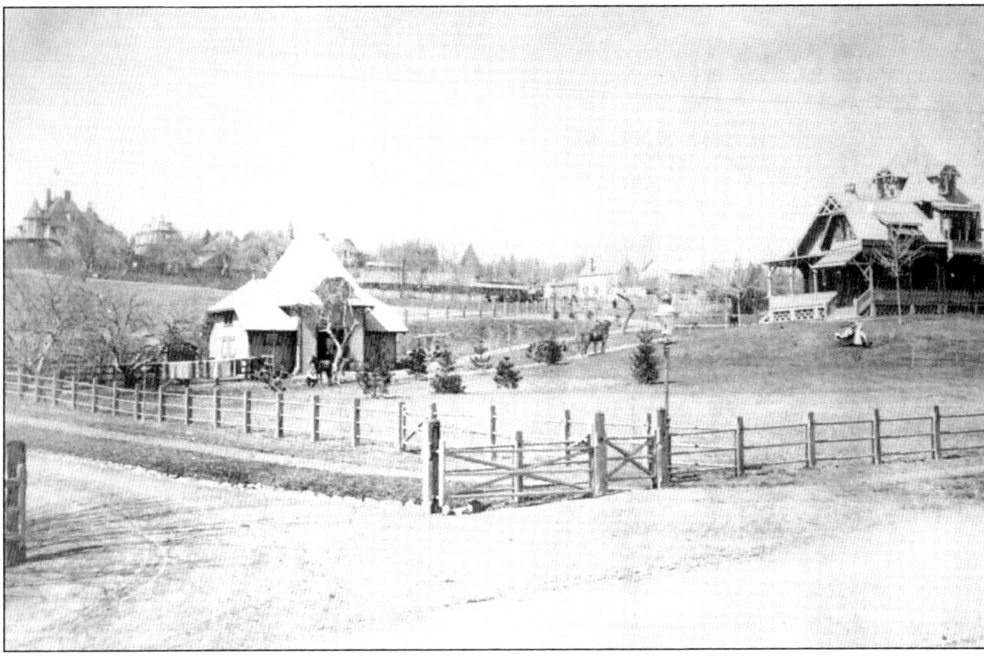

An image from an 1875 stereoview offers an early look at what is now Main Street when it was still a rural dirt road. It shows the property opposite the location where Edison built his laboratory 12 years later. The houses seen in the distance are in Llewellyn Park, and this is today a parking lot for the National Park Service across from Thomas Edison National Historical Park. The searchlight vehicle of the Edison Storage Battery Company is pictured below in a photograph taken on November 3, 1915, from almost the same camera angle and location as seen above. The house to the right above is the same house pictured here on the left. Trolley tracks are shown on Main Street (then known as Valley Road), which had now been paved with cobblestones.

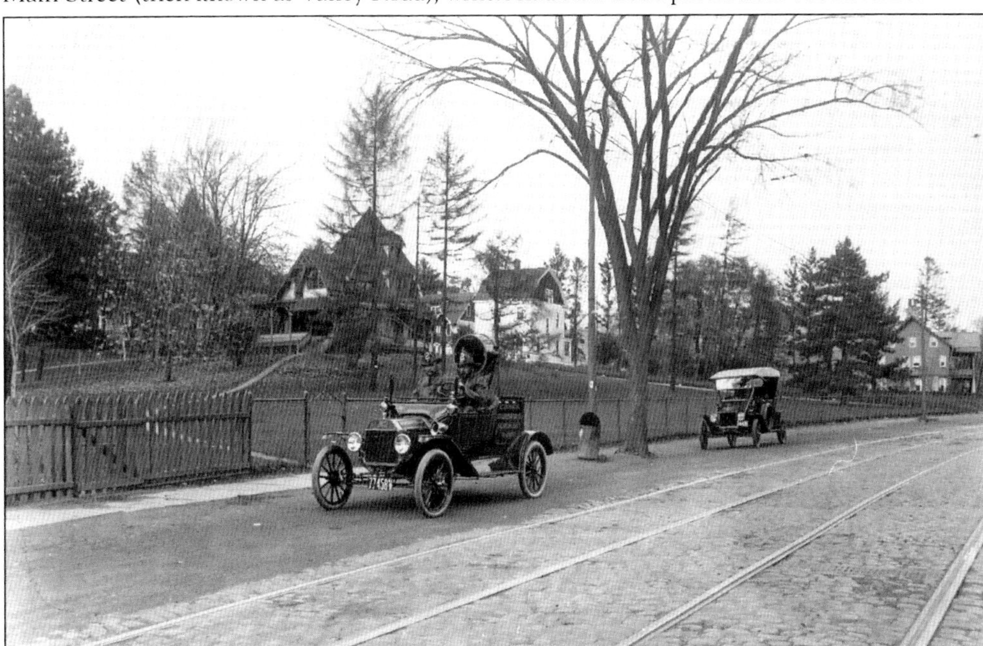

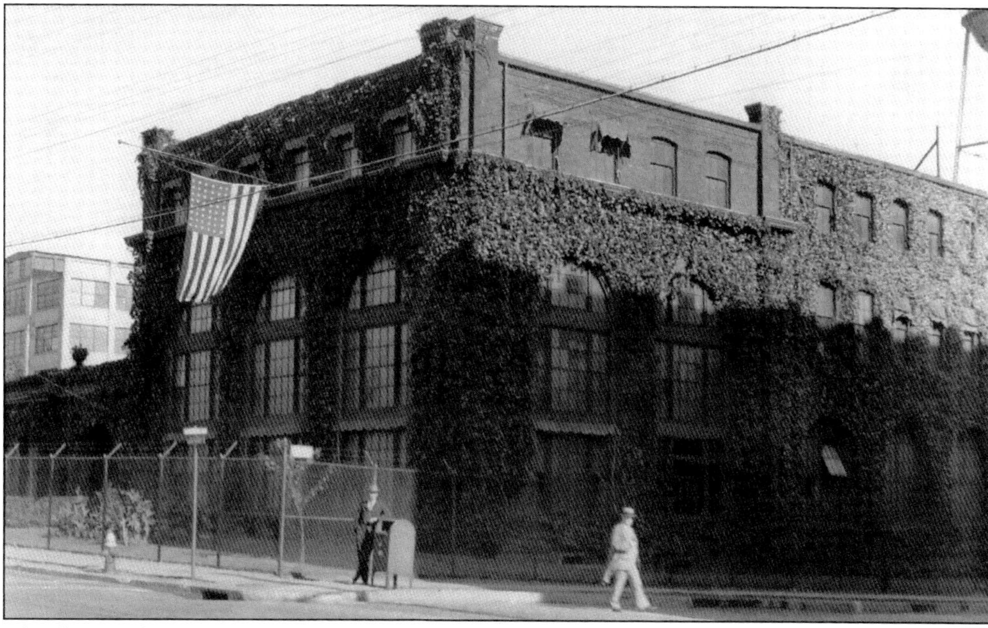

The flag was lowered to half-staff at Edison's laboratory on October 18, 1931, in remembrance of Thomas Edison, who had passed away only hours before. When it became apparent Edison was fading away, his family was quickly summoned to his bedside inside his Llewellyn Park home. West Orange mayor Simeon Rollinson also ordered all flags in town to be flown at half-staff in his honor.

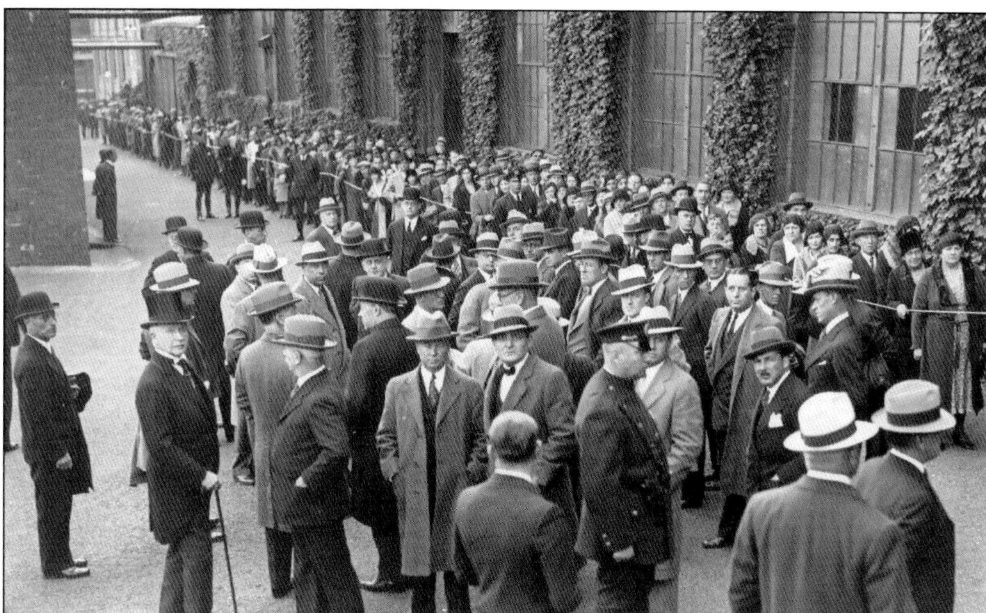

Seen here on October 20, 1931, is the line to view Thomas Edison lying in state at his Main Street laboratory. An estimated crowd of 10,000 people had gathered, and the public viewing had been intended to remain open for only one day. His widow, Mina Edison, decided to leave it open all night, and an estimated crowd of 50,000 people viewed Edison's coffin at his West Orange laboratory.

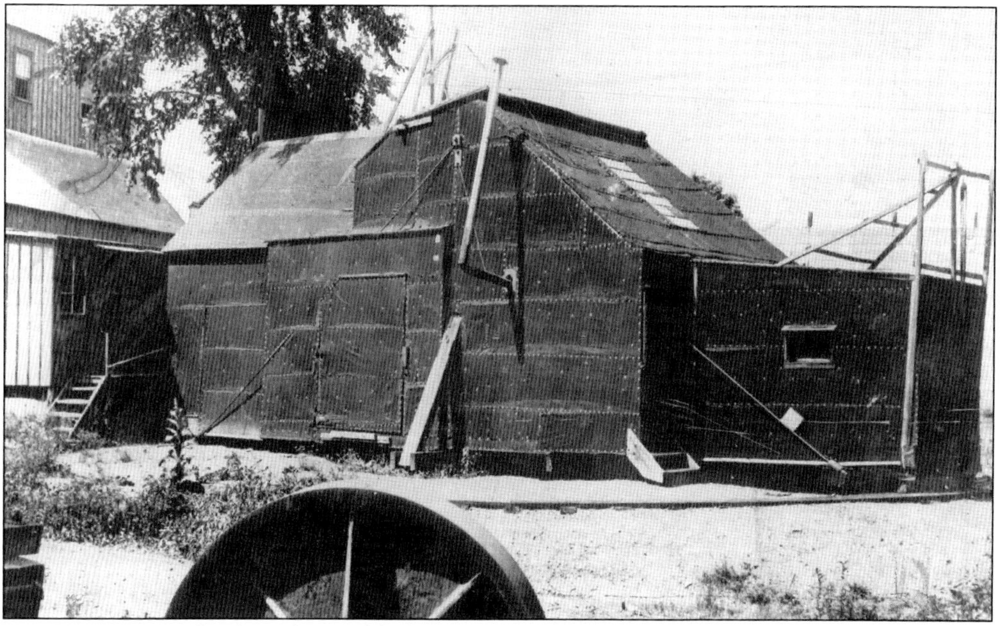

West Orange gave birth to the world's first motion picture studio, known as the Black Maria. It is seen here shortly after it was constructed in 1893 and was torn down sometime around 1903. Over 75 motion pictures were made here during 1894 exclusively for use in Edison's Kinetoscope. Short silent films featured many vaudeville performers and dancers and some notable celebrities, such as "Buffalo Bill" Cody and Annie Oakley.

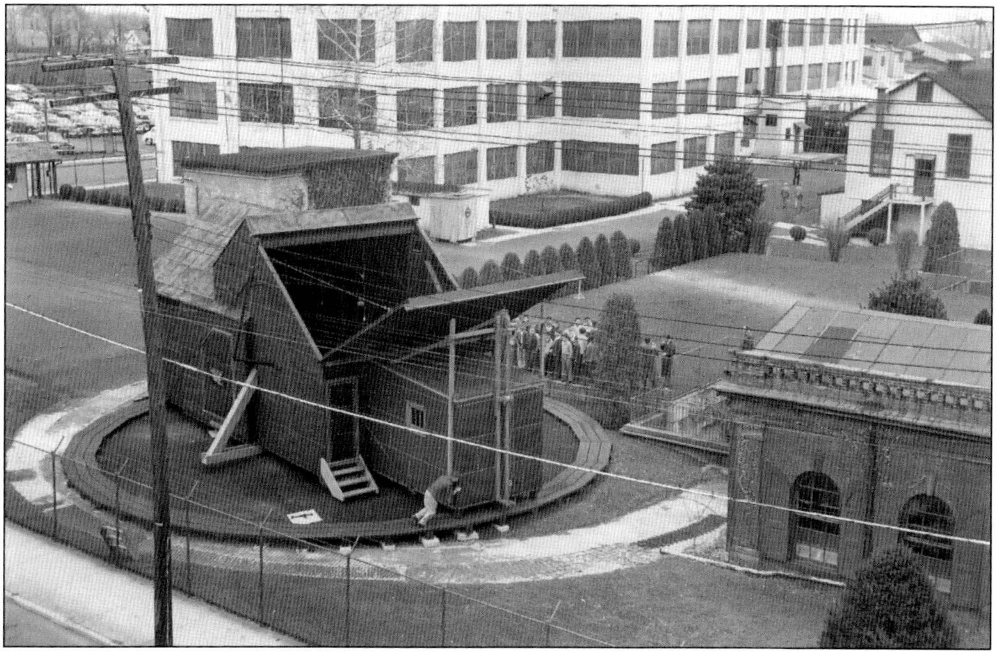

A photograph from February 27, 1955, shows the reproduction of the Black Maria studio constructed the previous year. The replica is still standing and is a fully functional example of how the studio once looked. It was specially designed on a track so it could be rotated with the roof open to keep it aligned with the sun. The film speed was so slow that only natural sunlight would work.

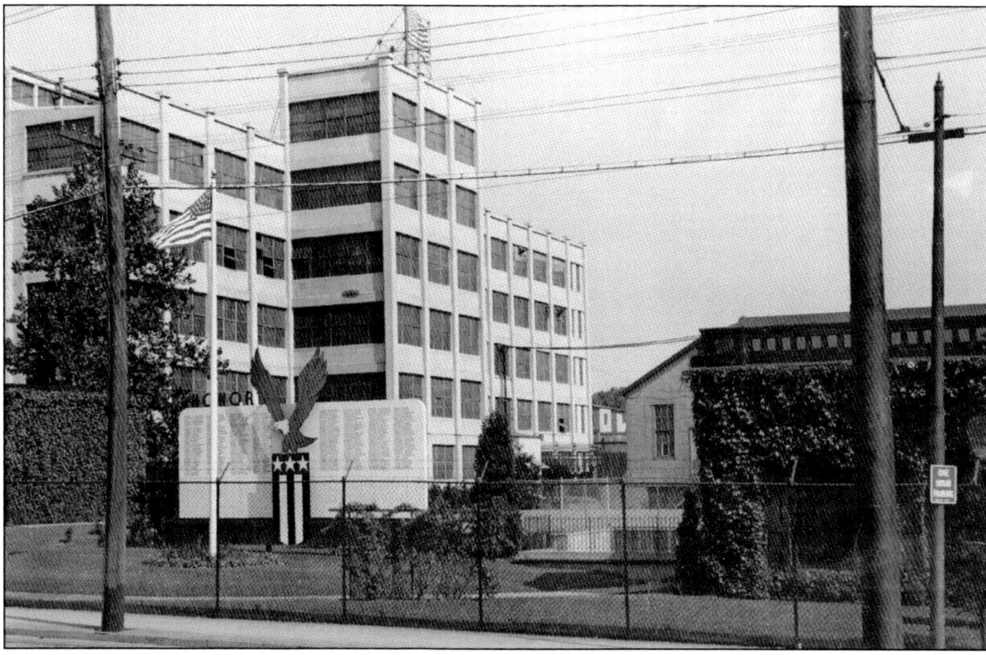

During the height of World War II, most companies posted honor rolls of employees who were enrolled in the armed forces. This billboard pictured in 1943 honors about 250 workers from the Edison plant who were serving in all branches of service. This billboard is no longer standing, and Edison's Black Maria replica was constructed here in 1954.

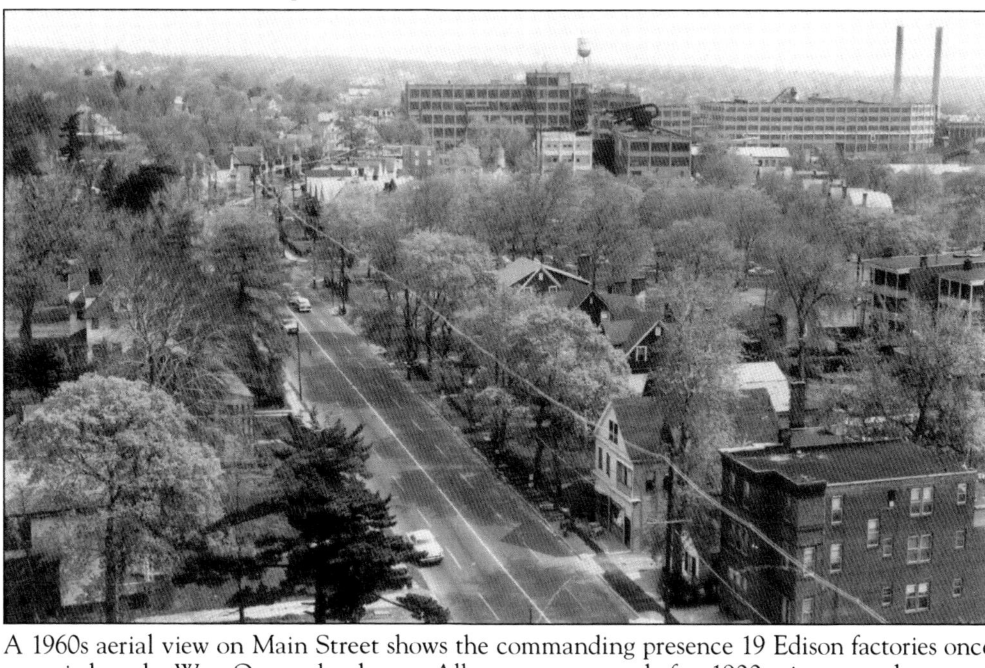

A 1960s aerial view on Main Street shows the commanding presence 19 Edison factories once occupied on the West Orange landscape. All were constructed after 1900 using poured concrete manufactured by Edison; the factories remained mostly intact following a 1914 fire. In 1974, they were owned by McGraw-Edison, and all but the storage battery building, which still remains, were demolished by implosion from July to October of that year.

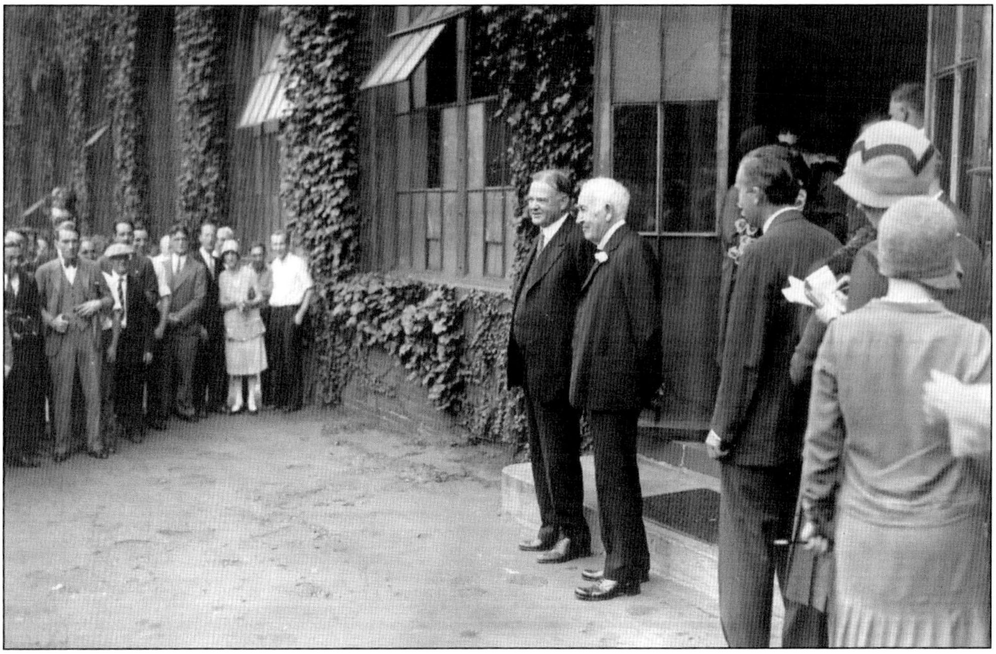

When Thomas Edison first arrived in West Orange in 1886, he was already world famous. Over the decades, he welcomed many famous persons and celebrities to both his laboratory and home. He is seen here on September 17, 1928, standing with Republican presidential candidate Herbert Hoover (left) while on his Eastern speaking tour. Hoover was a friend of Edison's and won the election the following year to become the nation's 31st president.

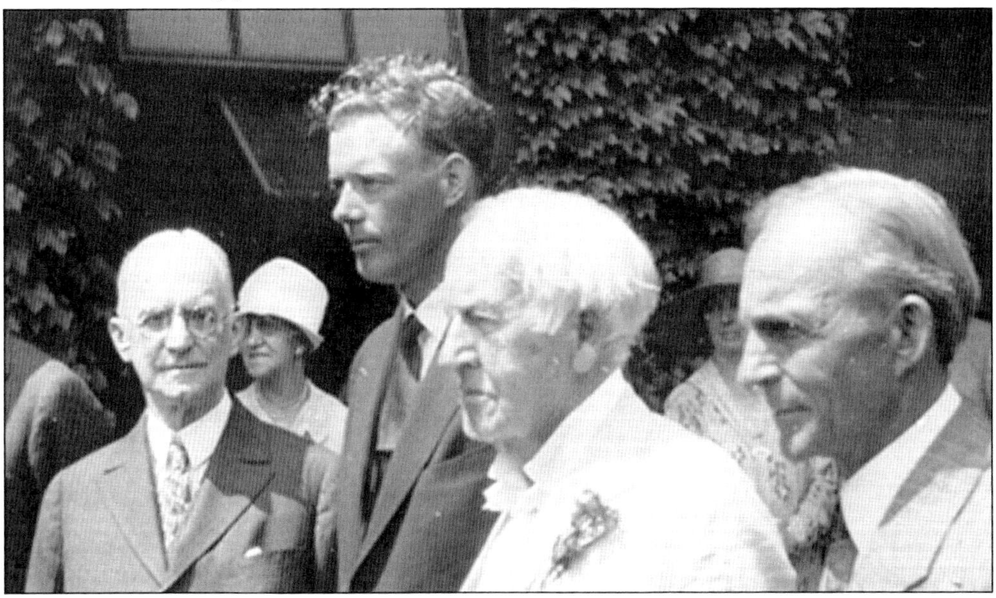

Pictured are, from left to right, George Eastman, Charles Lindbergh, Thomas Edison, and Henry Ford as invited judges for Edison's 1929 scholarship contest held in West Orange. They helped judge 49 candidates from around the country to select a winner who might be encouraged to follow in Edison's footsteps. The contest also created publicity for the golden anniversary of Edison's first successful lightbulb experiment, which occurred in 1879 at Menlo Park.

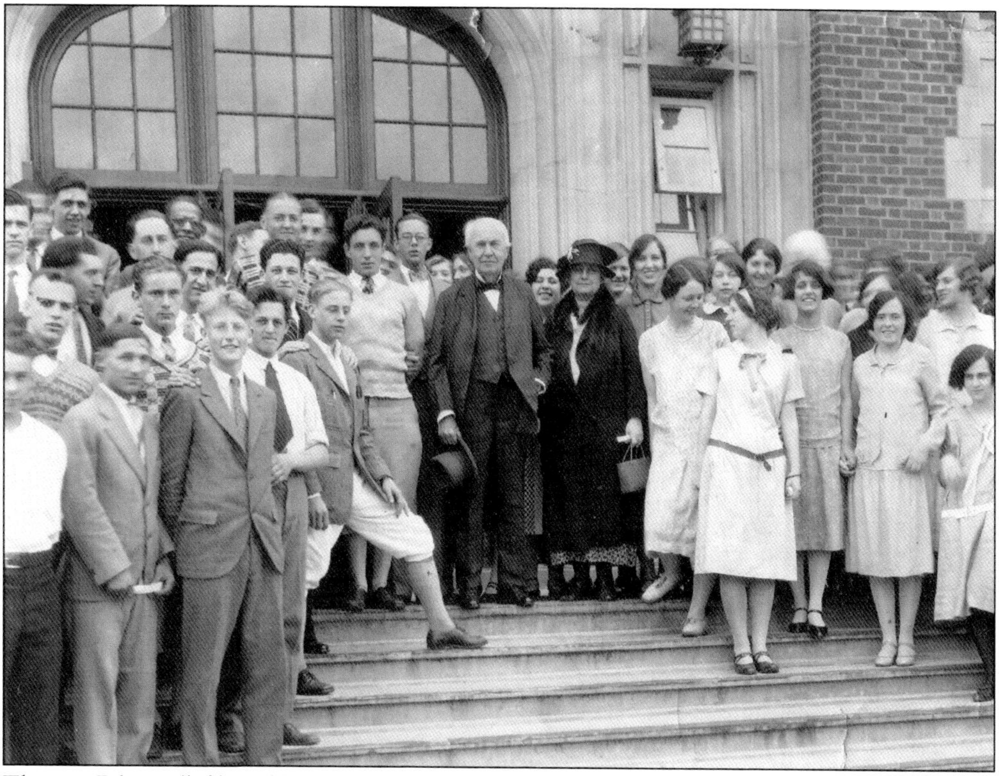

Thomas Edison (left) and his wife, Mina, pose with excited students after an assembly on the steps of the new West Orange High School with the first graduating class in 1926. The school had opened on Northfield Avenue four years earlier, and Eleanor Ramage was part of the graduating class. Her father, William, was working for Edison at the time and likely persuaded Edison to visit the school.

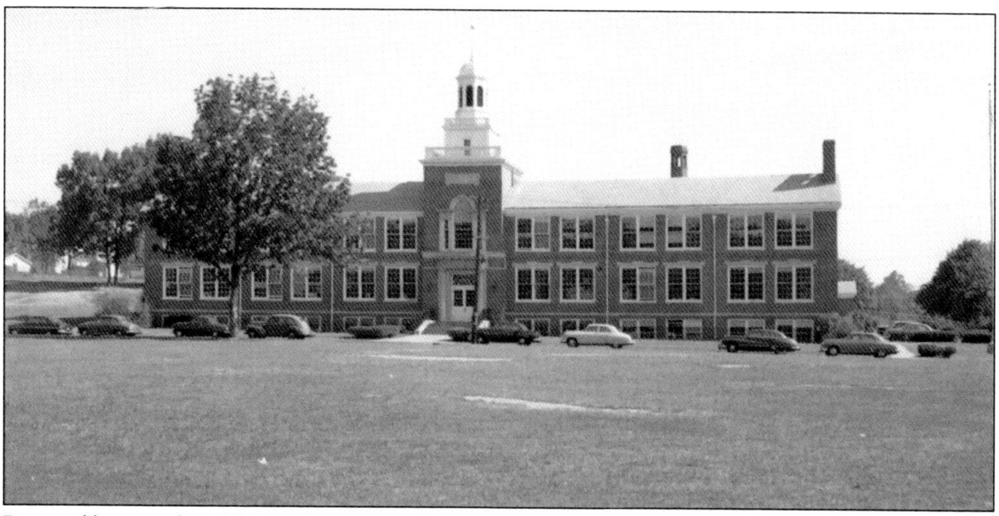

Pictured here in the 1950s is Thomas A. Edison Junior High School, named for the world-renowned inventor. It was dedicated on October 11, 1929, with Edison in attendance. The Wigwam Brook name dates to 1686, and the stream passes in front of the school; it was piped underground in the 1930s. In 2005, the school was renamed the Thomas A. Edison Middle School.

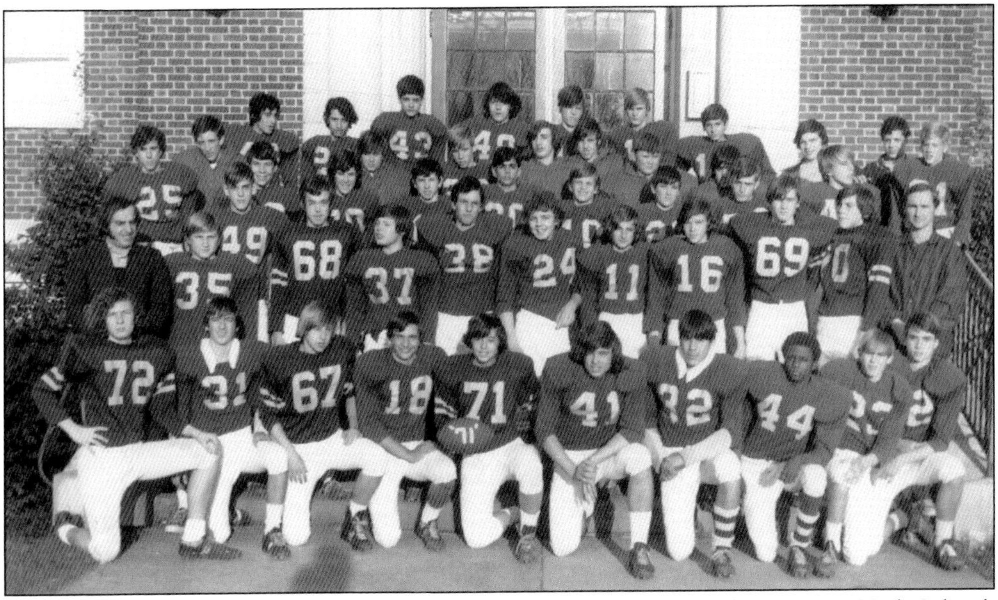

Pictured on the school steps is the 1971 football team of Thomas A. Edison Junior High School. At this time, the three West Orange junior high schools—Edison, Roosevelt, and Lincoln—all faced one another on their schedules. All three programs were combined in 1983 to form the first freshman team for the new West Orange High School that merged the following year with Mountain High School.

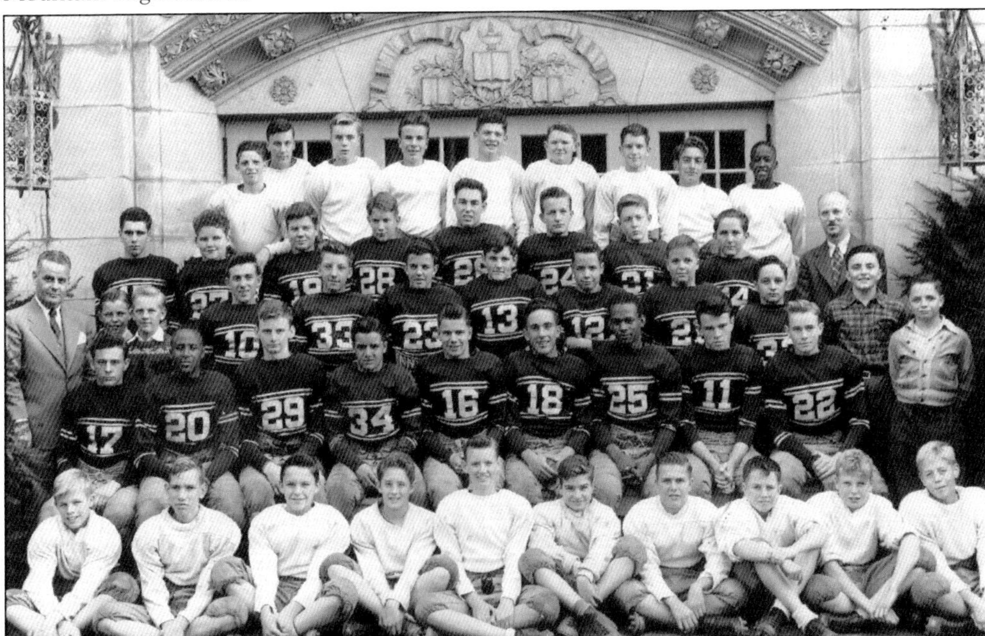

A new junior high school opened in 1933 named for Pres. Theodore Roosevelt. Its 1944 football team, pictured here, went 7-0 in an undefeated season. Uniforms and equipment are in stark contrast to that used by the 1971 Edison team seen at the top of the page. In 1909, when protective headgear and rules regulating safe play were less stringent, Albert Wibiralske, a West Orange High School senior, was killed during a game.

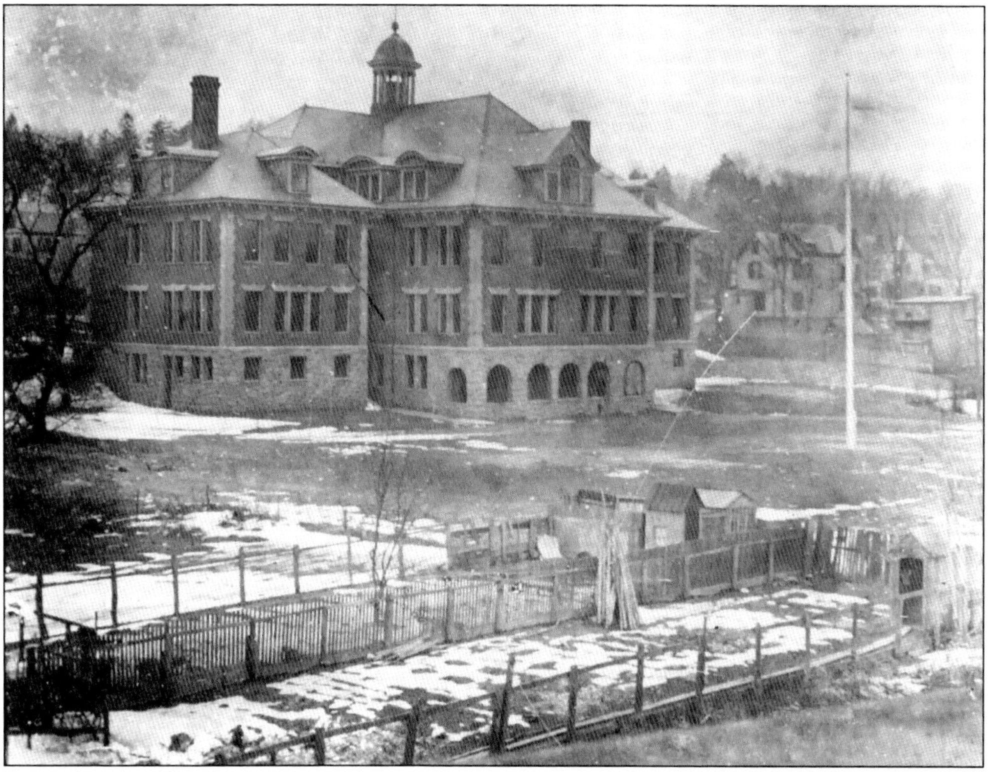

Most photographs show a front profile, but this one offers a rare rear view of the first West Orange High School that opened on Gaston Street in 1898. The Fairmount School was constructed directly behind this building in 1912, and its absence from the photograph helps date the picture. Vice Pres. Theodore Roosevelt visited here on July 1, 1901, and it was destroyed by fire on February 27, 1913. (BR.)

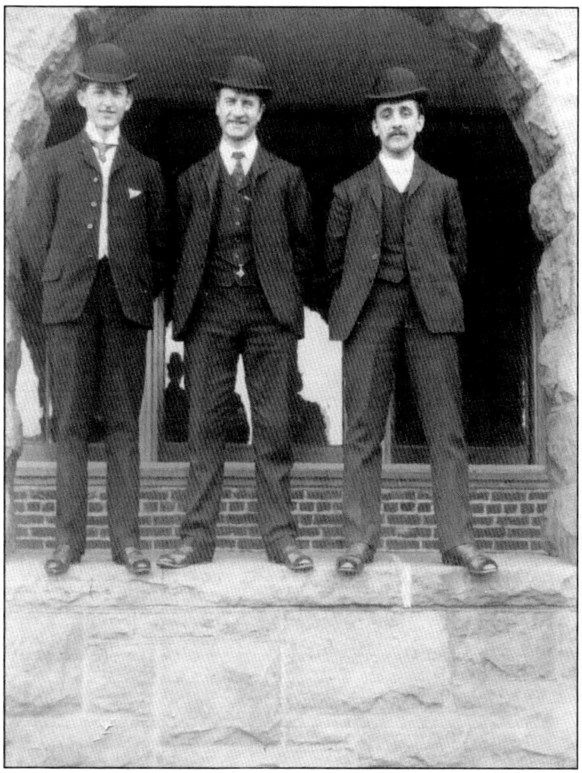

Two unidentified men stand with Fred Seibel (right) in the rear arches of West Orange High School. Seibel lived nearby on Longview Street, and his daughter Florence Elsie, born in 1905, attended this school after it was rebuilt from the 1913 fire. A new high school opened on Northfield Avenue in 1922, and the rebuilt school became known as Gaston Street Junior High School. (BR.)

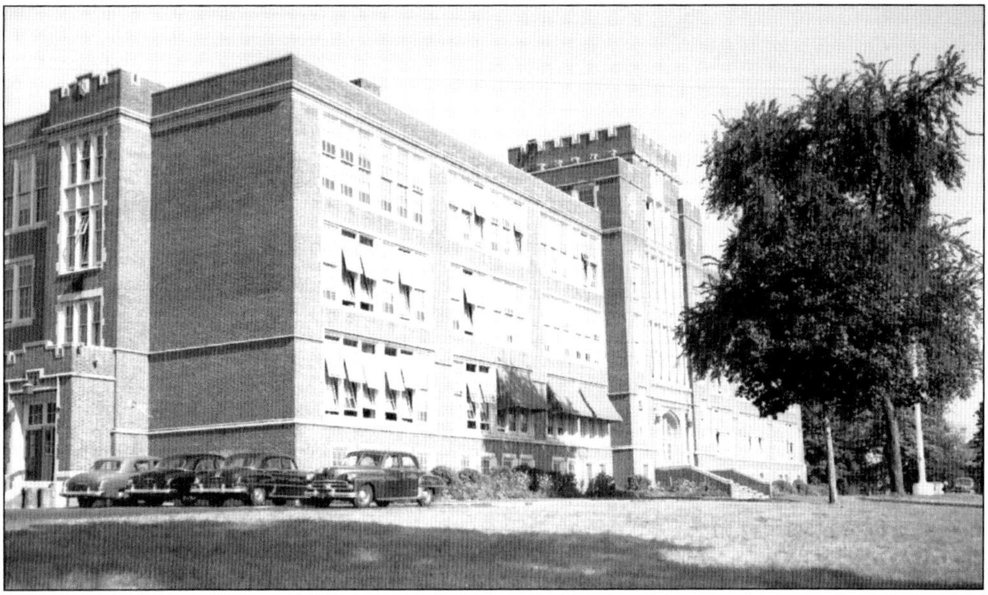

In 1922, a new West Orange High School, seen here in the 1950s, opened on Northfield Avenue. The original high school, which opened on Gaston Street in 1898 and was subsequently rebuilt following the 1913 fire, became a junior high school. This was the only high school in town until West Orange Mountain High School opened in 1960, but they were merged into a single West Orange High School in 1984.

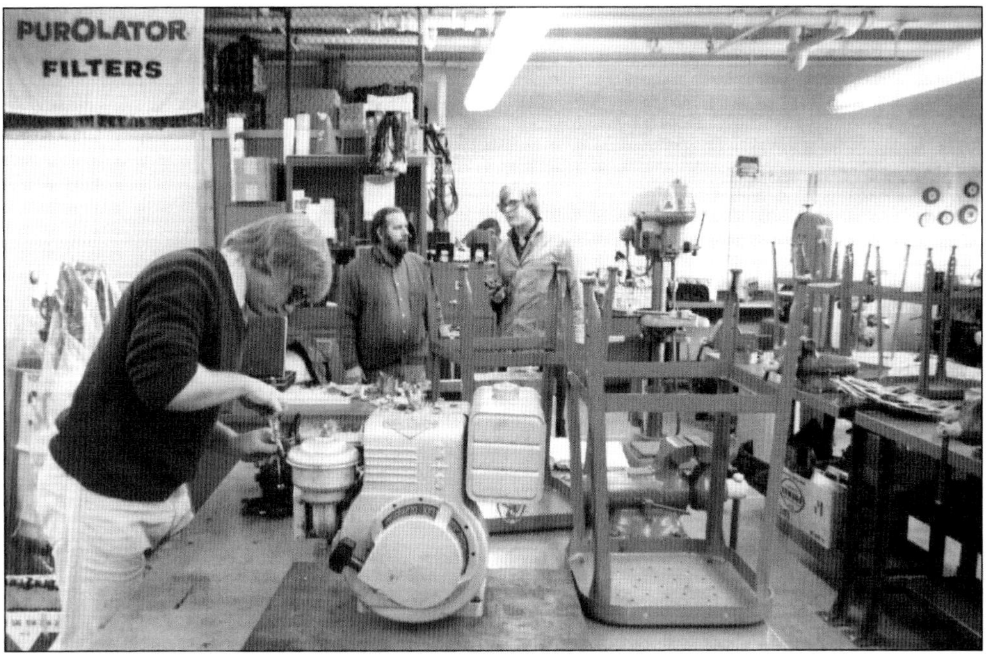

West Orange Mountain High School opened in 1960 and was the second high school in town. West Orange was able to sustain two high schools for over two decades, but declining enrollment eventually led to consolidation of both West Orange high schools in 1984. The original Mountain auto shop is seen here in 1975, and from left to right are Joe Fagan, Jack Brooks, and shop teacher Pete Harrington.

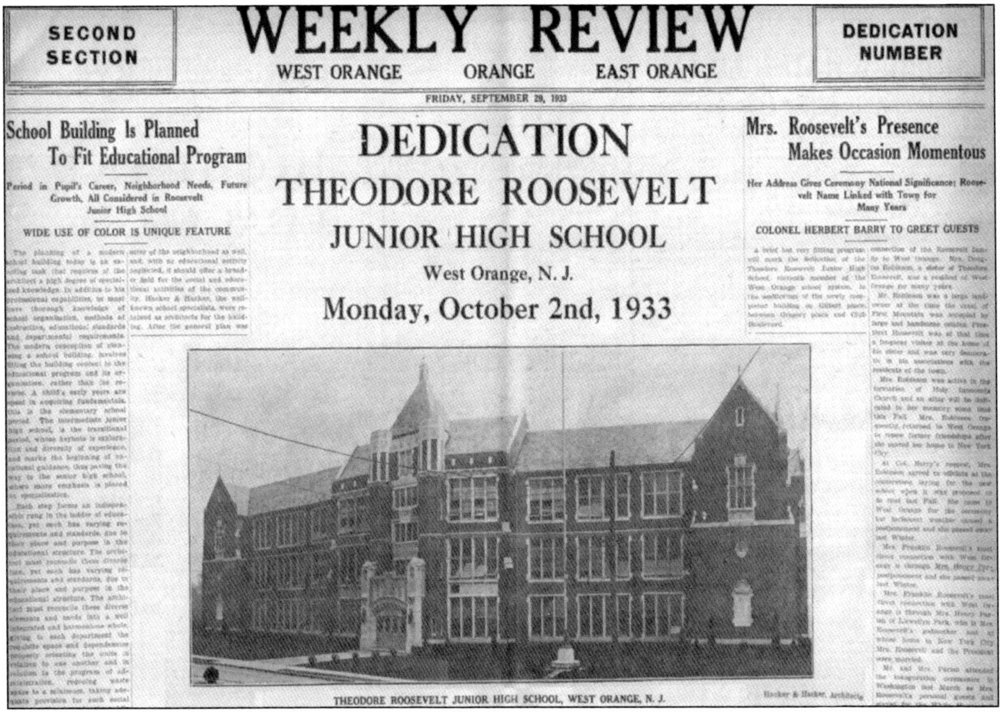

SECOND SECTION

WEEKLY REVIEW

WEST ORANGE ORANGE EAST ORANGE

DEDICATION NUMBER

FRIDAY, SEPTEMBER 29, 1933

School Building Is Planned To Fit Educational Program

Period in Pupil's Career, Neighborhood Needs, Future Growth, All Considered in Roosevelt Junior High School

WIDE USE OF COLOR IS UNIQUE FEATURE

DEDICATION
THEODORE ROOSEVELT
JUNIOR HIGH SCHOOL
West Orange, N. J.

Monday, October 2nd, 1933

Mrs. Roosevelt's Presence Makes Occasion Momentous

Her Address Gives Ceremony National Significance; Roosevelt Name Linked with Town for Many Years

COLONEL HERBERT BARRY TO GREET GUESTS

THEODORE ROOSEVELT JUNIOR HIGH SCHOOL, WEST ORANGE, N. J.

Hacker & Hacker, Architects

The second section of the local newspaper welcomed the opening of Roosevelt Junior High School in 1933. The school was named after Pres. Theodore Roosevelt, and his sister Corinne Roosevelt Robinson, a former resident of West Orange, was originally scheduled to attend the dedication. She unfortunately passed away prior to the opening, so his niece First Lady Eleanor Roosevelt attended the ceremonies on October 2, 1933, in her place.

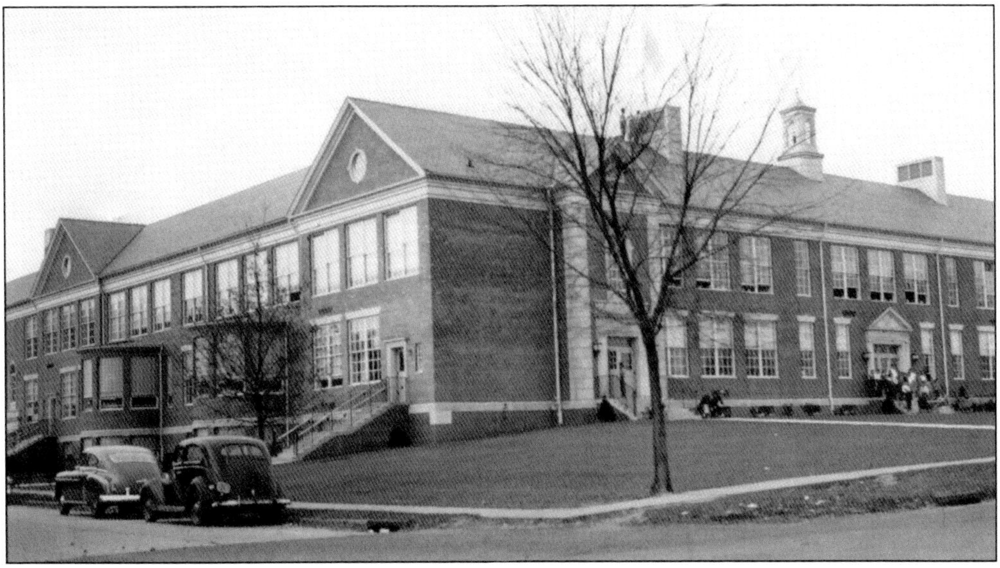

The first Pleasantdale School was built during the 1870s on Eagle Rock Avenue next to the Pleasantdale Cemetery. It was believed that decaying corpses from the neighboring graveyard had contaminated the well water for the school. A new school was built in 1902 a short distance away on Pleasant Valley Way and is seen here in the 1950s.

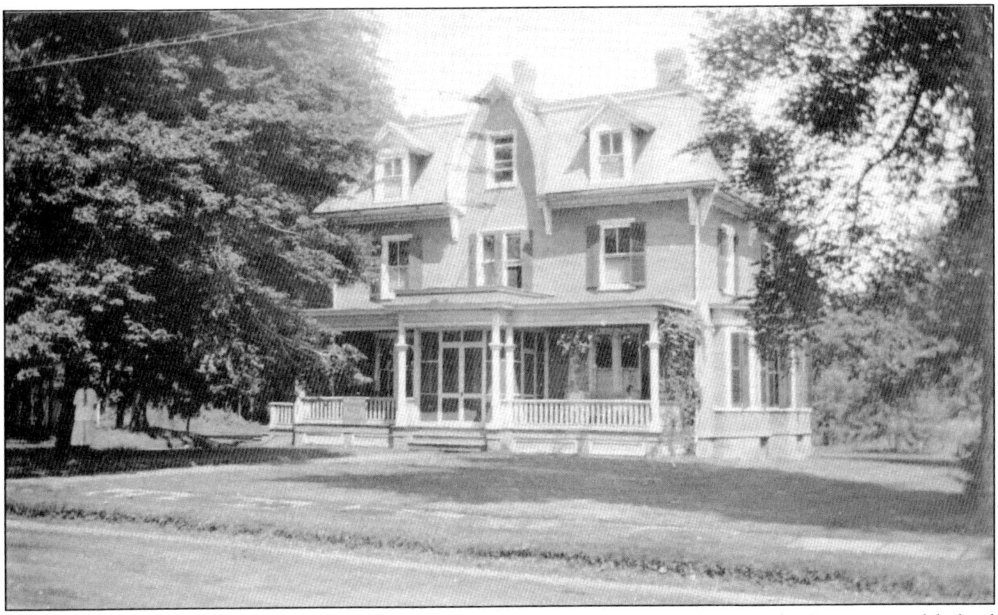

This Fairview Avenue home is pictured in 1919. New York banker John Crosby Brown established it as the Brownery, a convalescent and rest home for nurses, in 1907. It operated until 1914. At the cost of $5 per week, it offered nurses a refreshing country setting as a therapeutic reprieve from their hectic work in New York City.

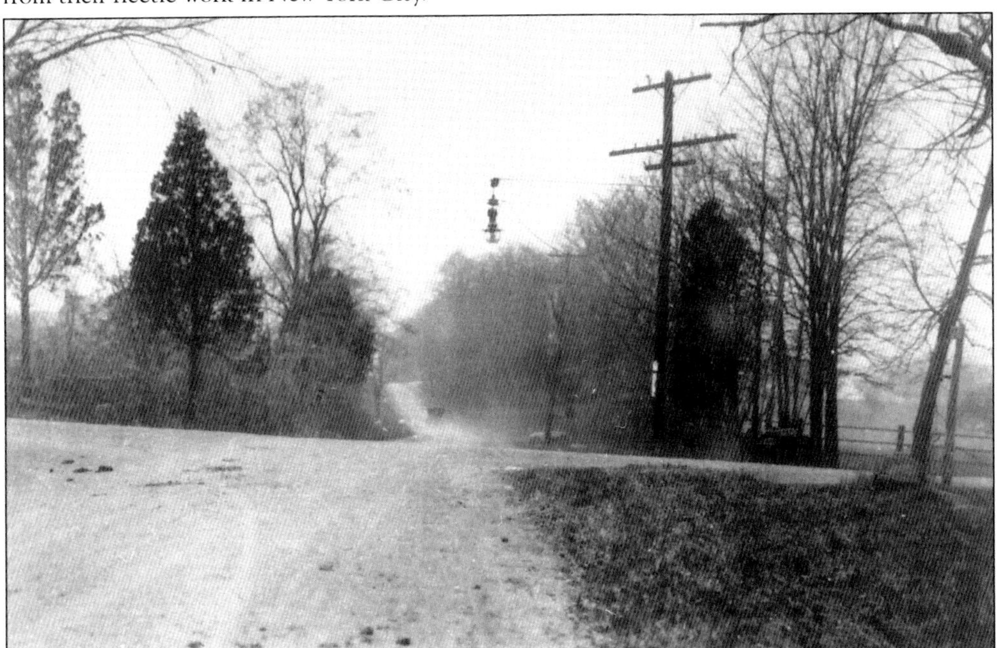

In 1806, the State of New Jersey chartered the Newark and Mount Pleasant Turnpike, and it passes through West Orange as present-day Mount Pleasant Avenue. The route was designated as New Jersey State Route 10 in 1927 and was officially defined in 1953 as beginning at the intersection with Prospect Avenue. The rural nature of Mount Pleasant Avenue is seen here, in a view looking west from the Prospect Avenue intersection around 1903.

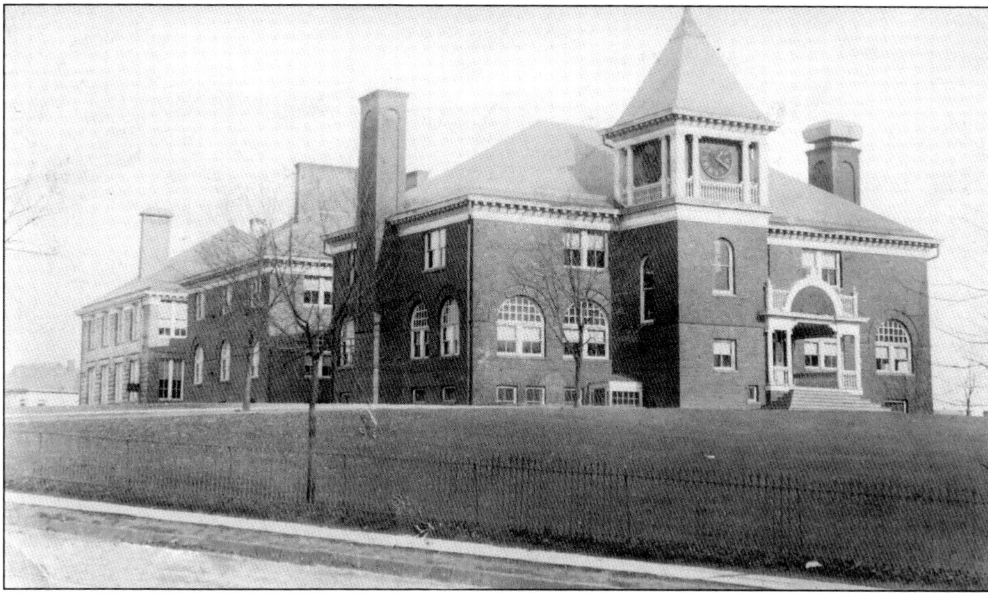

The Washington Street School opened in February 1895, and by the time this photograph was taken in 1915, it had already undergone several additions. The original brick building was completed at a total cost of about $18,000, and its main feature was an ornamental facade with a tower above the main entrance showcasing what was then considered to be the new town clock.

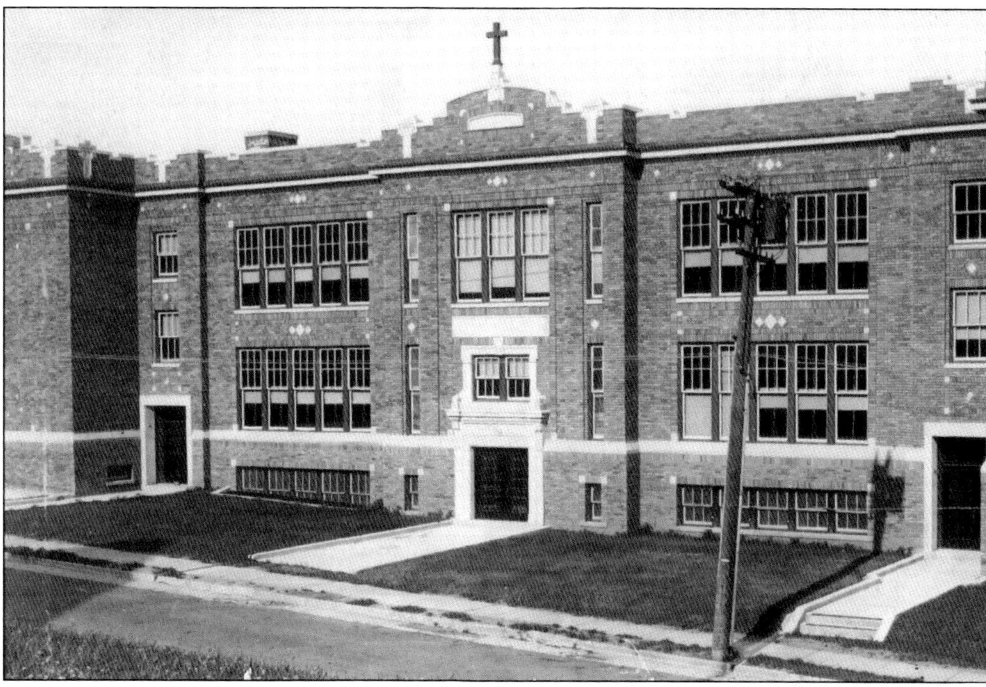

Our Lady of Lourdes parochial grammar school is seen here shortly after it opened on September 8, 1925, on Valley Way across from the Eagle Rock School. Only three years after opening, the school was already inadequate due to swelling numbers of enrollment, and four classrooms and an auditorium were added. The grammar school closed in 2006, and the Mount Carmel Guild Academy now leases classroom space here.

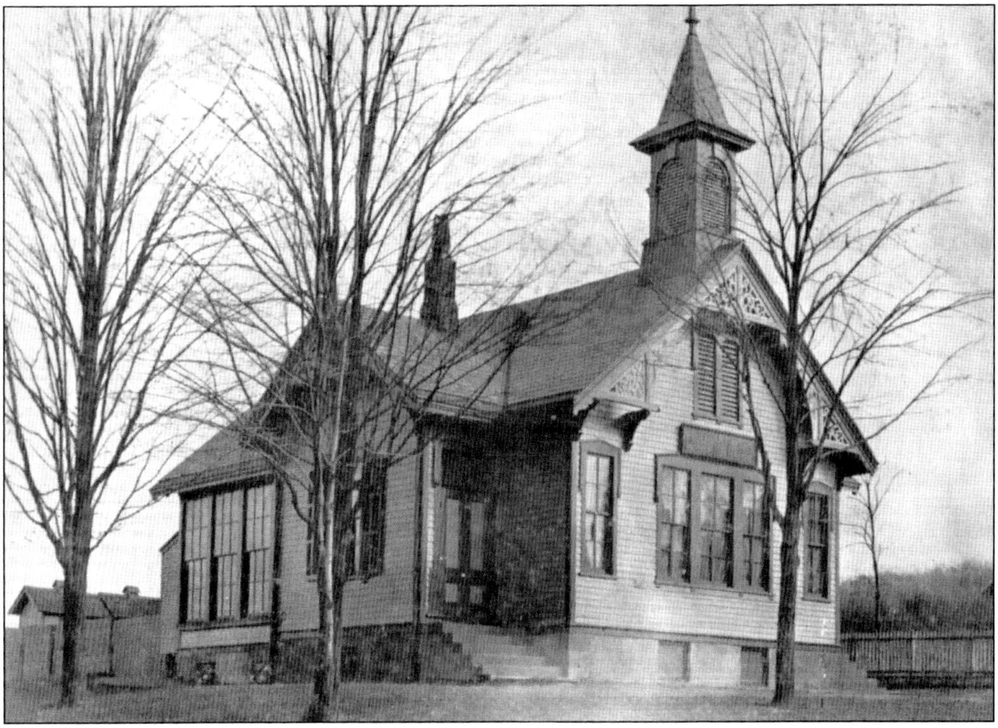

It remains unclear when the Mount Pleasant School, seen here, was first constructed, but it appeared on maps as early as 1881. This building is no longer standing but was once located near the site of the former West Orange First Aid Squad Building on Mount Pleasant Place. In 1911, there were two teachers and one janitor for 56 students in grades one through six.

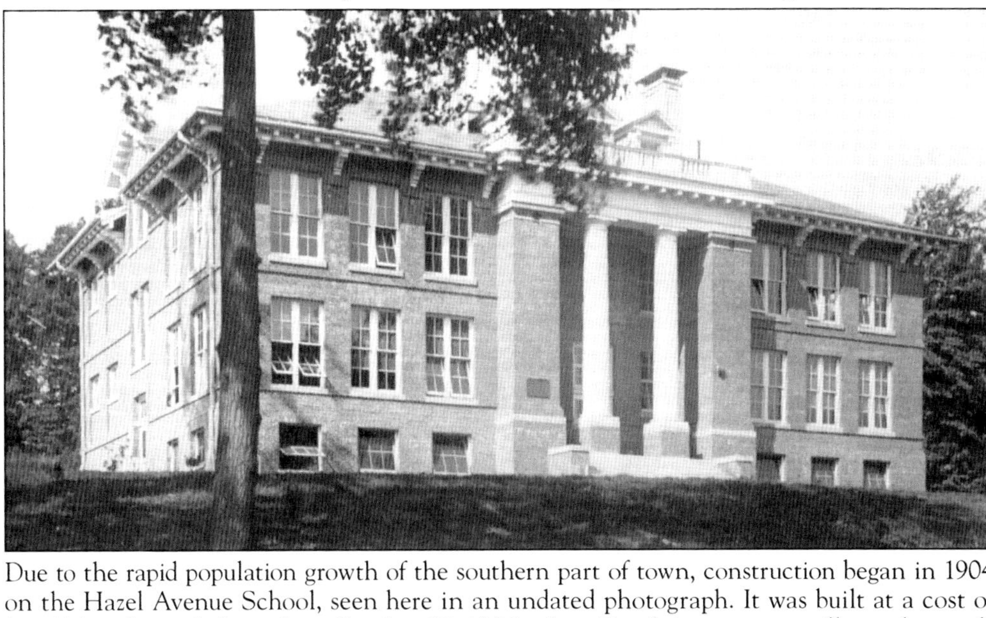

Due to the rapid population growth of the southern part of town, construction began in 1904 on the Hazel Avenue School, seen here in an undated photograph. It was built at a cost of $94,000 and was dedicated on October 19, 1906, when Hazel Avenue was still mostly woods and farmland. An addition was built in 1917, and the school still exists today with kindergarten through fifth grade.

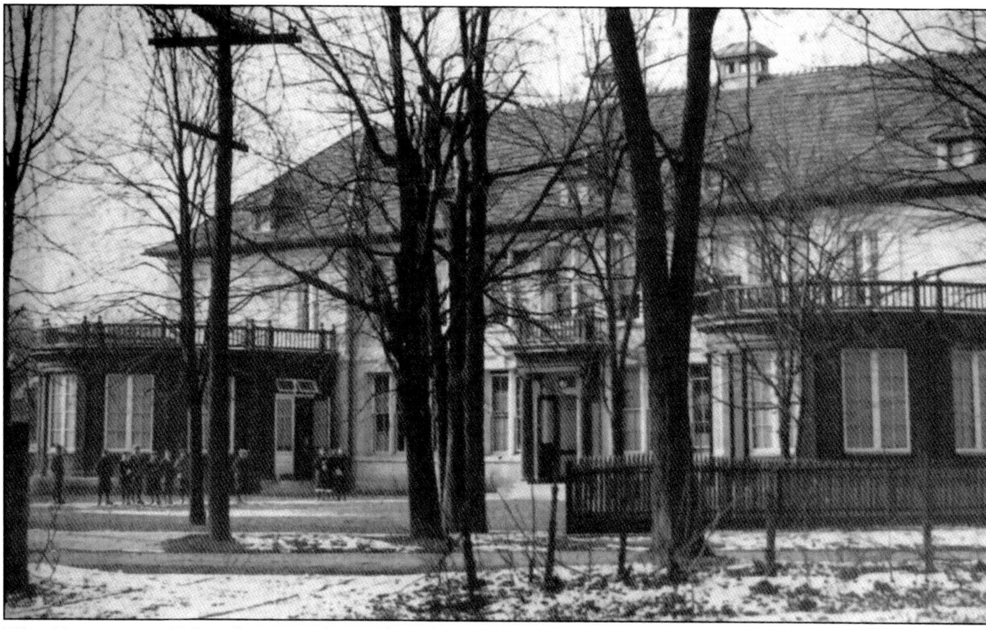

The Fairmount School is seen here shortly after in opened in 1912. It was located only 40 yards behind the high school on Gaston Street that was destroyed by fire in 1913. Fairmount School fortunately was not damaged and temporarily served as a high school until a new high school was constructed. Both were demolished in 1972 to make way for the John P. Renna Jr. House for senior citizens, which occupies the site today.

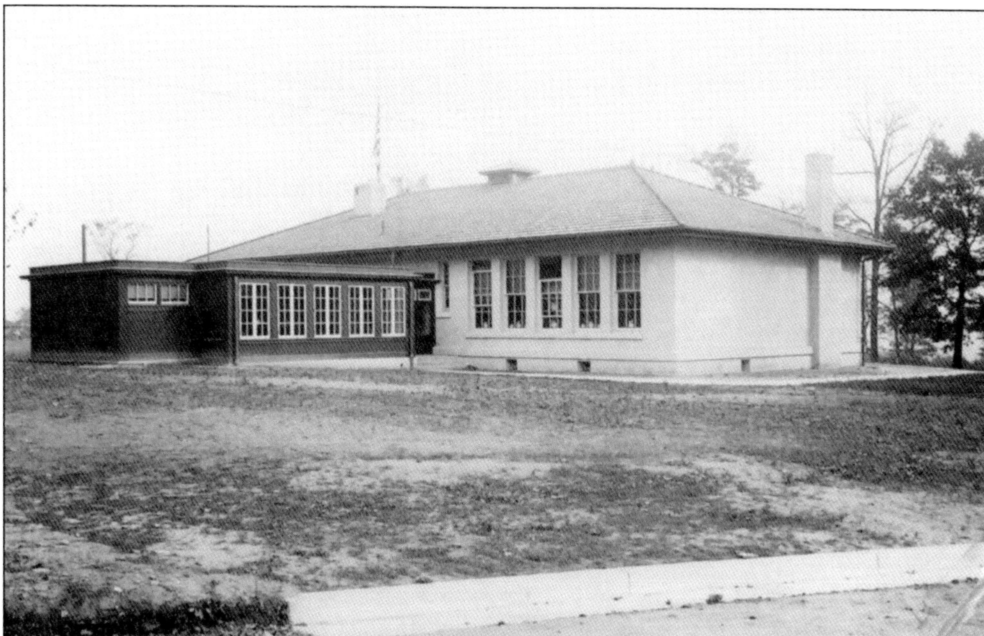

Helen Woodward lead an effort by several local mothers to get Andrew Allen from the Gregory neighborhood elected to the West Orange Board of Education in 1913. Allen subsequently pushed through a referendum that appropriated funds to build the Gregory School on the corner of Gregory Avenue and Walker Road, seen here shortly after it opened in 1914. (GS.)

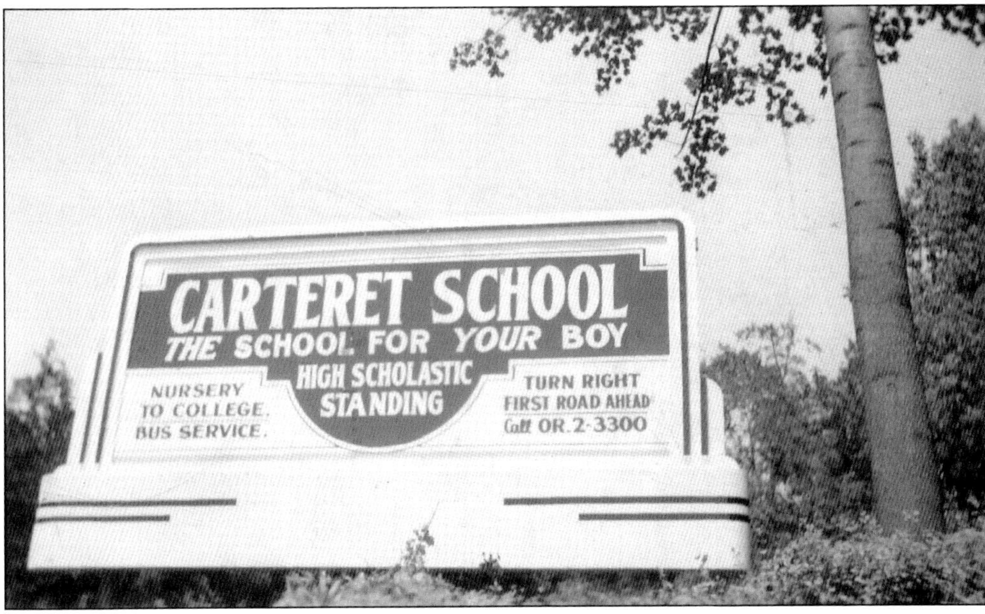

The Carteret Academy opened on September 25, 1901, in Orange, and by the 1920s, it was nearing the limit of any further potential expansion. Property was eventually purchased in West Orange, and a new school was erected. With the move, the school also changed its name from the Carteret Academy to the Carteret School. This billboard once sat on Northfield Avenue.

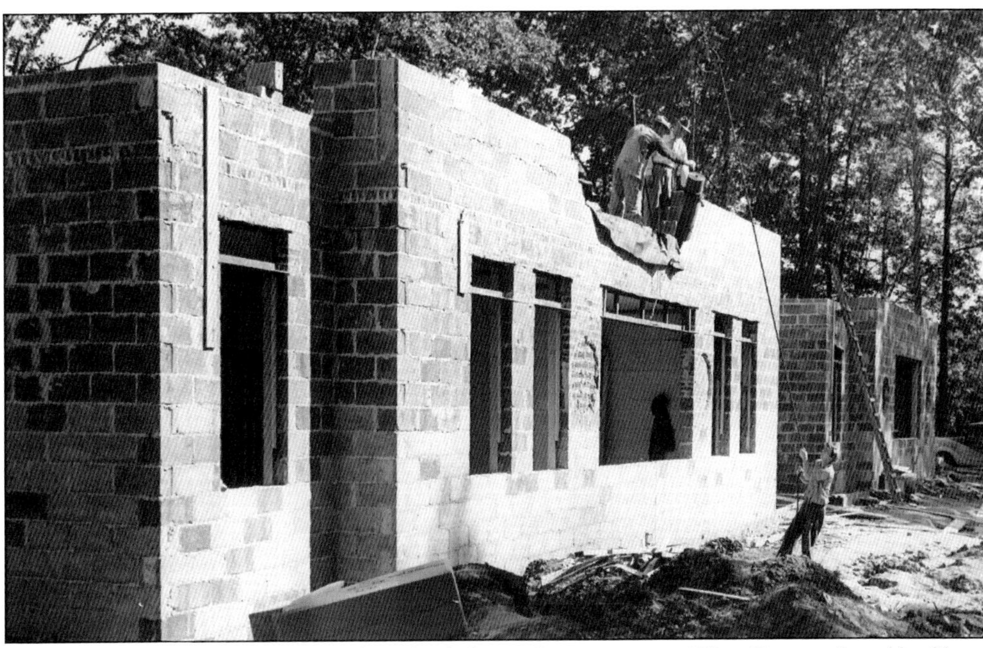

As early as 1930, the Carteret Academy had planned on moving to West Orange. Land had been purchased that year near the site of the current-day Rock Spring Country Club, and construction was set to begin. Legal matters developed over its tax-exempt status, and plans were abandoned and the property sold. A new site on Prospect Avenue was eventually purchased, and by 1939, construction can be seen nearing completion.

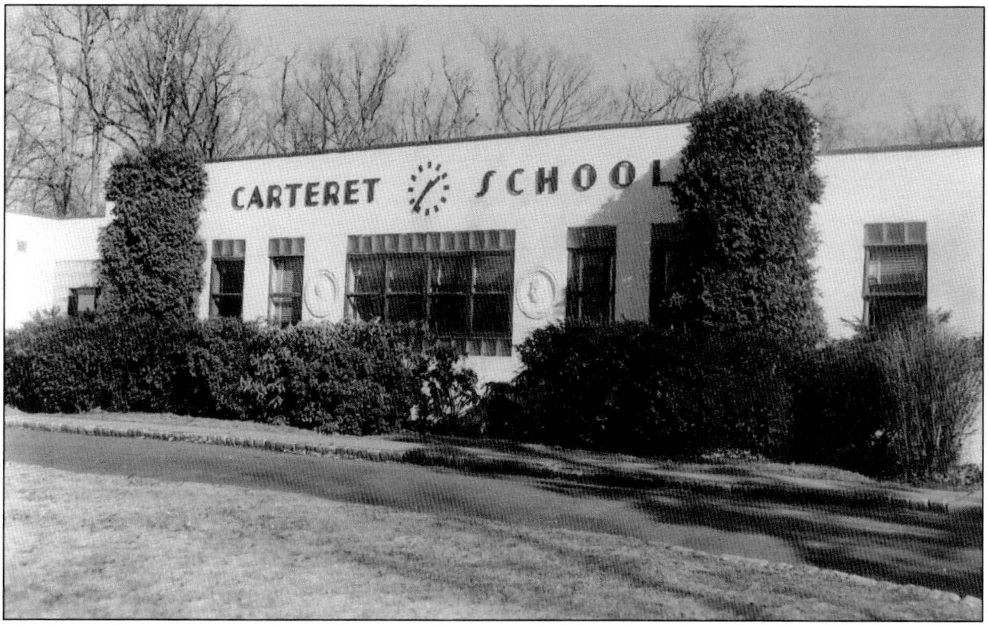

The Carteret School was a private boys' school that opened on January 6, 1940. The school was constructed on the former property of John Crosby Brown (see page 38), and his son William Adams Brown, pastor, was invited to the school's opening. In his letter of acceptance to the invitation, he expresses that his late father would have highly approved of the schools construction on their former land.

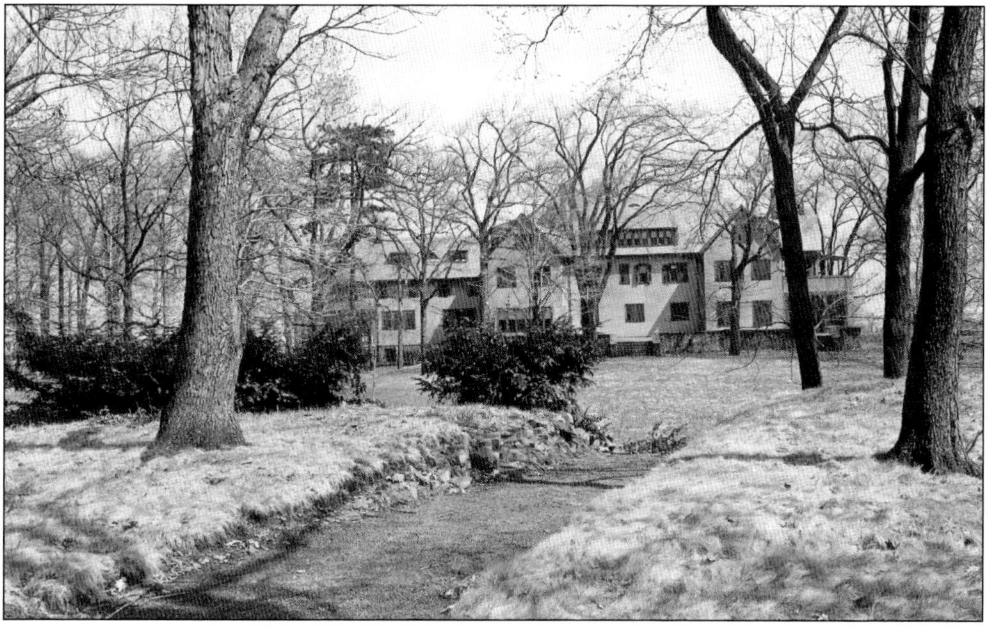

Leonor Loree was a wealthy railroad executive who purchased property on Ridge Road off Mount Pleasant Avenue in 1918 and built this mansion on a sprawling 31-acre estate. Known as Bowood, it had 27 rooms with 8 bathrooms and many outbuildings, riding stables, farm buildings, greenhouses, tennis courts, a caretaker's cottage, and various garages. Bowood is seen here shortly after Loree passed away on September 6, 1940, at age 82.

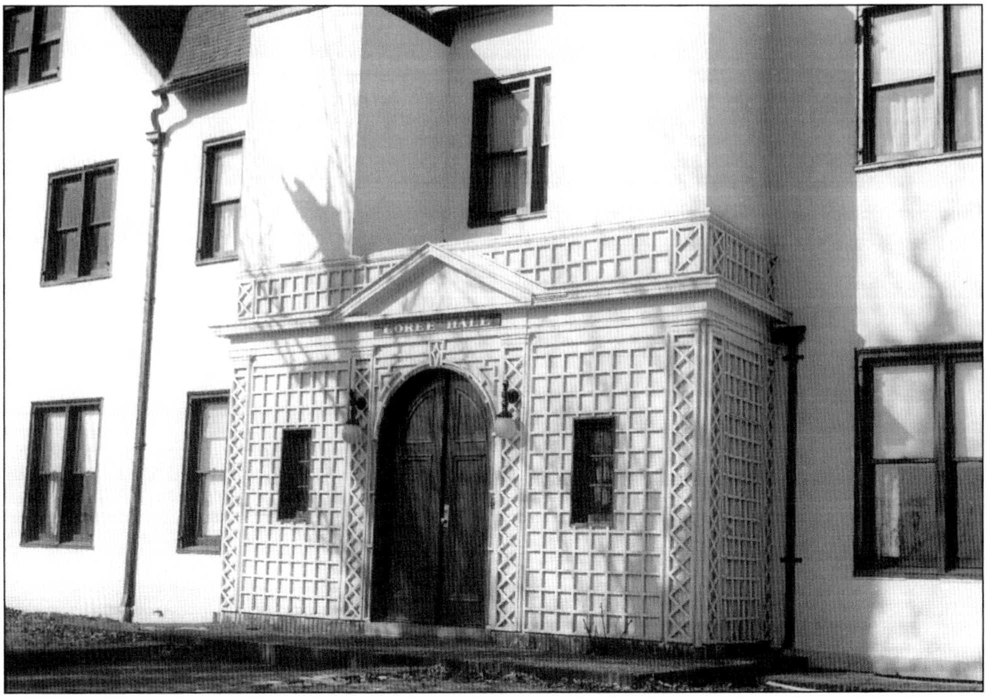

Shortly after the Carteret School opened in 1940, it purchased the Delano estate adjoining its property. The school acquired the nearby Loree estate in 1943, increasing its property from 40 to 71 acres. Bowood was converted into a dormitory and renamed Loree Hall, seen here in 1944. The Carteret School closed in 1970, and all the buildings on the former Loree property once used by the school were eventually demolished.

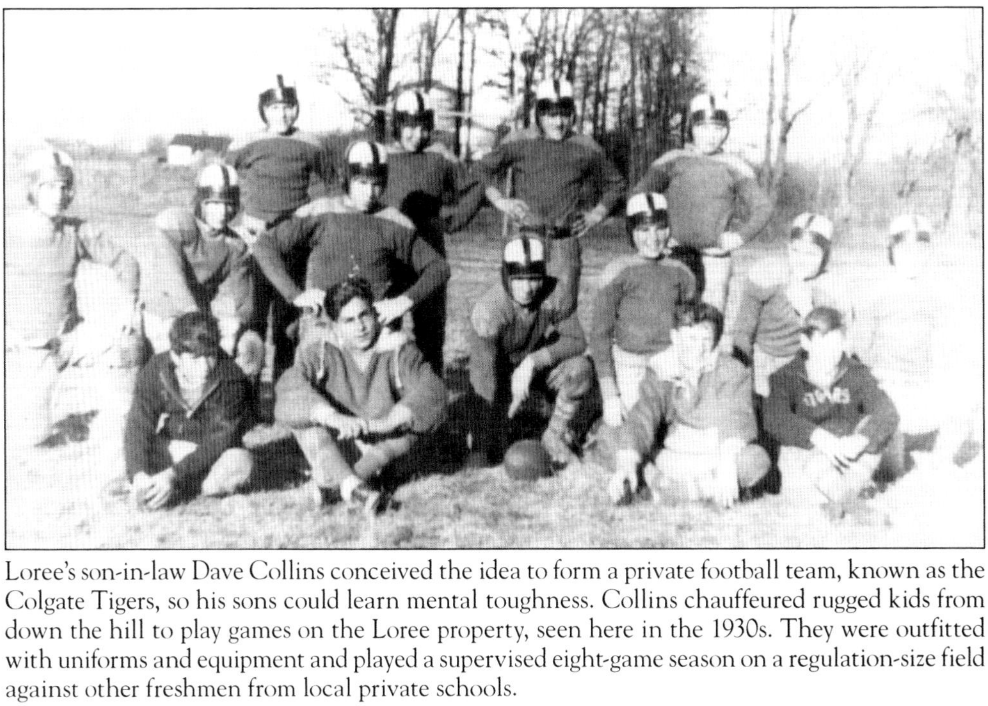

Loree's son-in-law Dave Collins conceived the idea to form a private football team, known as the Colgate Tigers, so his sons could learn mental toughness. Collins chauffeured rugged kids from down the hill to play games on the Loree property, seen here in the 1930s. They were outfitted with uniforms and equipment and played a supervised eight-game season on a regulation-size field against other freshmen from local private schools.

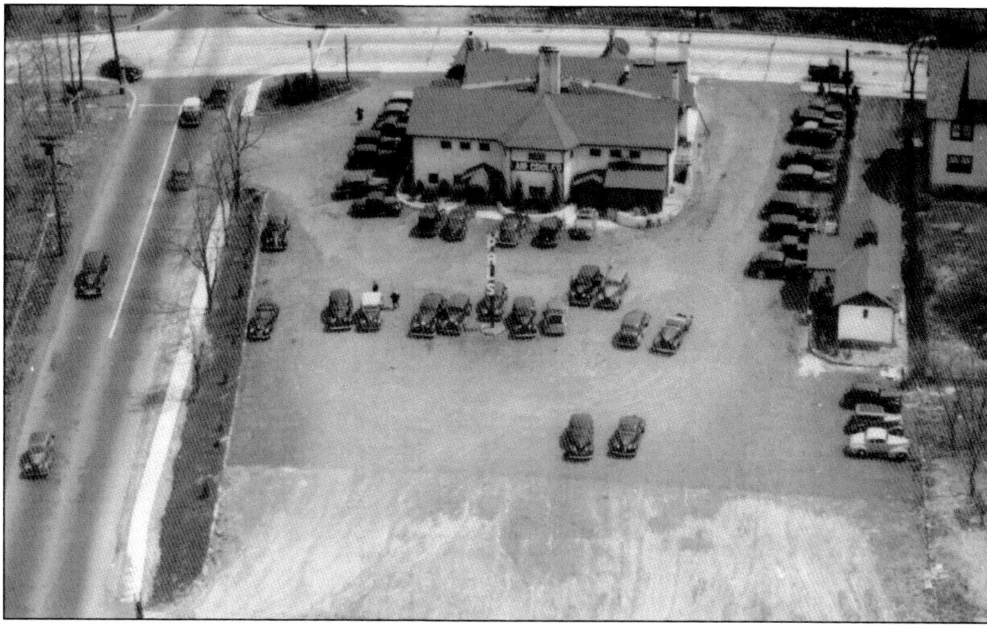

Childhood pals Marty Horn and Roy Sale first opened a small hot dog stand near the corner of Prospect and Eagle Rock Avenues on May 18, 1932. It eventually expanded to a restaurant known as Pal's Cabin, whose name was inspired by them being longtime friends. The restaurant can be seen in this aerial view from the late 1930s that captures the once rural nature of the now busy intersection.

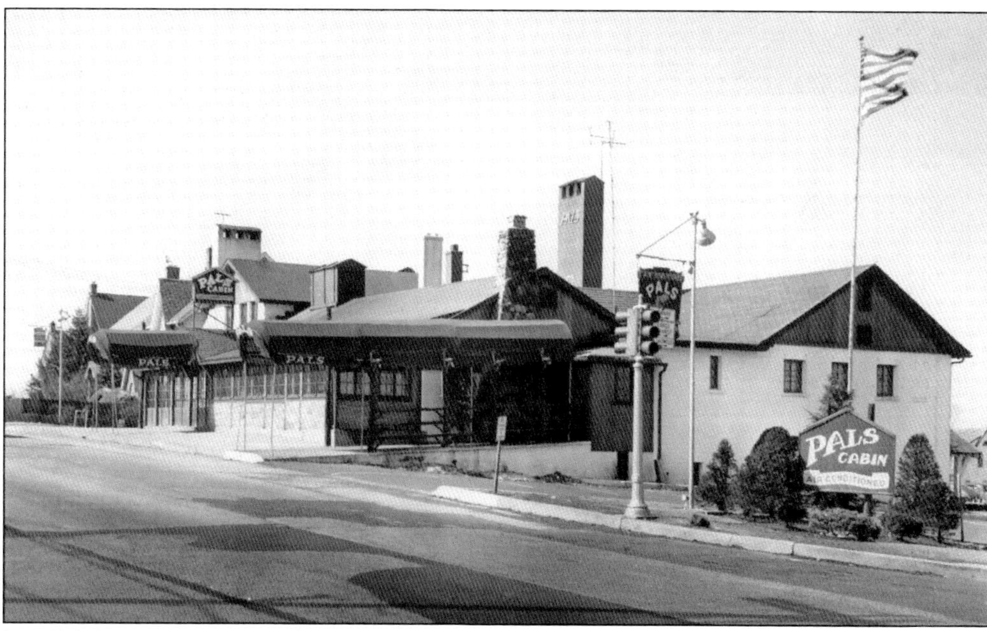

In 1936, Marty's sister Josephine Horn Simmons joined them as a third pal, and business grew with a series of additions to the restaurant. Roy Sale was killed in an automobile accident in 1941, and Josephine passed away in 1953. At that time, Horn's sons Don and Marty Jr. with sister Carol became involved in one of New Jersey's most famous charcoal-broiled steak houses, seen here around 1945.

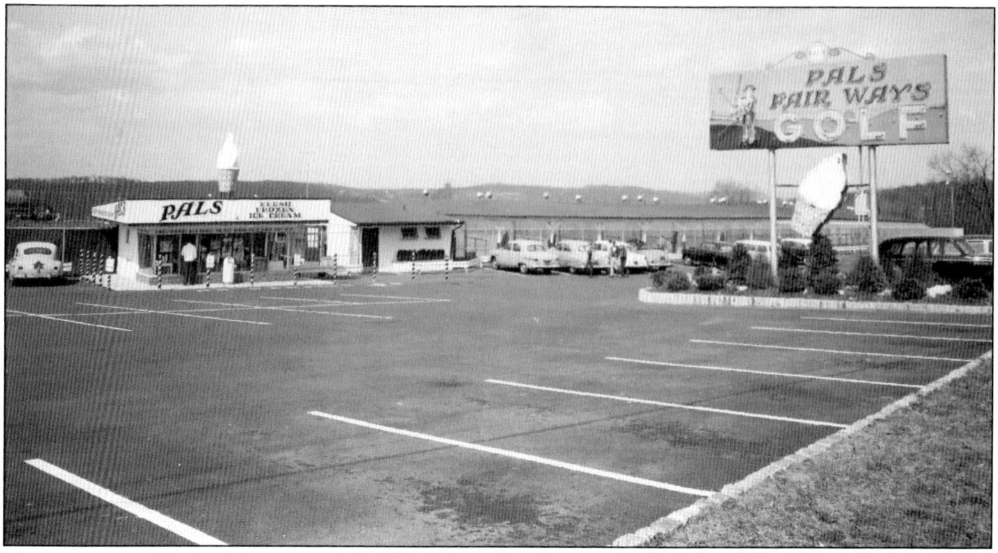

The owners of Pal's Cabin opened a driving range opposite the restaurant in 1953 called Pal's Fairways. On September 25, 1957, a New Mexico businessman successfully landed his Piper Tri-Pacer airplane here after running out of fuel—with only minor injuries and damage. In the early 1960s, a large shopping center was constructed on this site at this intersection of Prospect and Eagle Rock Avenues; it still remains today.

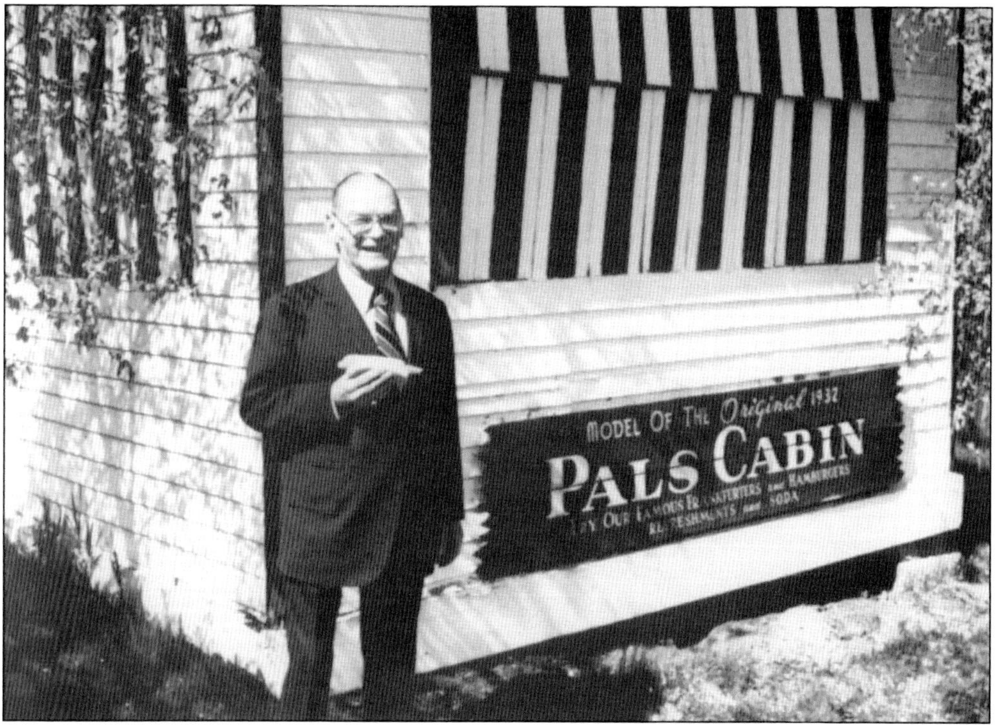

Marty Horn Sr. is seen on May 8, 1982, in a publicity shot to commemorate the restaurant's 50th anniversary. Marty Sr. passed away in 1984, but his legacy continued until May 18, 2013, when the restaurant celebrated its 81st and last anniversary. Pal's Cabin closed its doors on June 1 that year and was soon demolished but remains as an inseparable part of West Orange's proud history.

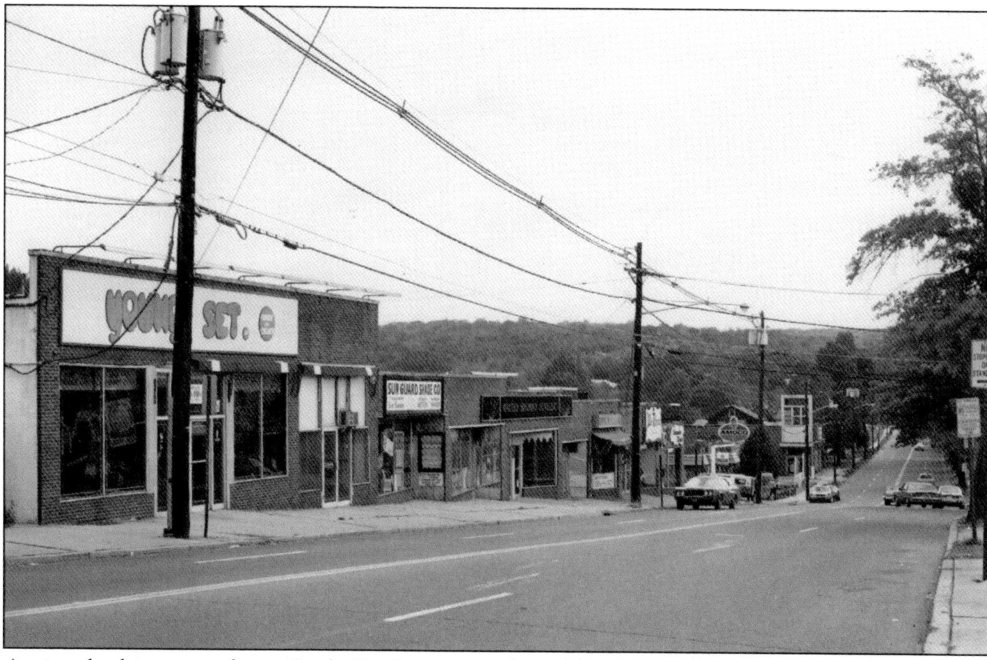

A view looking east down Eagle Rock Avenue from Pleasant Valley Way in the 1970s is very recognizable to a similar view in the Pleasantdale section of town today. The earliest documented history of Pleasantdale dates to the diary of a young girl Jemima Condict, who lived opposite this location where she was born on the family farm on August 24, 1754.

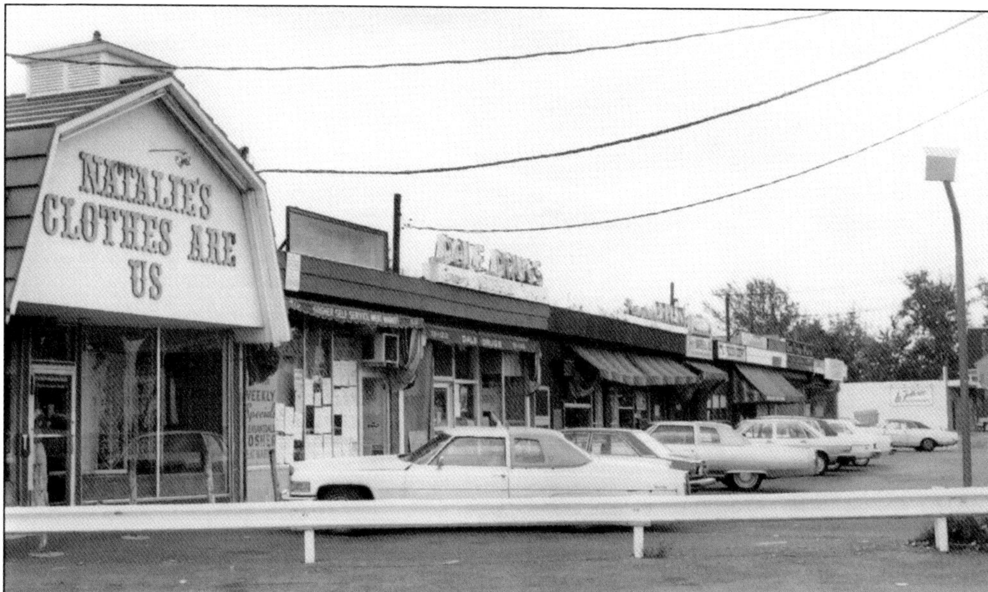

This 1970s view of what is commonly referred to as the Pleasantdale center near the intersection of Eagle Rock Avenue and Pleasant Valley Way is practically identical today. The buildings are still standing, and only the names of the businesses have changed. This main thoroughfare between the first and second mountains of West Orange derives its name from the pleasant valley through which it passes from Verona to Milburn.

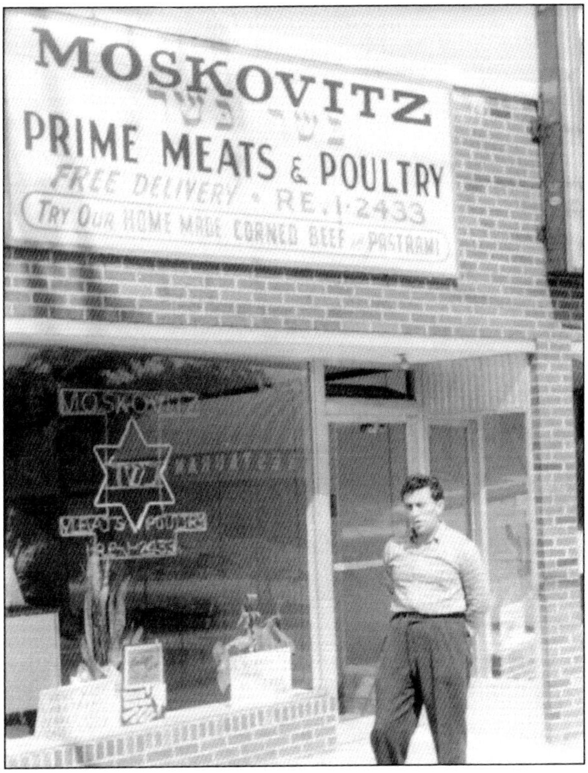

Irving Moskovitz fled his native Czechoslovakia from the horrors of the Nazis and the holocaust during World War II and eventually came to West Orange. He is seen here in an undated photograph at the kosher butcher shop he opened in 1955 at 643 Eagle Rock Avenue. He retired in 1975 and was tragically killed crossing Pleasant Valley Way on October 15, 1997. (RMB.)

The smoldering wreckage of the Trimotor biplane that crashed near the Pleasantdale Cemetery on Eagle Rock Avenue can be seen on June 10, 1942. It exploded on impact and plunged 10 feet into the ground, and the pilot Richard Behrens was tragically killed in the crash. This is the present-day location of the Crestmont Gardens Condominium complex on Conforti Avenue.

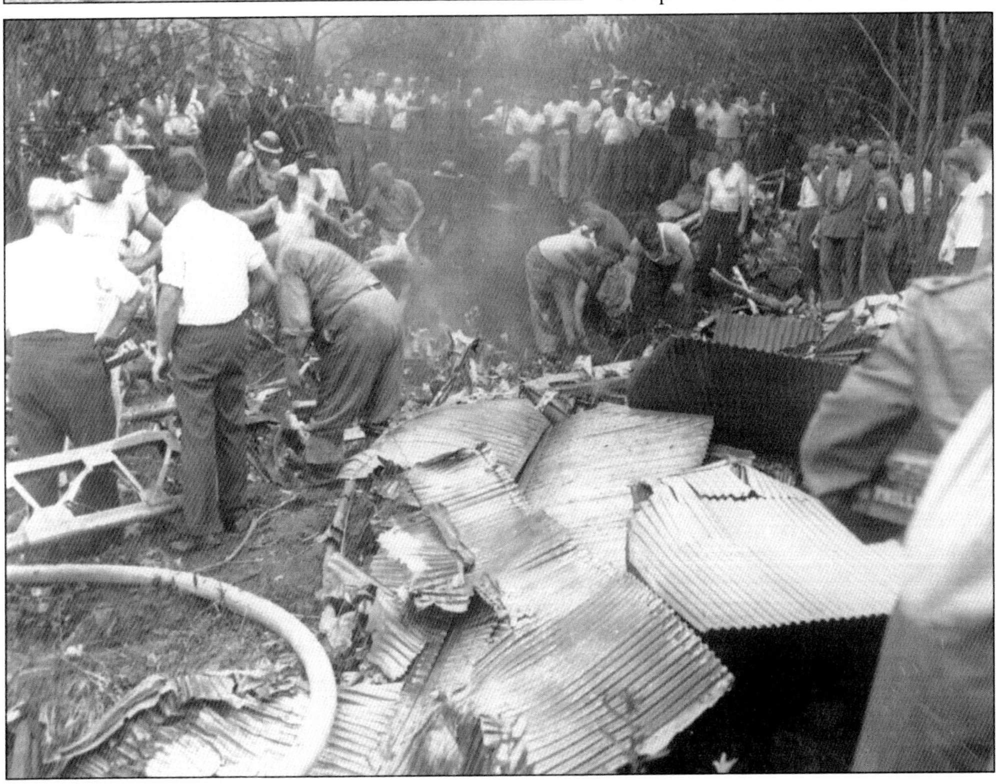

The West Orange Water Company was formed in 1892 as a separate commercial venture that shared the town name but had no connection to the town government. It installed the first water supply system in town, which it completed by the end of 1893. Company offices are seen around 1905 on Valley Road, and were relocated to 20 Northfield Avenue in 1915.

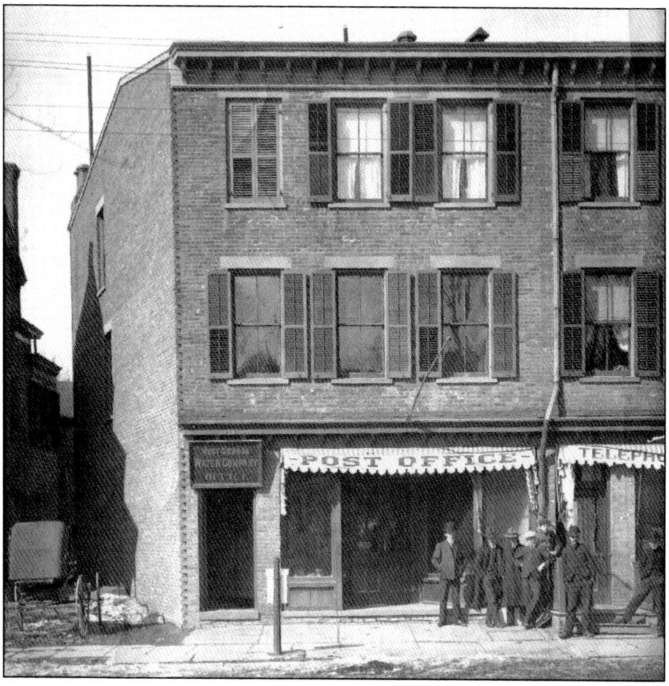

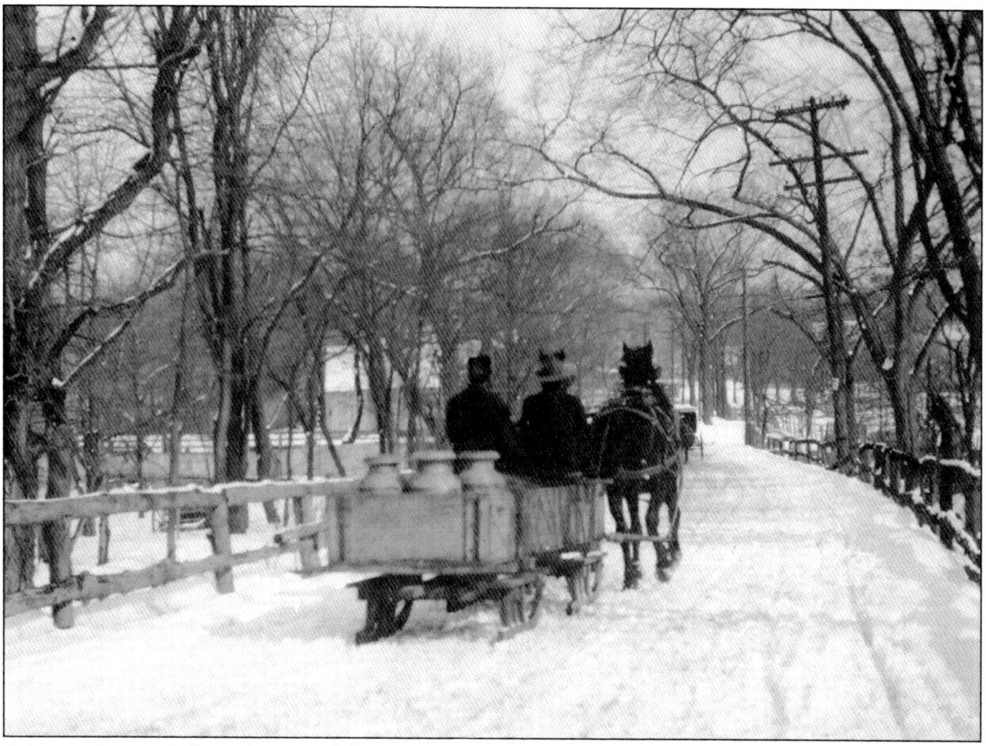

A horse-drawn sled can be seen delivering milk cans while revealing the once rural surroundings near the bottom of Northfield Avenue on March 5, 1907. Many farms still existed in the area at the time, and sleds were a common sight and nearly a necessity during winter months when snow removal from roads was not immediately forthcoming, if at all.

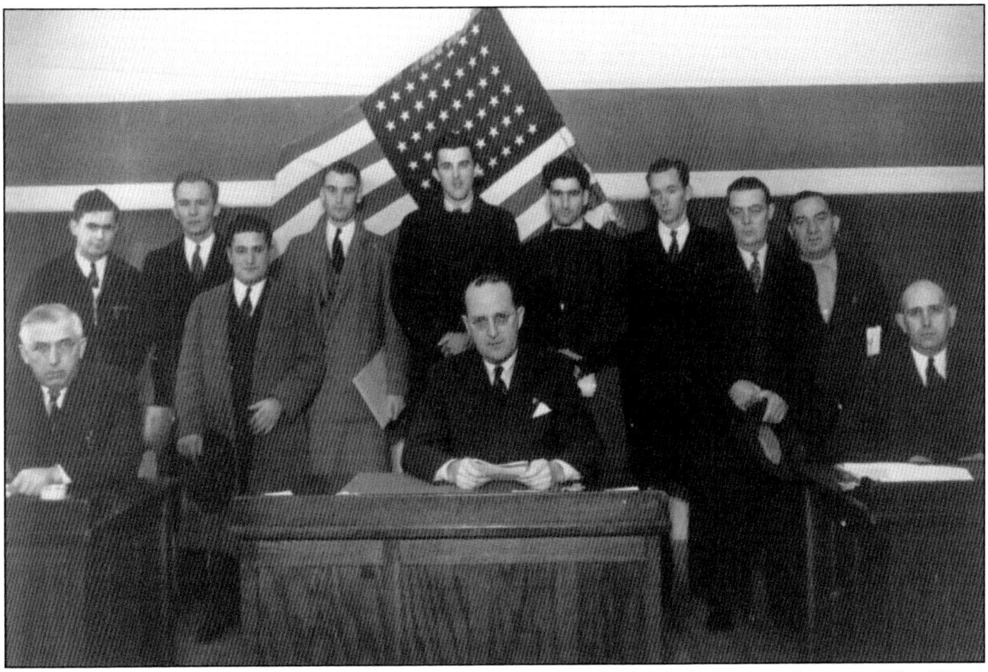

In 1940, Congress enacted into law the first peacetime draft in American history. The West Orange draft board administrators seen here on November 27, 1940, are (seated from left to right) Verner Davis, Frank Moran, and Thomas Reagan. Standing behind them in the board office in the Macintosh Building at 14 Northfield Avenue is the first group of inductees to enter service from West Orange into various branches of the military.

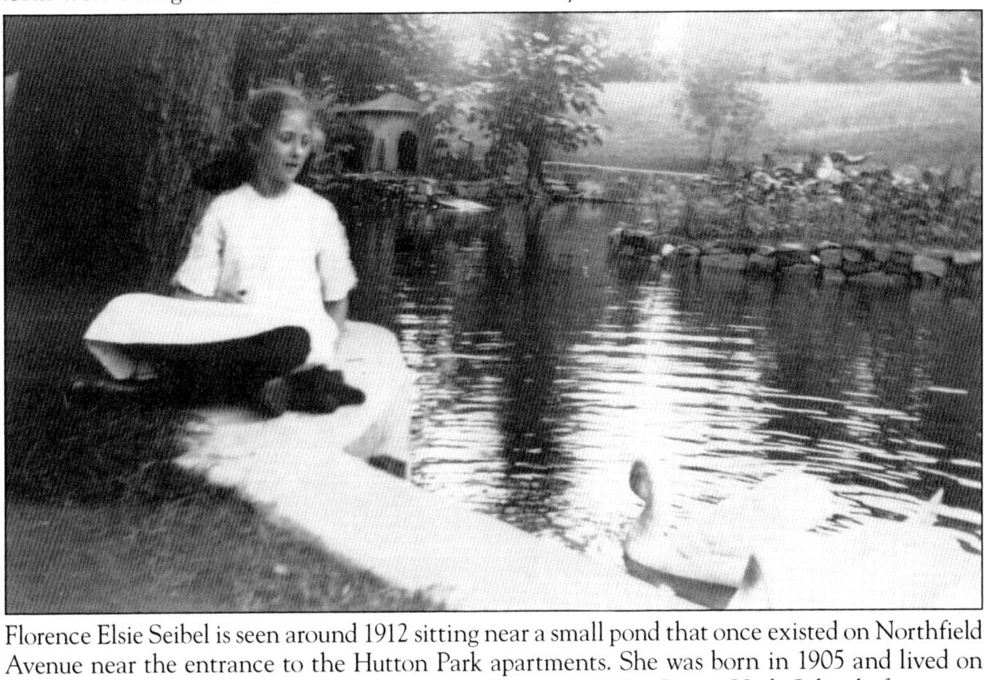

Florence Elsie Seibel is seen around 1912 sitting near a small pond that once existed on Northfield Avenue near the entrance to the Hutton Park apartments. She was born in 1905 and lived on nearby Longview Street. Florence Elsie attended Gaston Street Junior High School after it was rebuilt following the 1913 fire. (BR.)

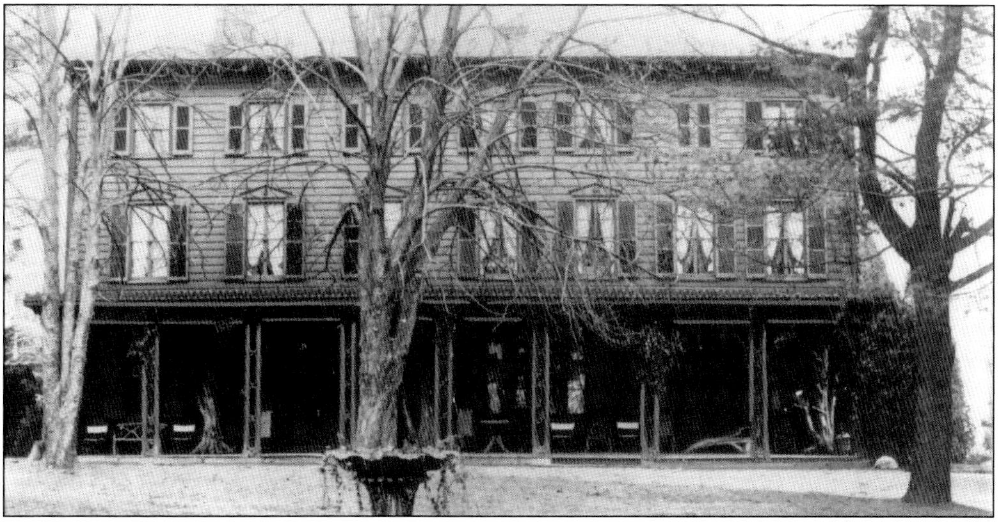

In 1820, a mineral spring was discovered on a farm off Northfield Avenue and found to have medicinal values. The following year, the Orange Springs Hotel was erected and became a resort, which prospered for about a decade. Following several owners and renovations, it became the new clubhouse for the Essex County Country Club in 1888. Seen here in an undated photograph, the structure was torn down in 1947.

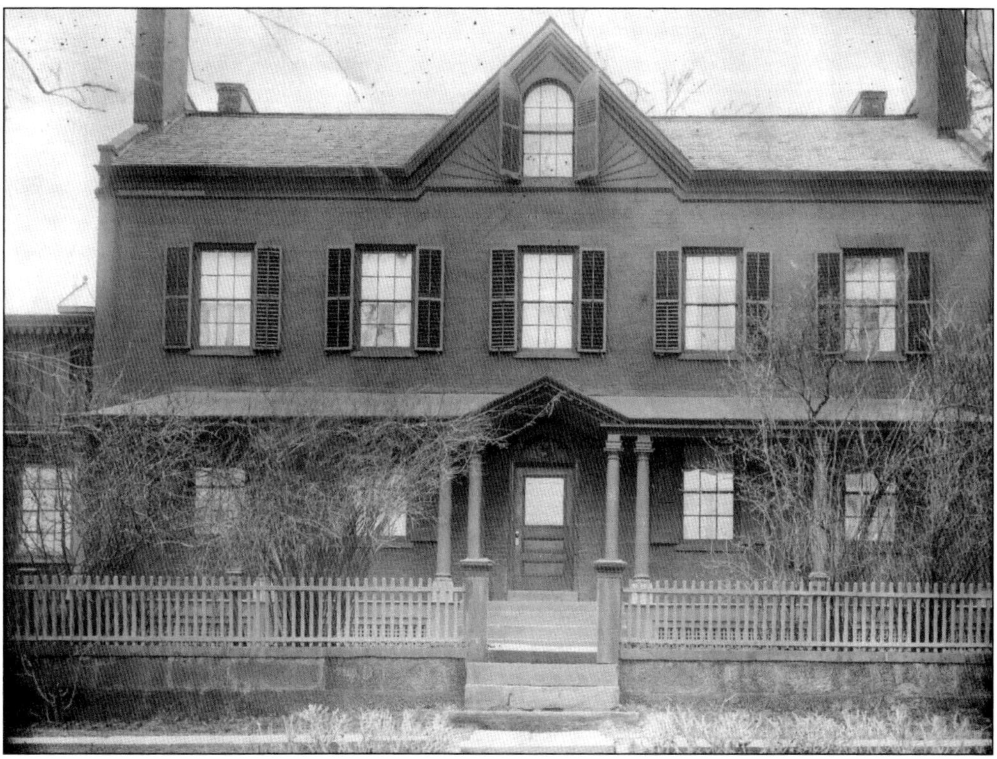

A 1920s photograph shows the brick mansion built by Caleb Harrison in 1808 on a large tract of land at the base of the mountain on Northfield Avenue. It was appropriately named Mountain Foot and considered to be an outstanding masterpiece of Colonial-style architecture. It was razed in 1969 when the current-day office building at 100 Northfield Avenue was built.

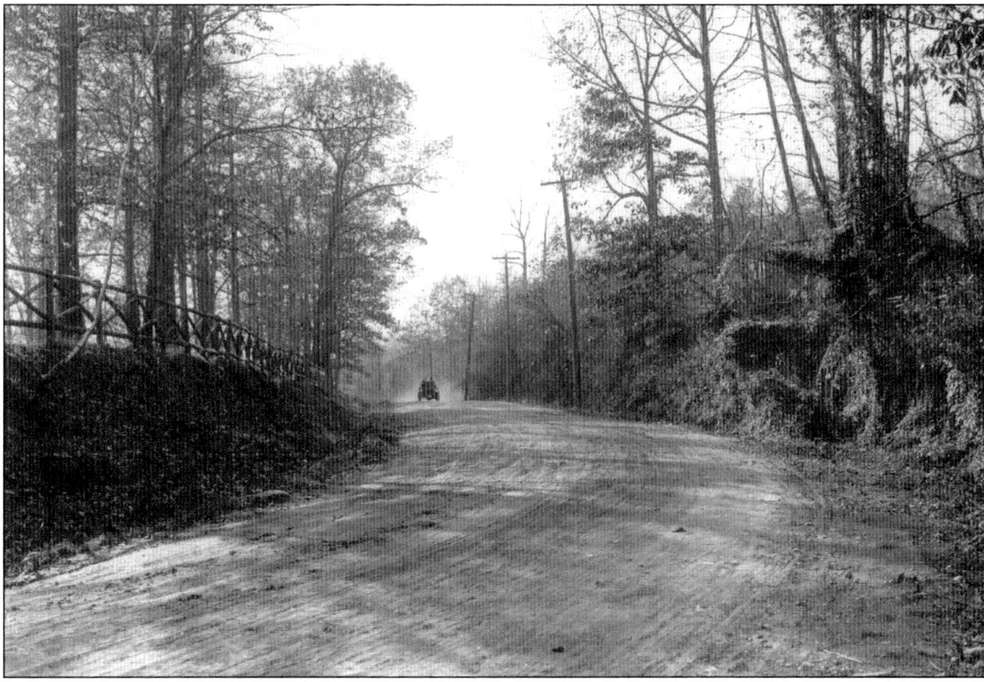

A lone automobile can be seen blazing a dusty trail on Northfield Avenue in 1908 when most traffic was still horse and wagon. This view looking west near the summit of the first mountain shows what was known for many years as Blue Birds Bend. The steep grade could make passage both difficult and dangerous, depending on road conditions.

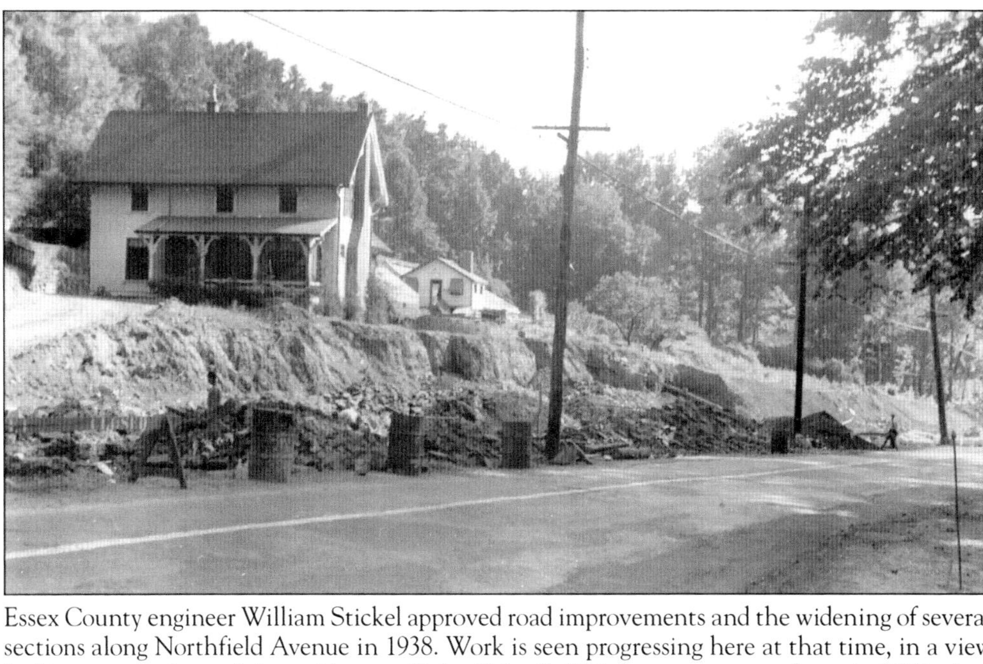

Essex County engineer William Stickel approved road improvements and the widening of several sections along Northfield Avenue in 1938. Work is seen progressing here at that time, in a view looking east in front of the residence of John Schroll. This house was torn down in 1958 when construction began on the present-day site of the Ronjolyn Apartments on Northfield Avenue.

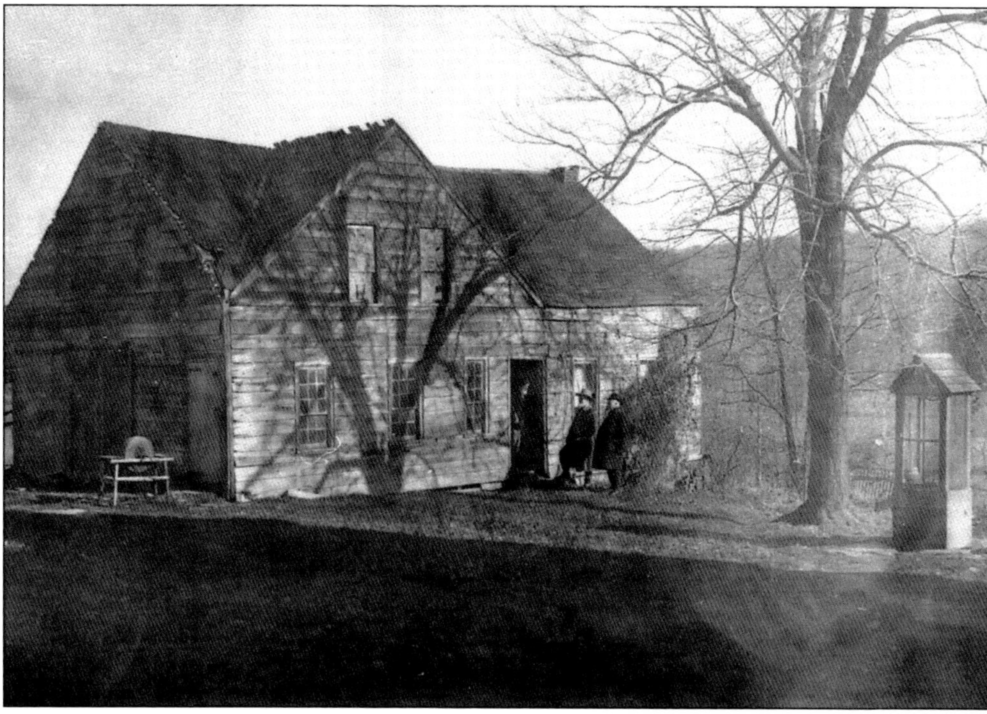

A gristmill and well, where water was hand drawn by a bucket and rope, can been at the old Condict homestead around 1903. This property is now part of the Francis Byrne Golf Course and once was near the intersection of Pleasant Valley Way and Old Indian Road, then known as Mountain Avenue.

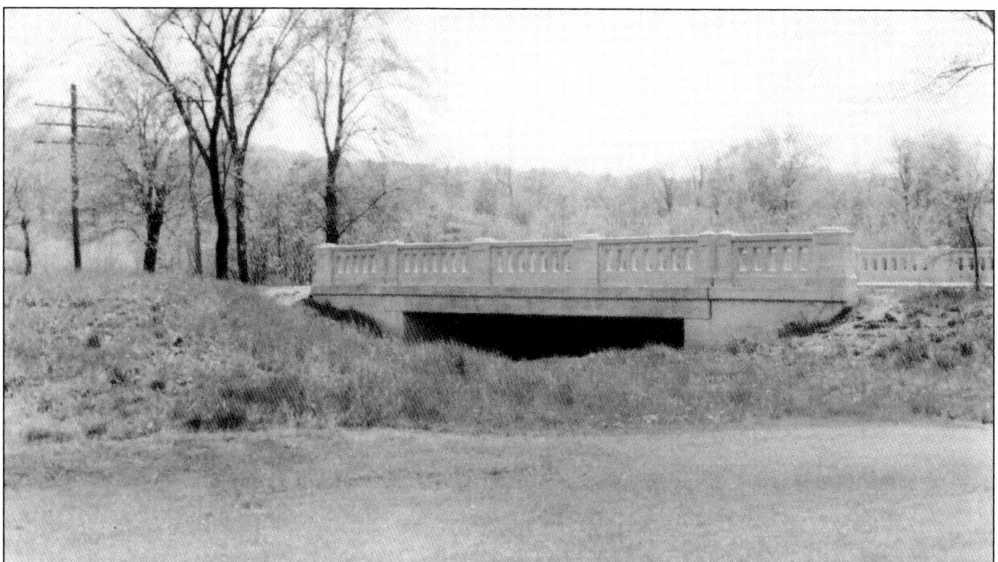

The newly constructed bridge is seen about 1928 over the West Branch of the Rahway River on Old Indian Road, then known as Mountain Avenue. The name was changed to Old Indian Road in 1937. This originally was the southernmost end of Pleasant Valley Way, where the road made a left turn onto Mountain Avenue. The bridge was most recently replaced in 1998.

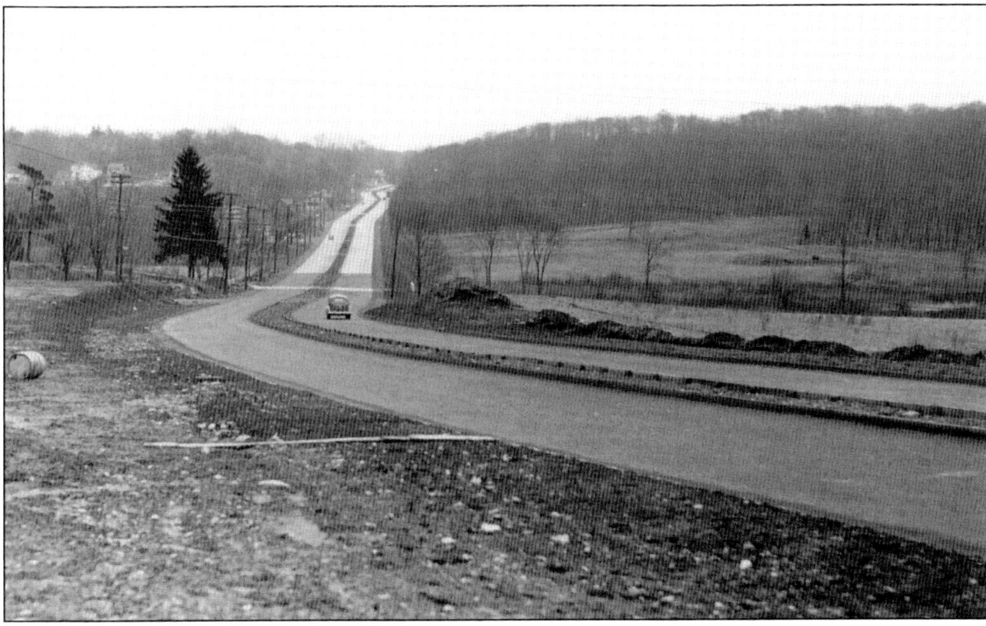

In 1937, Pleasant Valley Way was extended south to connect with Northfield Avenue. Prior to that time, it only went as far as today's Old Indian Road, then known as Mountain Avenue. A view looking east from the newly opened connection with Pleasant Valley Way shows a mostly barren Northfield Avenue at that time. The vacant land seen in the distance to the right is occupied by the South Mountain Recreation Complex today.

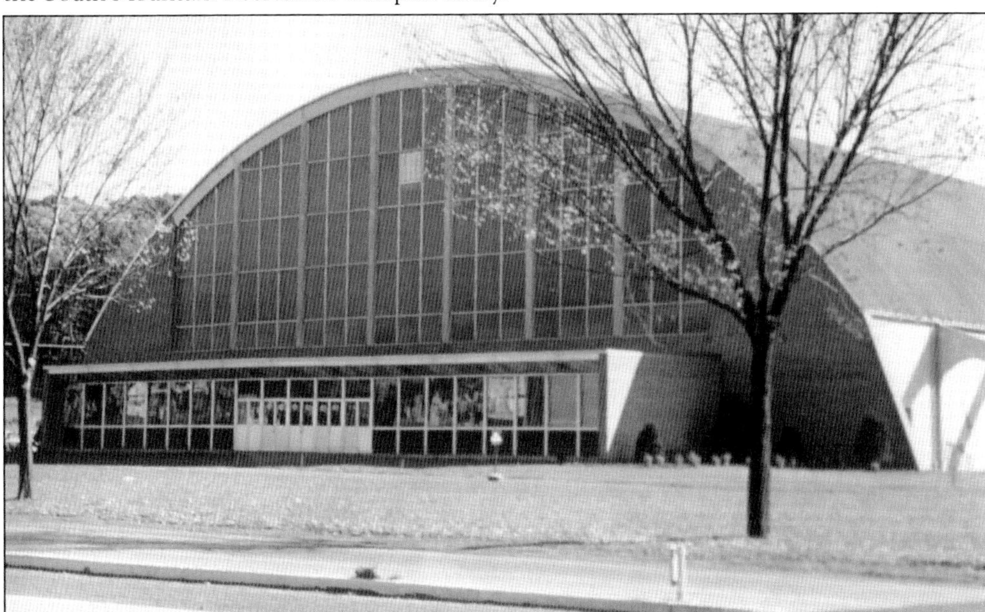

The South Mountain Arena is seen here shortly after it first opened in November 1958 on Northfield Avenue. The first interscholastic hockey league in New Jersey was formed the same year and played ice hockey here. The arena underwent major renovations in 2004 but kept the recognizable arched roof. When it reopened the following year, it was renamed the Richard J. Codey Arena.

Three

PARKS AND RECREATION

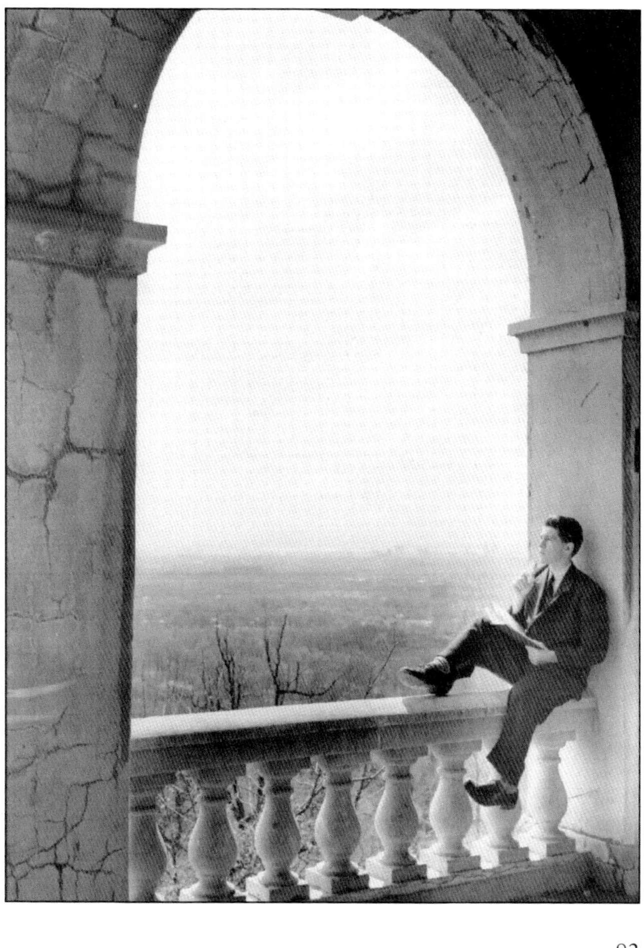

Gilbert Dixon looks out in a moment of self-reflection while doing homework on May 1, 1953, at the "Casino" building that opened in 1910 at Eagle Rock. The building fell into a state of disrepair and was almost torn down. It was spared by renovation and opened on December 19, 1986, as the Highlawn Pavilion restaurant that operates today with this arch as part of the restaurant's interior.

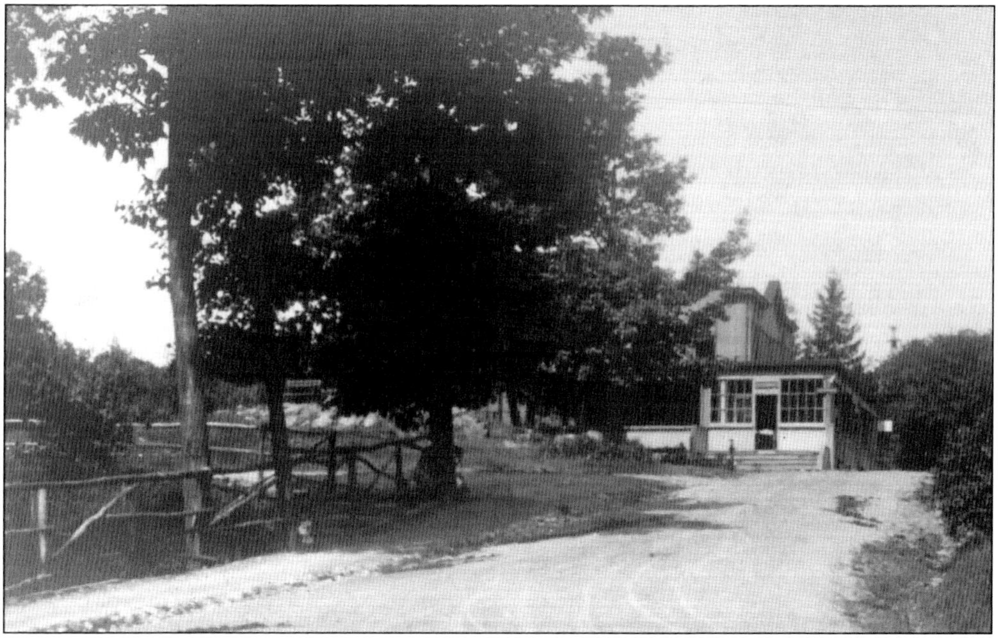

A photograph from 1900 shows one of several buildings dating to the Eagle Rock resort first built by A.T. Compton in 1874. The current road alignment is nearly identical today, and this onetime café, which is last seen on a 1911 map, sat just south of the site of the present-day gazebo at the Eagle Rock Reservation.

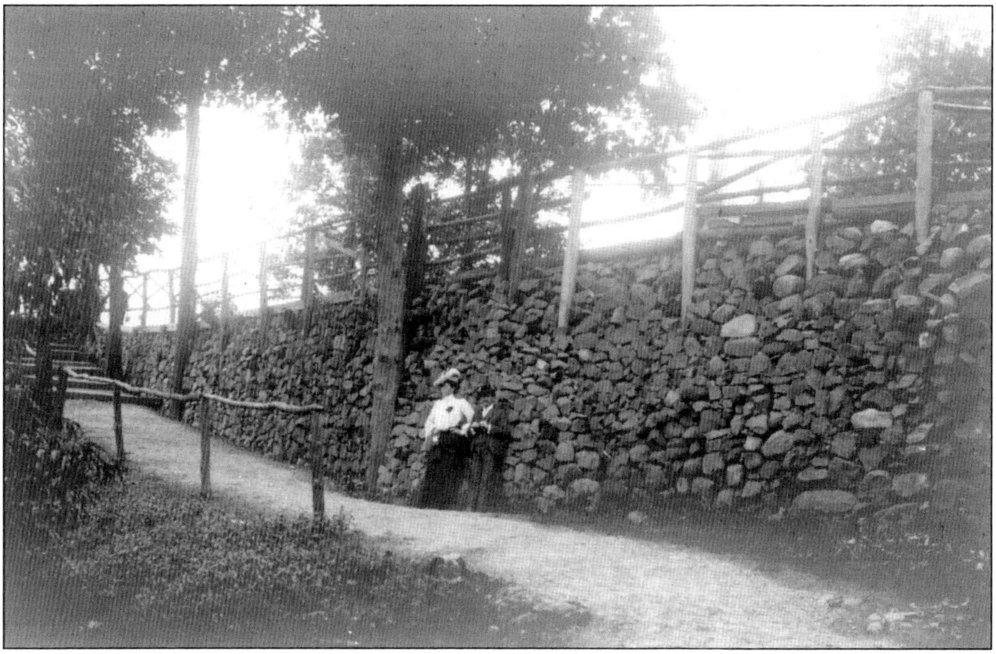

This photograph, likely taken at the same time, shows an unidentified couple posing on the path leading directly to the café at Eagle Rock. It would have been just up the steps to the left, and this is the same wooden fence seen in the previous image. In 1907, it was replaced by a 450-foot concrete wall with iron spikes at the Eagle Rock Reservation that is still there today.

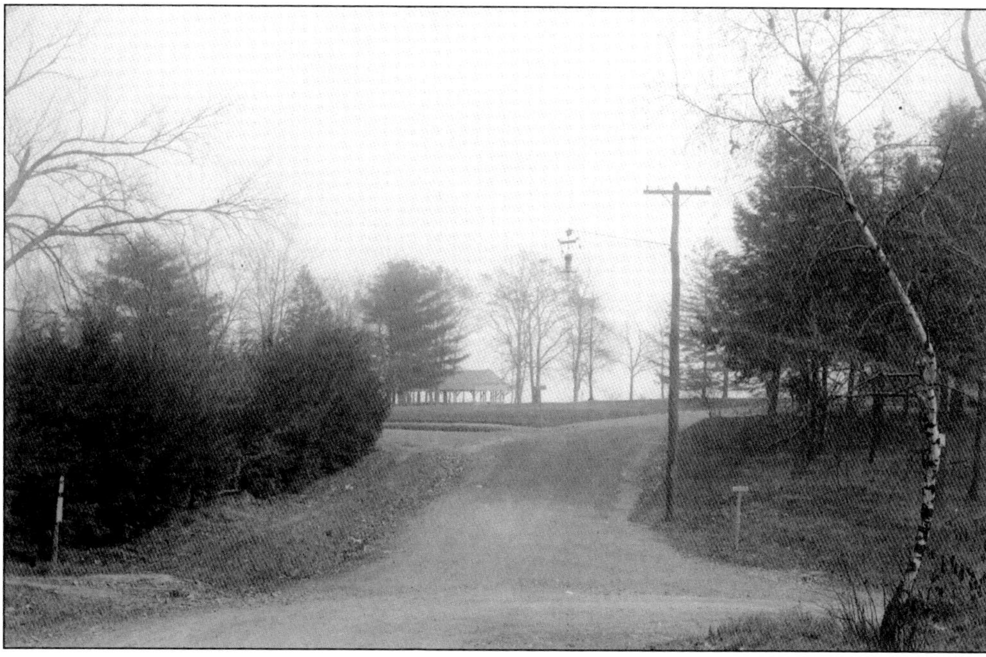

The road coming from the right is Eagle Rock Avenue, which in 1900 made a sharp left and passed directly through the Eagle Rock Reservation. The café seen at the top of the opposite page is out of view here but would be directly straight ahead and around the bend to the right. In 1957, Eagle Rock Avenue was realigned and a new entrance into the park was created.

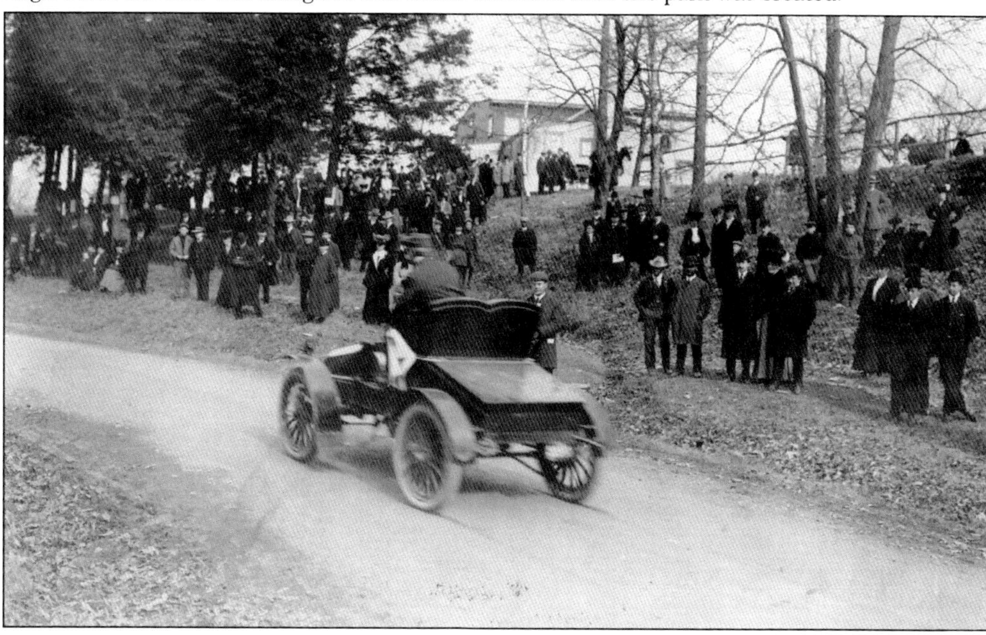

This view shows an automobile ascending Eagle Rock Avenue just before entering the Eagle Rock Reservation on the road seen in the previous photograph. The rear of the café pictured at the top of the opposite page also can be seen here, adding perspective to the location. The crowd has gathered to watch the Eagle Rock Hill Climb automobile race on November 24, 1904, that ended inside the Eagle Rock Reservation. (DPL.)

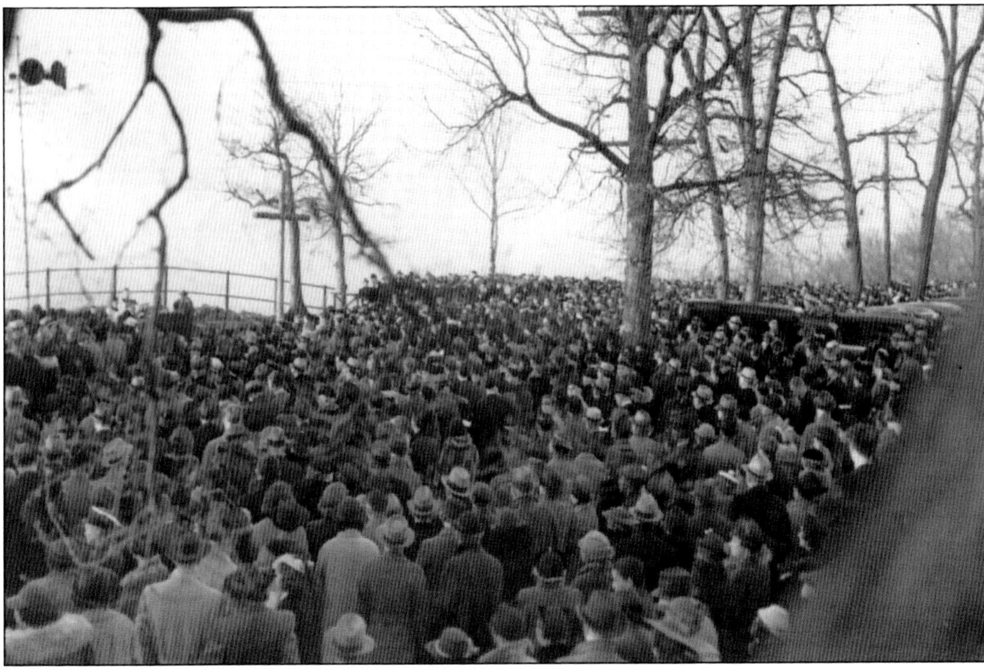

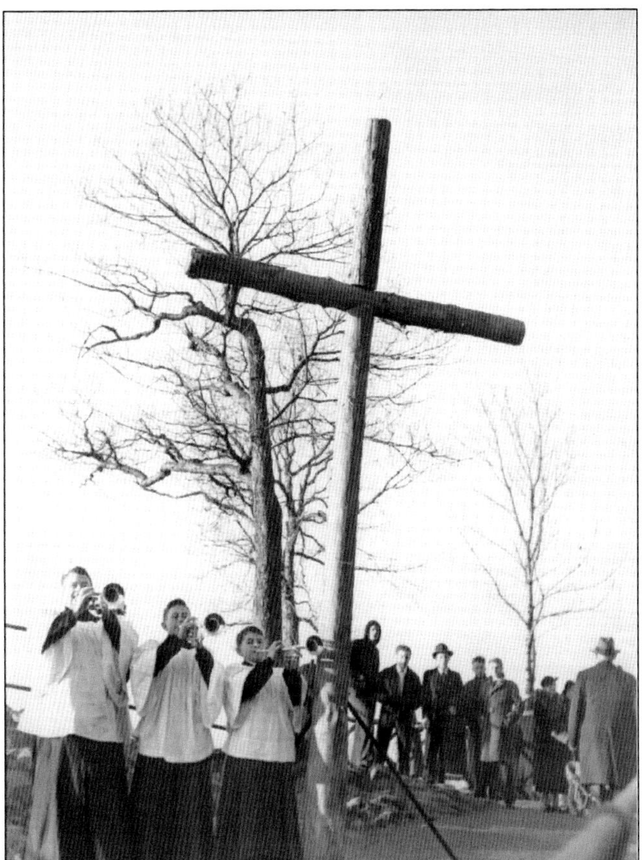

Easter services originally were held at Cable Lake near the Rock Spring Country Club. It began as a small group of fathers and sons hiking an annual pilgrimage at dawn to the mountaintop. It had become so popular that services were moved to the Eagle Rock Reservation to accommodate larger crowds. An estimated 10,000 people are seen here for Easter services at dawn on April 17, 1938.

Seen here performing at Easter services at Eagle Rock on April 17, 1938, are the Cummins' Trumpeters, a trio made up of a father and his two sons. A feature of this year's service was the addition of church organ music played live by organist Stanley Pinhero of Elizabeth and amplified over a public address system. The annual worship service continued for many years and was nondenominational.

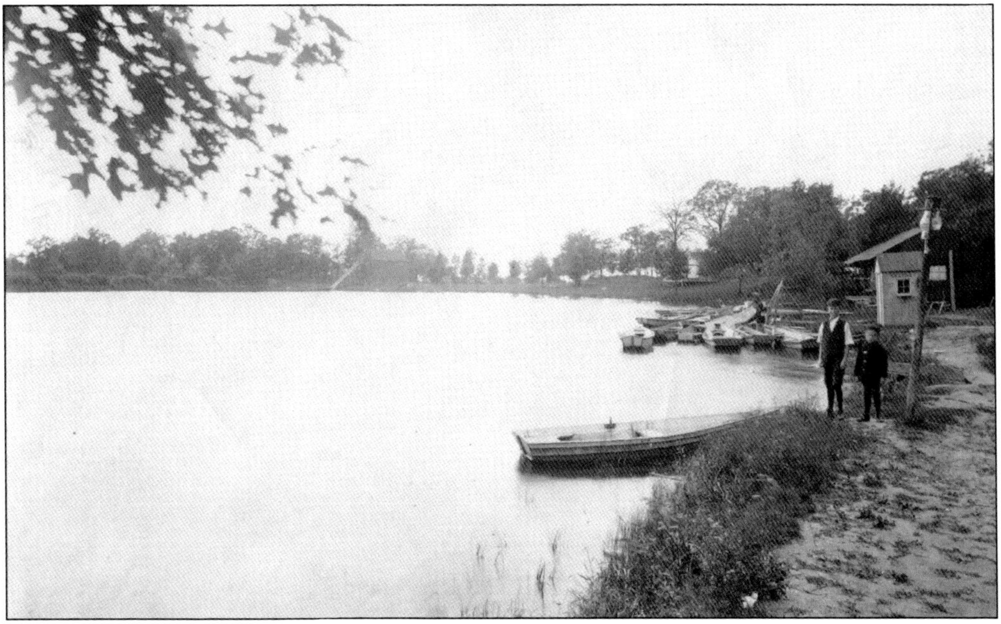

Two young boys are seen around 1900 at Crystal Lake, which was just a short walking distance from the Eagle Rock Reservation. The icehouse in the distance dates to around 1890 and was captured on film by William Heise of the Edison Manufacturing Company. *Hockey Match on the Ice* was shot nearly from this same perspective on February 24, 1898, and was the first hockey film in history.

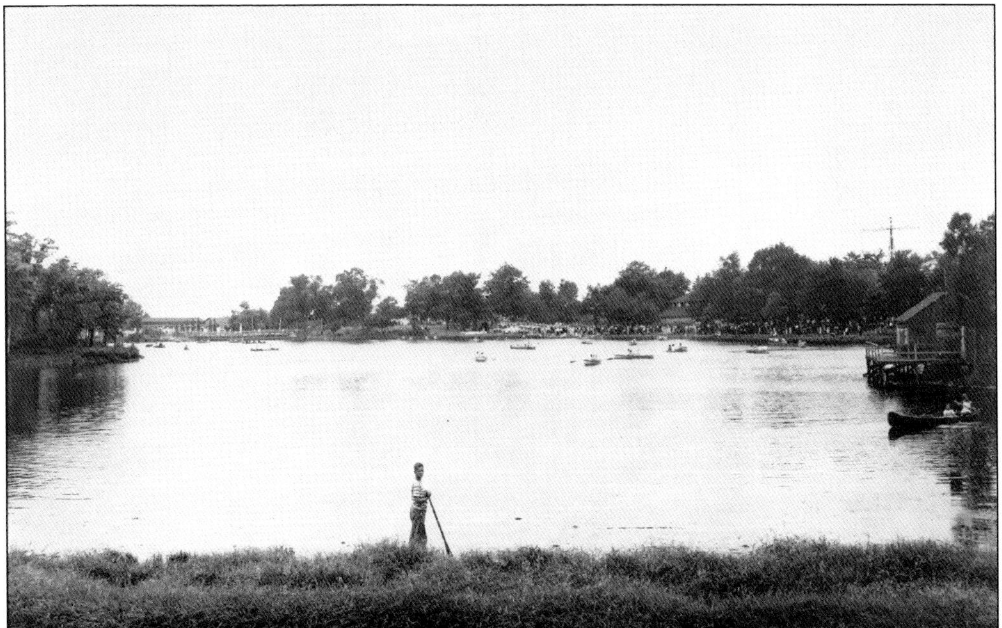

By the 1940s, a similar camera angle that Crystal Lake had grown as an amusement park destination. The carousel peeking from behind the trees in the distance to the right first appeared on maps in 1904 and featured wooded horses reported to have been hand carved in Italy. Another popular ride, called the airplane swings, can be seen towering above the trees at the right.

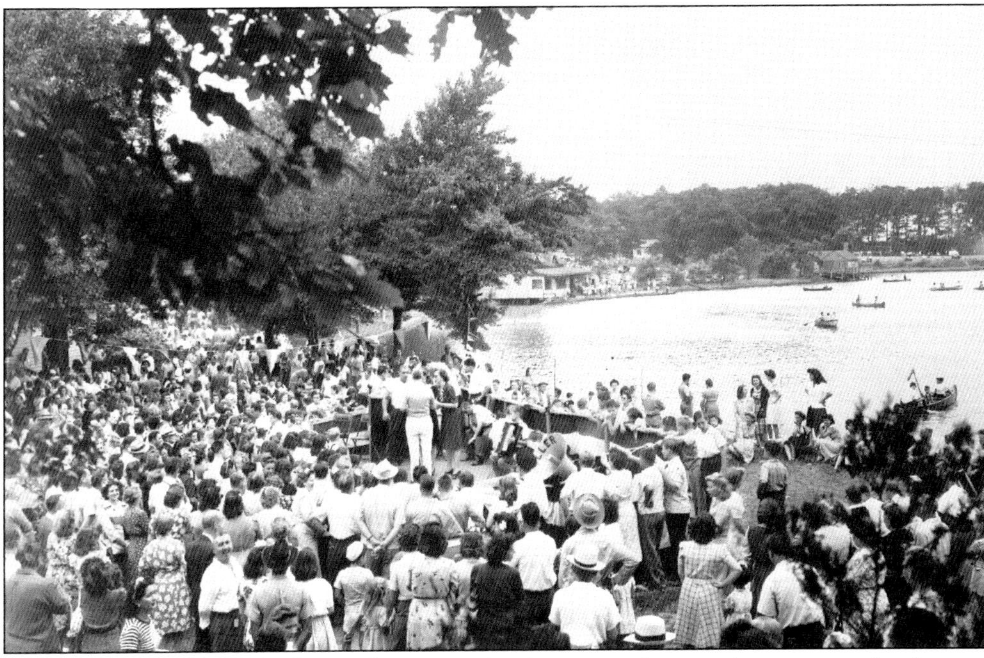

In addition to boating, which was always popular, live musical entertainment was also featured at Crystal Lake during its peak of popularity in the 1940s. This view looking east would be very near the grounds of the current-day Oskar Schindler Performing Arts Center where the sound of music from concerts still continues to be heard around the lake.

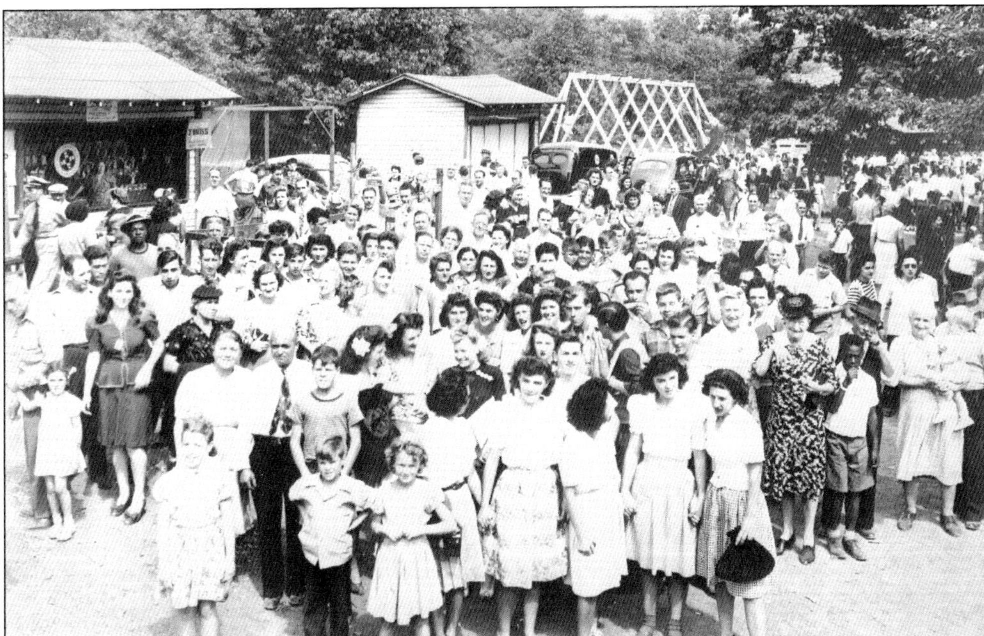

Pictured here during the 1940s is Crystal Lake's version of a promenade; its popularity is evident from the crowds it once drew. It ran from the lake's parking area, near today's bowling alley off Eagle Rock Avenue, through the center of the amusement park. At the stand to the left, it cost a nickel for two chances to throw balls at the wooden bottles to win a prize.

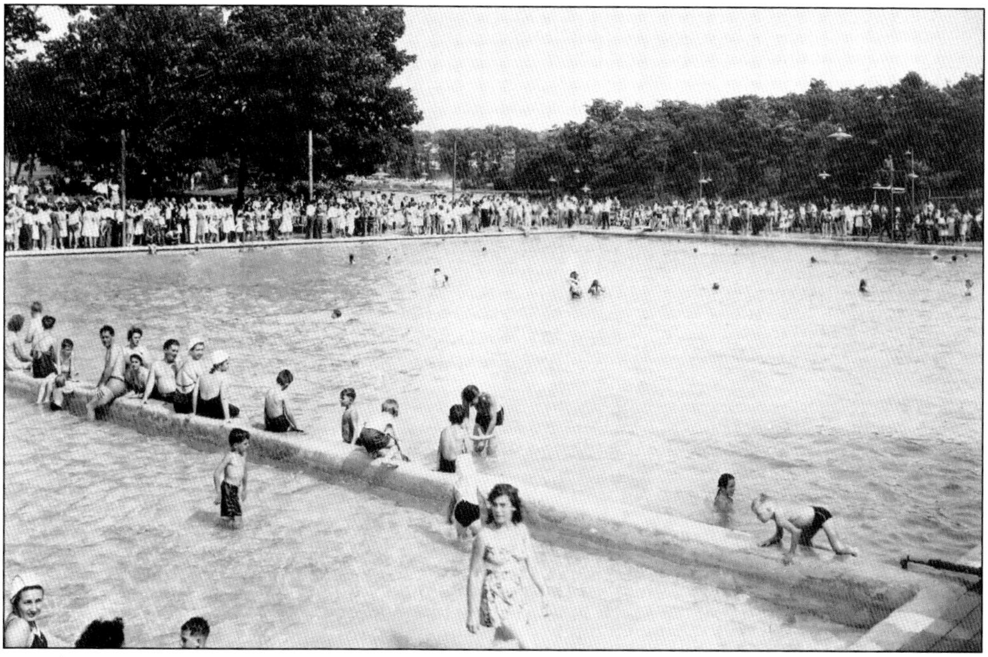

Another popular attraction at Crystal Lake was the pool at the far end of the lake, near Prospect Avenue, seen here during the 1940s. The pool used filtered water taken directly from the spring-fed lake and offered a refreshing reprieve during the hot summer months. Years after the amusement park closed, the pool became part of a private swim club that lasted into the 1970s.

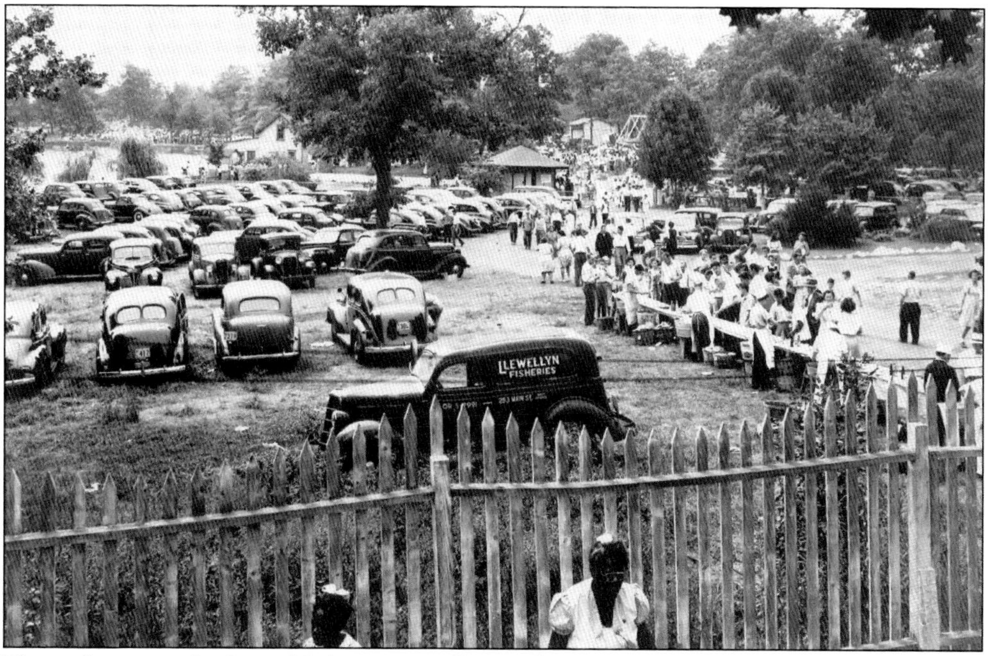

The parking area for Crystal Lake was usually overflowing with vehicles parked in a haphazard fashion on unpaved grass fields. This same location from the 1940s coincidentally is a paved parking lot today near the bowling alley off Eagle Rock Avenue. The Llewellyn Fisheries truck is providing food for a catered outing that was commonplace during this time.

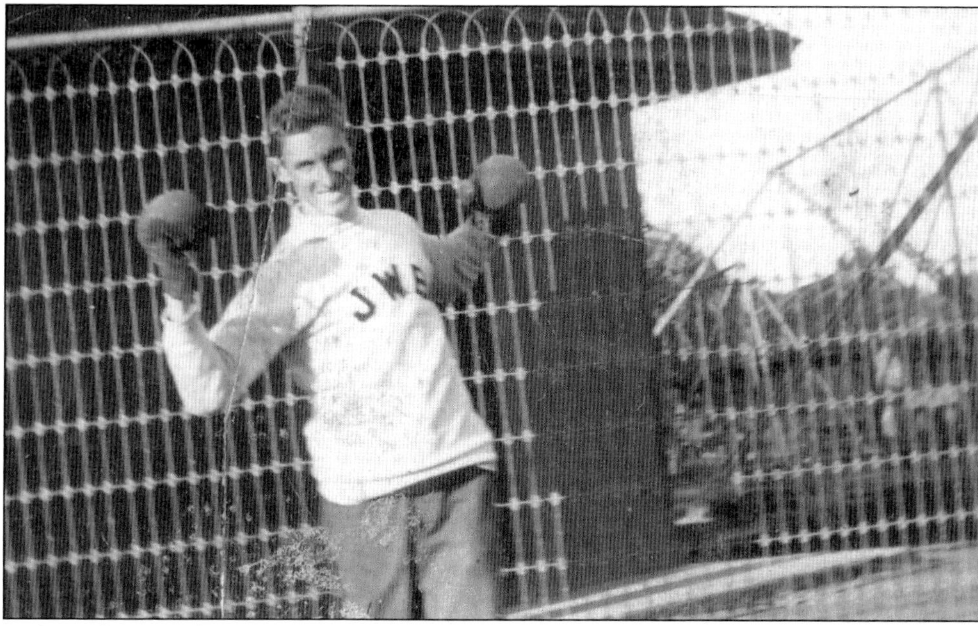

Jenkins Playground was the first playground in West Orange and opened on June 16, 1911, on Valley Road. Joseph W. Byrne Sr., seen here in 1913 wearing boxing gloves, was appointed the first supervisor of recreation for West Orange playgrounds that same year. During World War I, he was gassed but survived and returned to his duties in West Orange. Byrne passed away in 1928 from his war injuries.

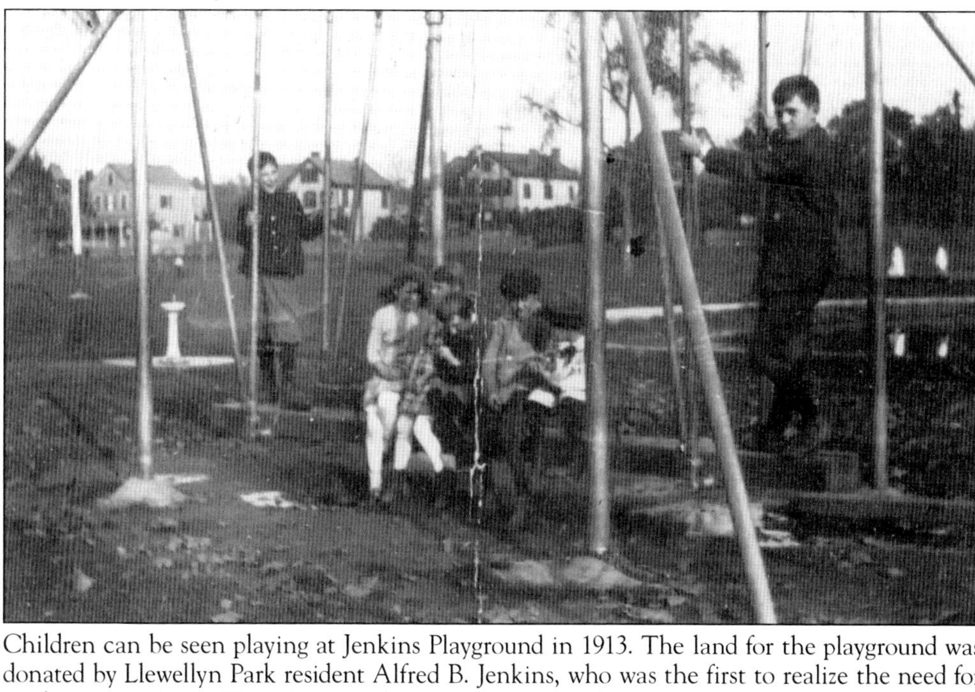

Children can be seen playing at Jenkins Playground in 1913. The land for the playground was donated by Llewellyn Park resident Alfred B. Jenkins, who was the first to realize the need for outdoor recreation in West Orange. The playground still exists today but has been greatly reduced in size because Interstate 280 and a firehouse, constructed during the 1970s, took land away from the playground.

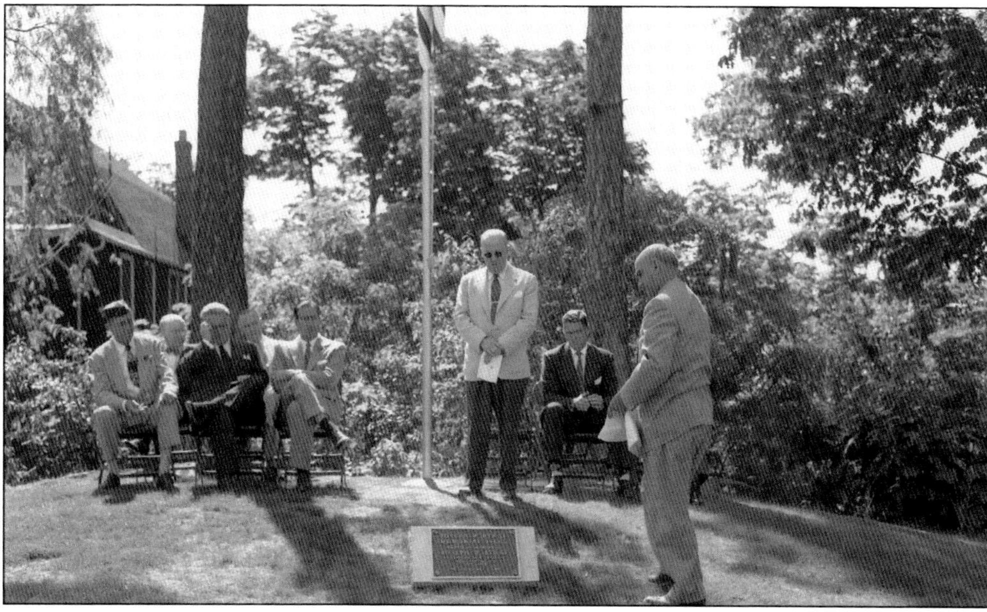

On May 31, 1954, a new playground on Liberty Street was dedicated to the memory of Joseph W. Byrne Sr., who was first supervisor of recreation for West Orange playgrounds. Frank Moran is standing next to the flagpole, and seated to the right is Joseph Byrne Jr., who followed in his father's footsteps by working for the recreation department. Lefty Boland unveils the plaque naming Joseph W. Byrne Memorial Field.

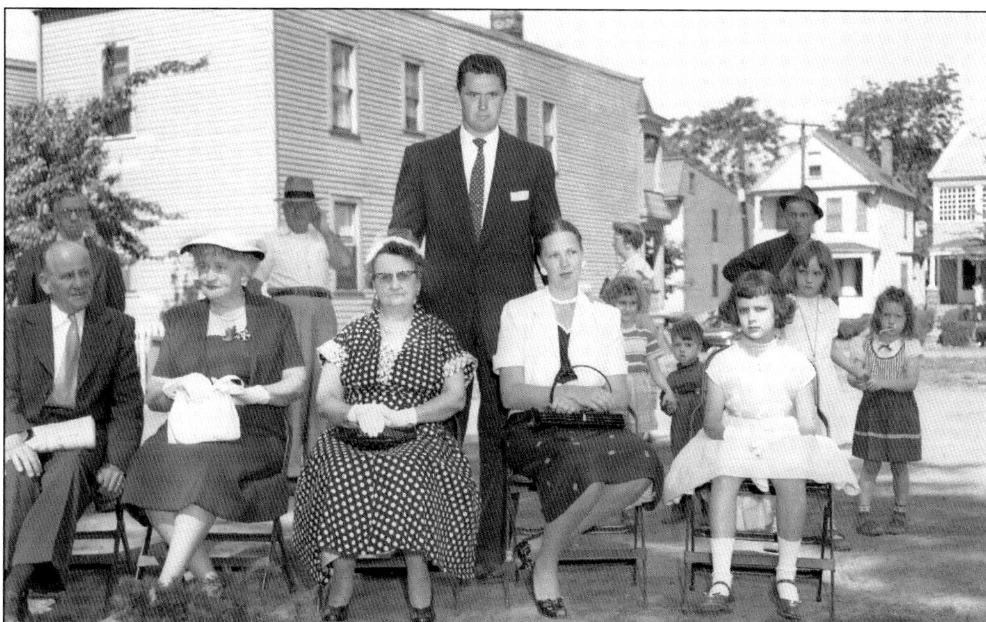

Joe Byrne Jr. is standing behind his sitting mother, Mary (left), and wife, Jean (right), at the playground named in his father's honor on May 31, 1954. Joe Jr. passed away in 2000 and a plaque was placed in his memory at Colgate Field in 2002 honoring him as the originator of the Old-Timer's Game, which began there in 1977 and continues today as an annual tradition to honor playground athletes.

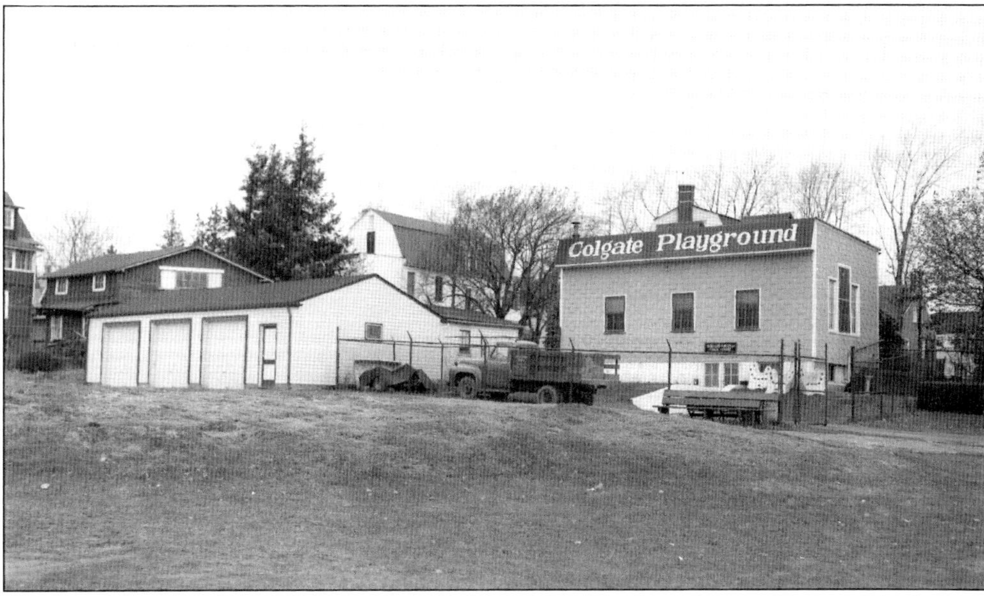

The first field house at the Colgate Playground is seen here in the 1950s. It was named for Bernard M. Degnan, who served as West Orange commissioner of parks and recreation from 1934 to 1937. Degnan later served as West Orange mayor from 1938 to 1951, and present-day Degnan Park in West Orange is named for him. This building was torn down in 2015.

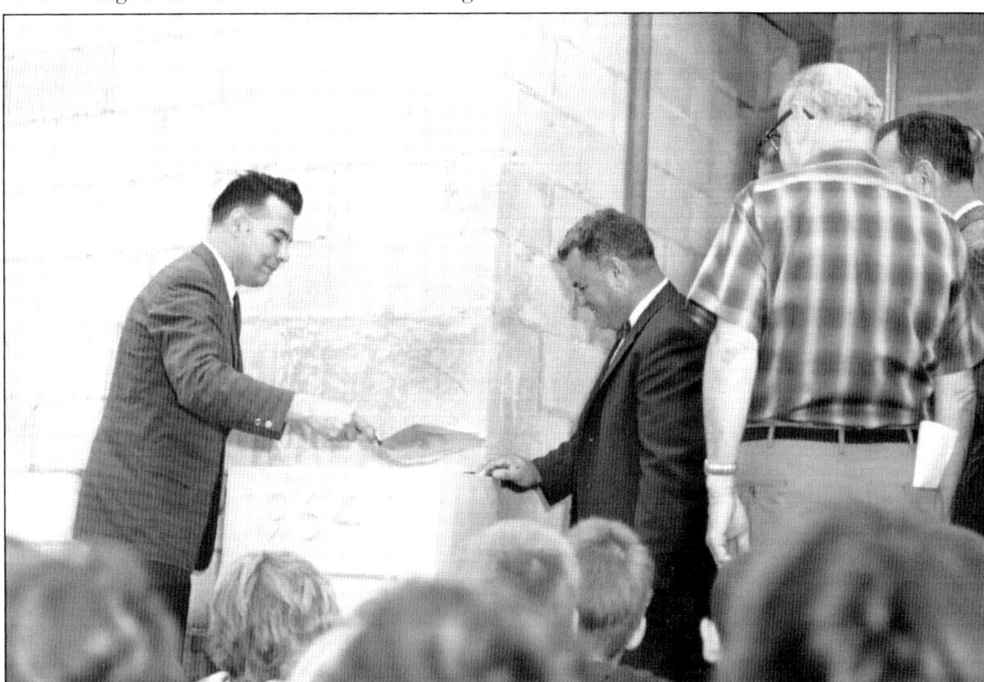

West Orange mayor James Sheeran is seen laying the cornerstone for the new field house at Colgate Field in 1964. Recreation director Lefty Boland is in the plaid shirt to the right with his back to the camera. Today, this building currently serves as offices for the West Orange Department of Recreation. (FM.)

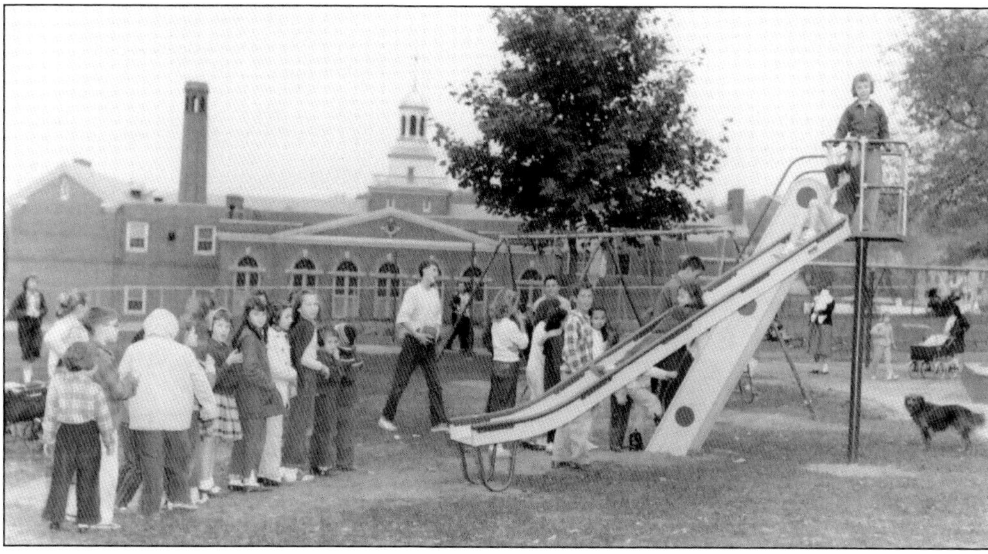

The Colgate Field playground, seen here around 1964, offers an interesting glimpse of social attitudes among children at that time. The playground was certainly not problem free, but kids generally understood that everyone benefited by patiently waiting in line to use the sliding board. Also, no one is seemingly alarmed by a friendly, unleashed dog from the neighborhood—whose name everyone probably knew—inside the playground, as seen on the right. (FM.)

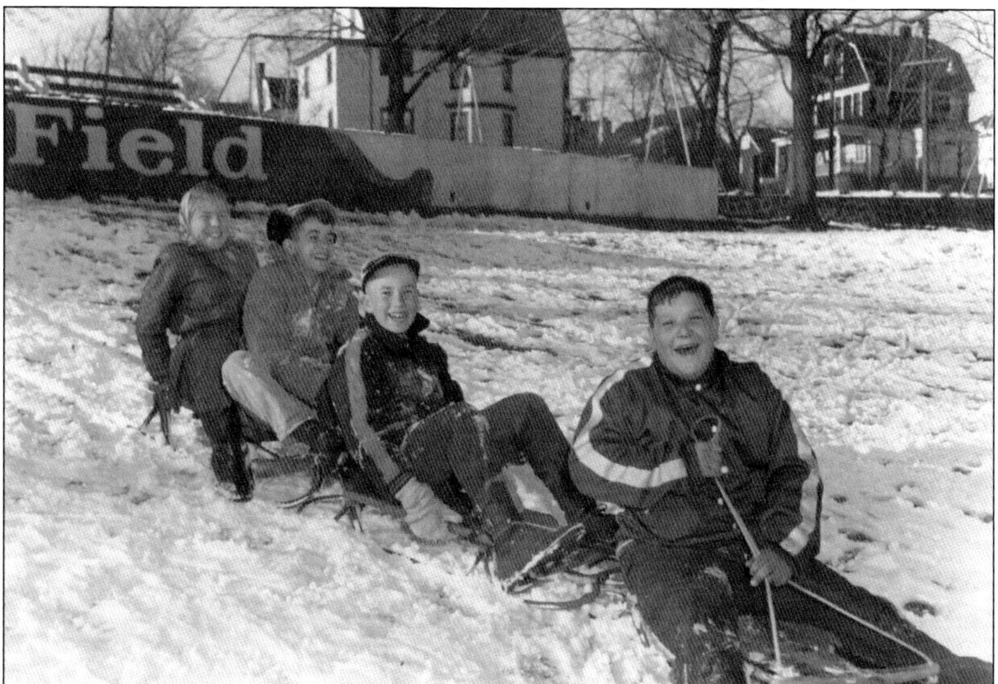

Unidentified youngsters are seen sledding at Colgate Field around 1960. The field was named after Richard Colgate, who deeded seven acres to the town bordering on Franklin Avenue and Cherry Street to create the town's second playground, which opened in September 1918. Colgate was the grandson of the founder of the Colgate Company, which at one time was the largest soap manufacturer in the United States. (FM.)

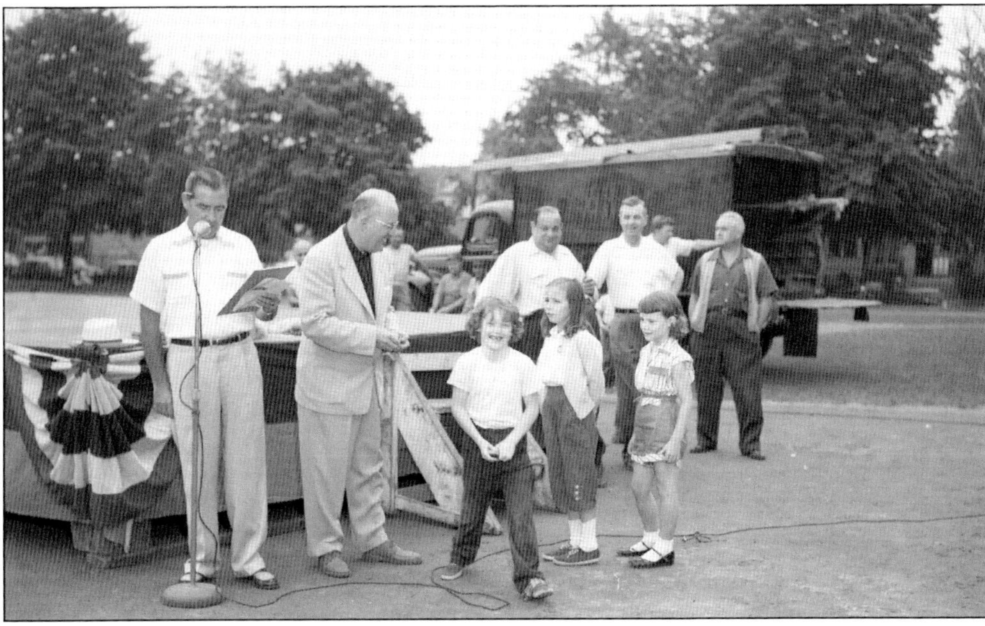

In 1938, a committee of private citizens began raising funds to hold annual Fourth of July races for township youngsters at Colgate Field that eventually were taken over by the recreation department. Phil McLaughlin is seen behind the microphone with Commissioner Frank Moran to the right handing out awards around 1956. McLaughlin was part of the original committee and emceed the annual event for 41 years, from 1938 to 1984.

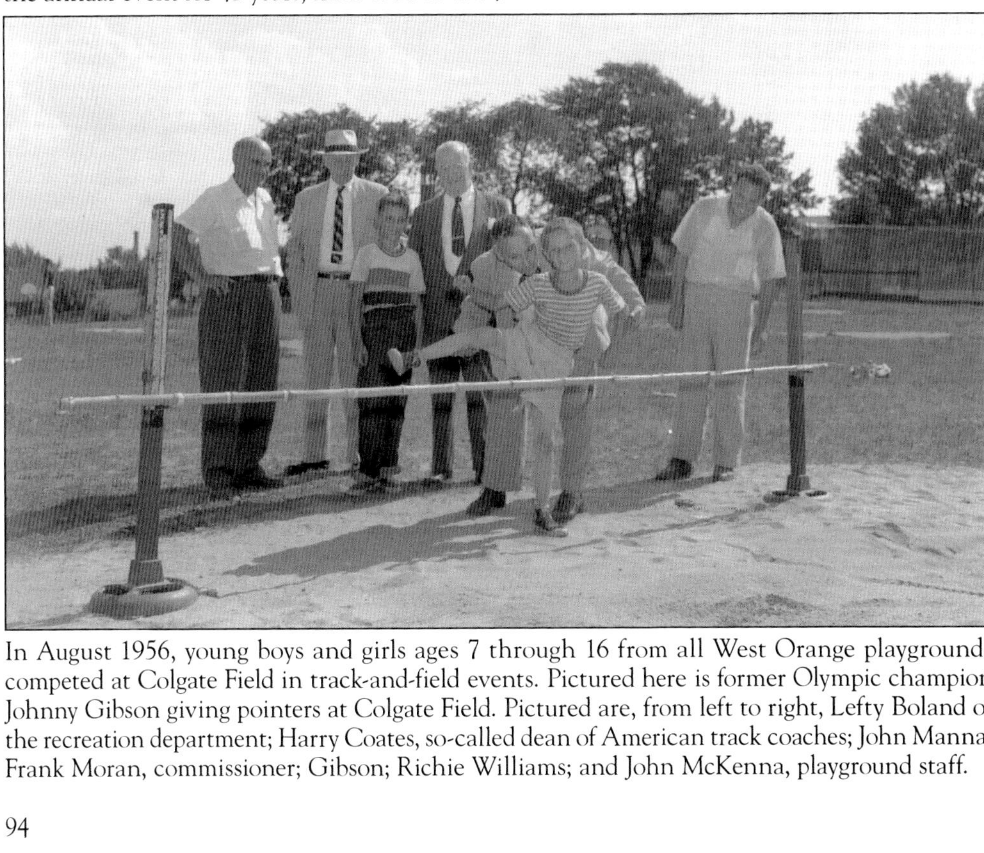

In August 1956, young boys and girls ages 7 through 16 from all West Orange playgrounds competed at Colgate Field in track-and-field events. Pictured here is former Olympic champion Johnny Gibson giving pointers at Colgate Field. Pictured are, from left to right, Lefty Boland of the recreation department; Harry Coates, so-called dean of American track coaches; John Manna; Frank Moran, commissioner; Gibson; Richie Williams; and John McKenna, playground staff.

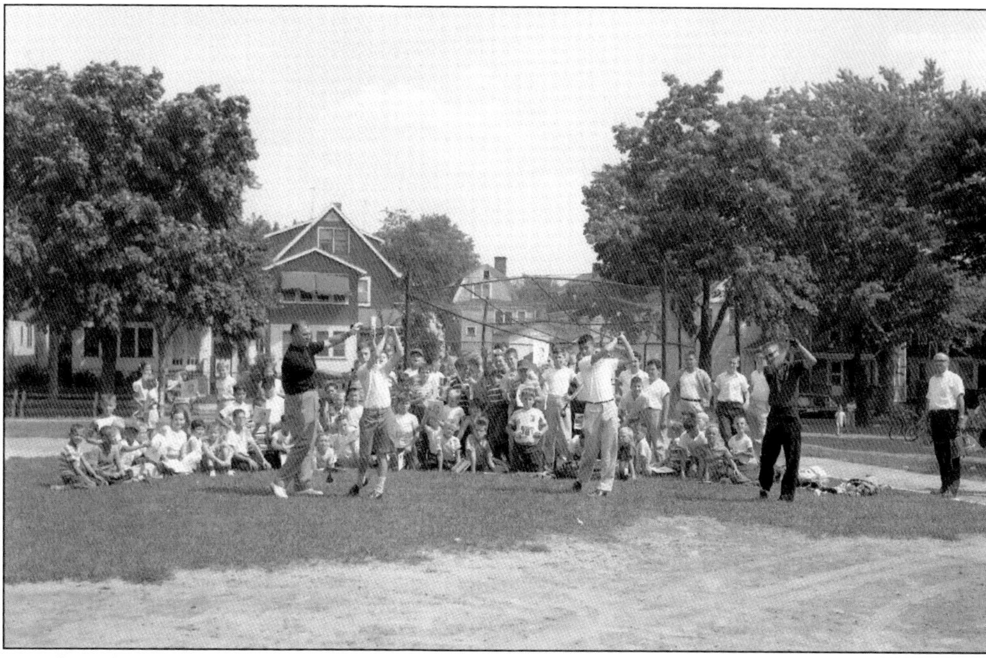

J. Bud Geohegan, the club pro from Crestmont Country Club in West Orange, is seen in the dark shirt on the left demonstrating the fundamentals of golf. He helped instruct over 200 youngsters at this golf clinic sponsored by the recreation department at Colgate Field in August 1959. Lefty Boland, head of the department, is seen holding the bag at the right.

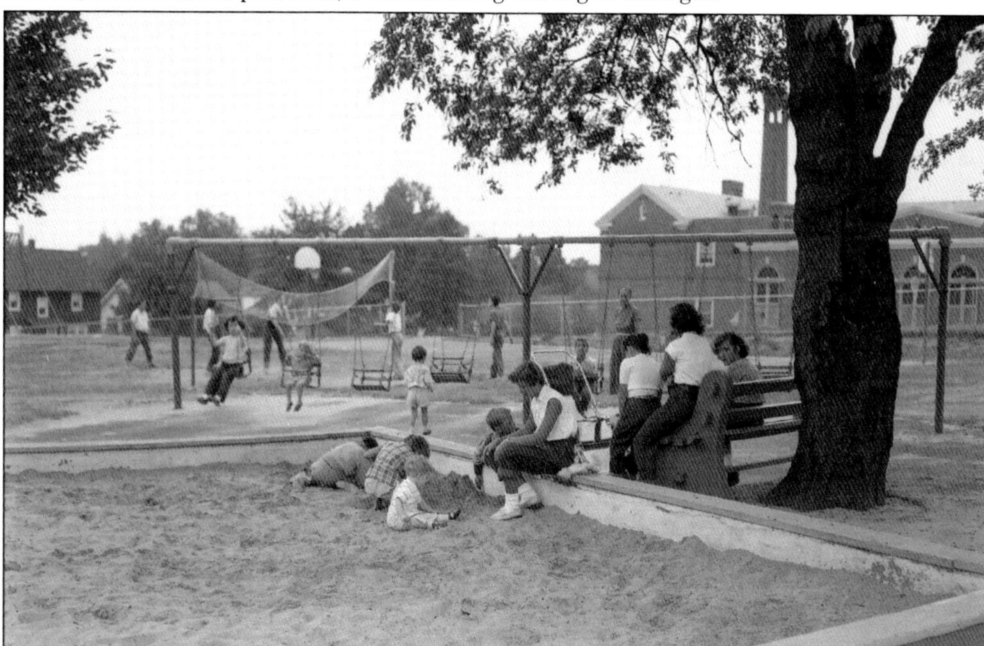

In an era before video games and computers, a popular summer outdoor activity for young kids was playing in a backyard sandbox. Colgate Field, seen here around 1964, featured a huge public sandbox that provided a fun activity for children, often occupying them for hours, as their parents looked on. The rear of Edison Junior High School is seen in the background to the right. (FM.)

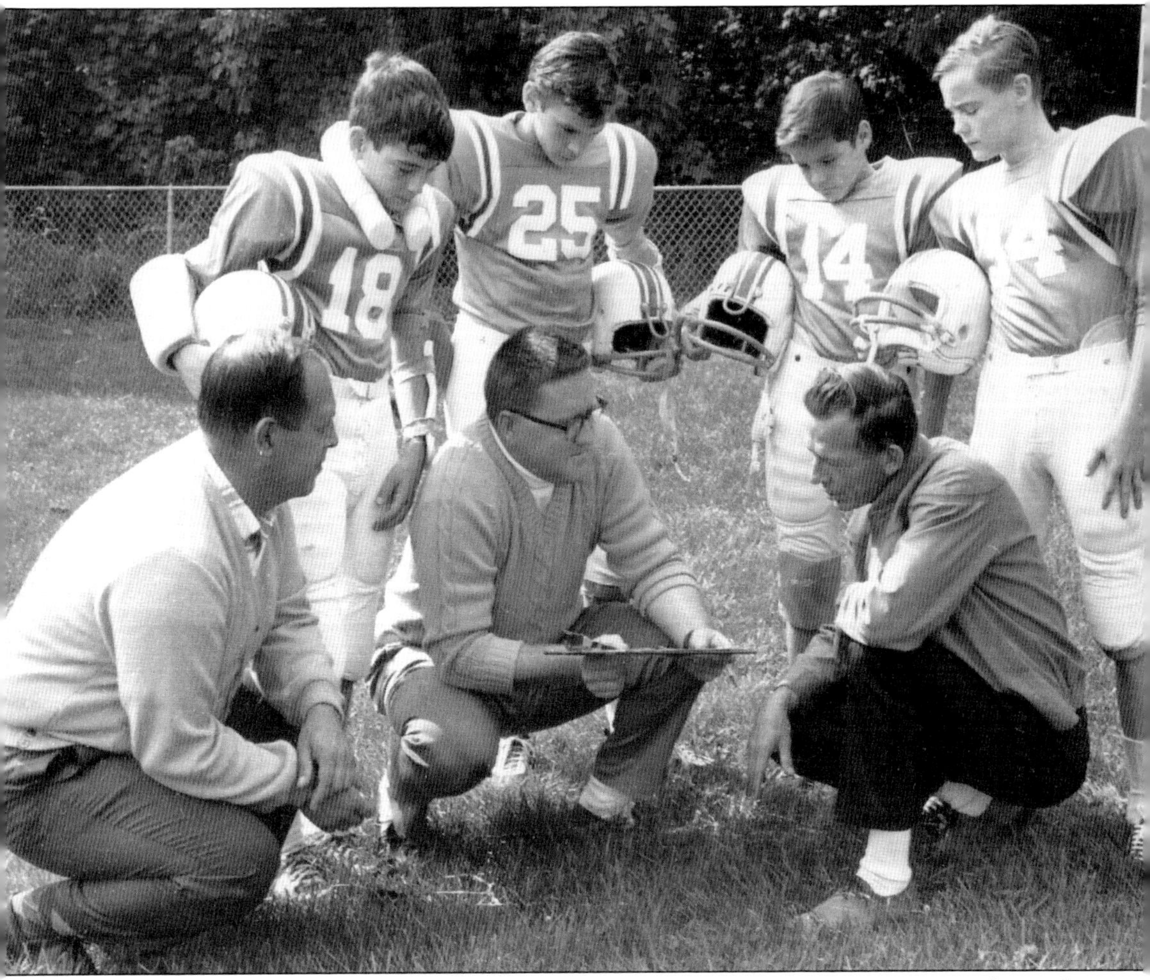

The West Orange Police Athletic League (PAL) was chartered on March 1, 1962, and since has continuously provided opportunities for young boys and girls to participate in sports. Pictured here are coaches and players of the 1968 football team, the Mustangs. Coaches are, from left to right, Joe Pansulla, Jim Ganning, and Harry Hofheing. Players are, from left to right, Larry Filan, Brian Trifiolis, Mike Fagan, and Kevin Robinson. These coaches and players were also part of the 1967 team that finished with a 5-2-1 record. In 1968, they experienced tremendous near flawless success and went undefeated in eight regular-season games, outscoring their opponents 261-18. They went on to defeat Orange 35-0 in the Inter Orange PAL Bowl later that year. They also scored two more wins in the playoffs for a season record of 11-0, and the West Orange Mustangs became the 1968 Western Division Champions of the Northern New Jersey Pop Warner Football Conference. Glenn "Pop" Warner, for whom youth football leagues around the country are named, was a contemporary of Amos Alonzo Stagg (see page 46).

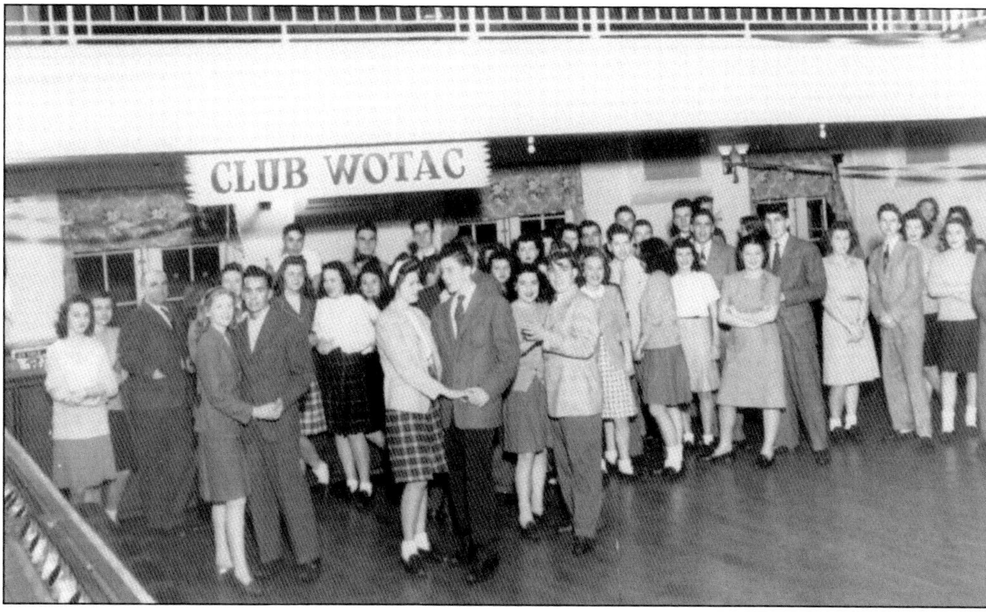

The West Orange Teen Age Canteen was held at the Gaston Street school auditorium seen here during the 1940s. It was the first canteen in New Jersey and was founded in 1944. It gave teenagers a place to socialize, attend dances, play games, and make new friends. It was regularly moderated by local religious, educational, and recreational leaders to help maintain a wholesome atmosphere.

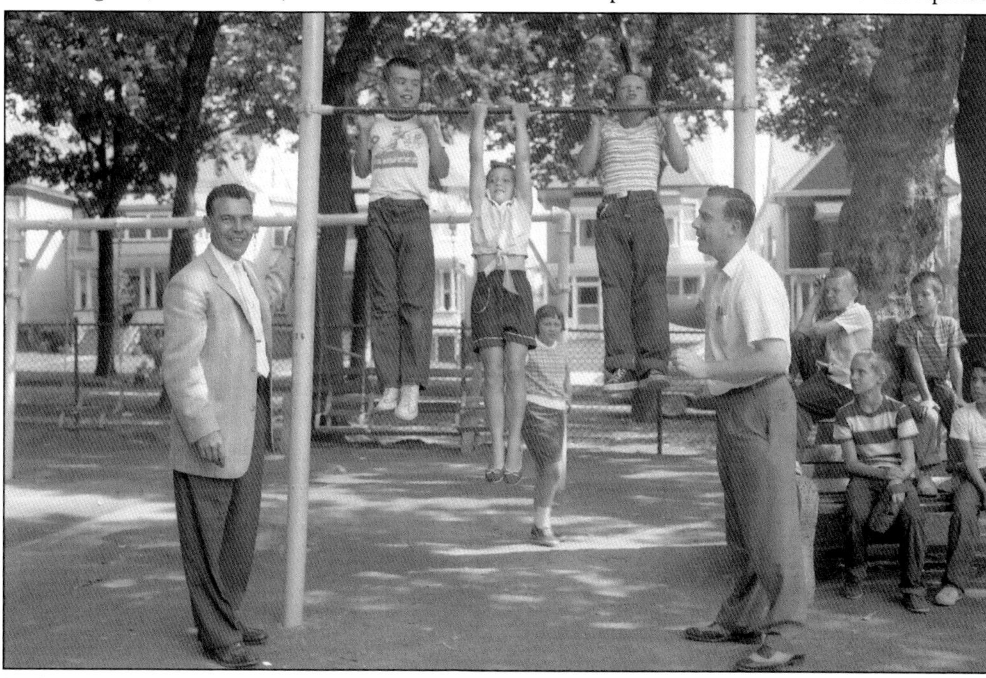
In August 1958, over 250 West Orange youngsters participated in a town-wide physical fitness program sponsored by the West Orange Junior Chamber of Commerce and the Sports Wheaties Federation. Pictured here at Lafayette Playground are, from left to right, Mayor James Sheeran, Robert Habbin, Valerie Gervasio, Robert Byer, and Jaycee chairman Allen Simonson. Unidentified children are to the right and in back. (FM.)

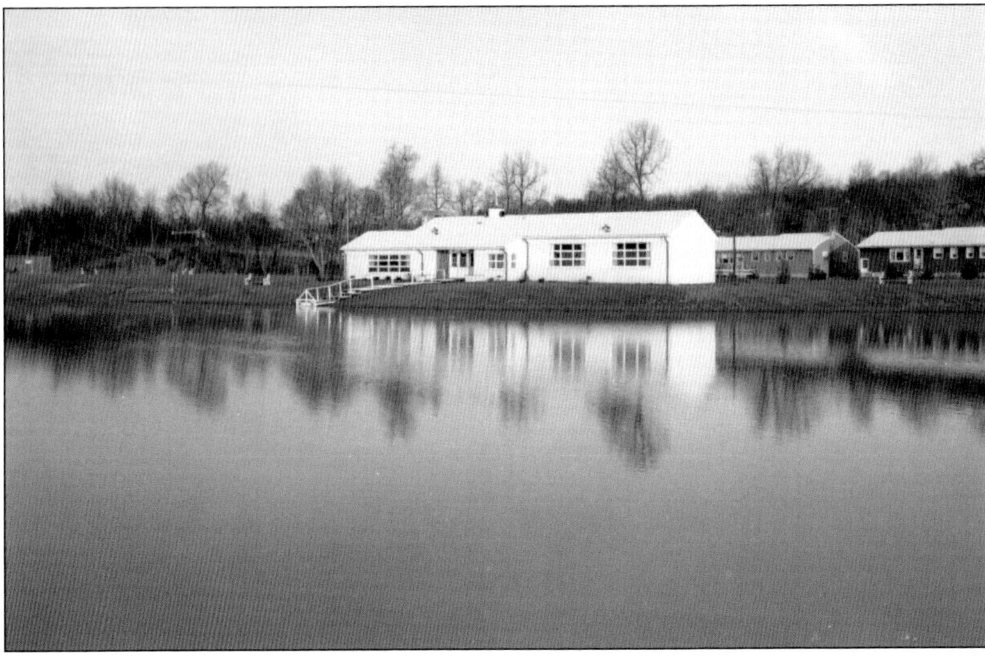

In November 1955, ground was broken for the construction of a new field house at the Lake Vincent playground on Pleasant Valley Way, seen here shortly following completion in the spring of 1956. Today, it is known as the Katz Civic Center, named in honor of Toby Katz, a former West Orange councilwoman, for her dedicated service to the residents of West Orange.

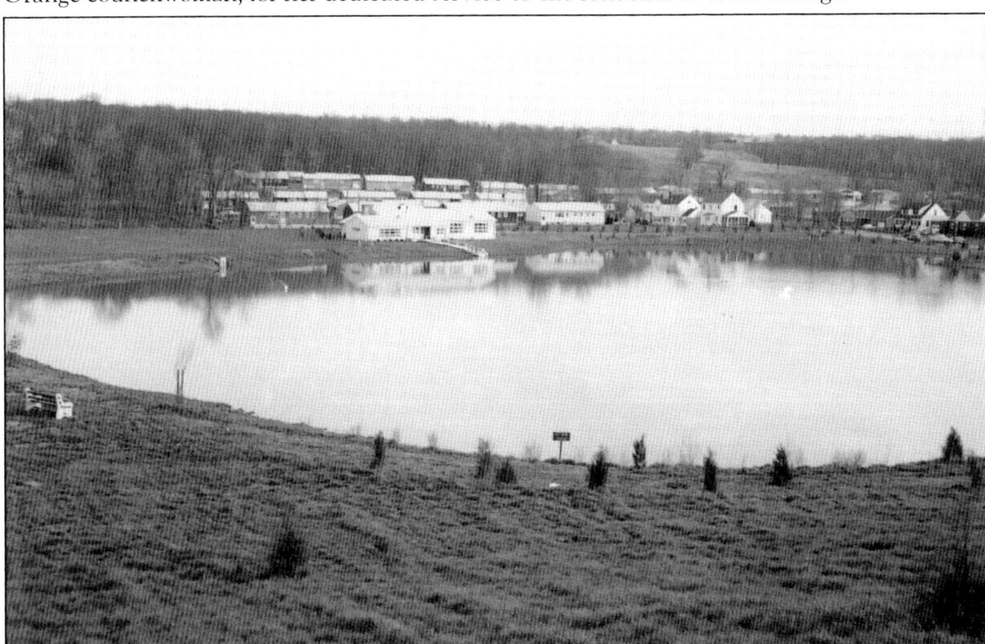

A wide-angle view of the field house, also from 1956, shows newly constructed homes on Carteret Street behind the field house. The small, freshly planted trees seen along the shoreline today obscure the view of the lake. The photograph also offers an unobstructed view of Hooper Avenue at the north end of the lake.

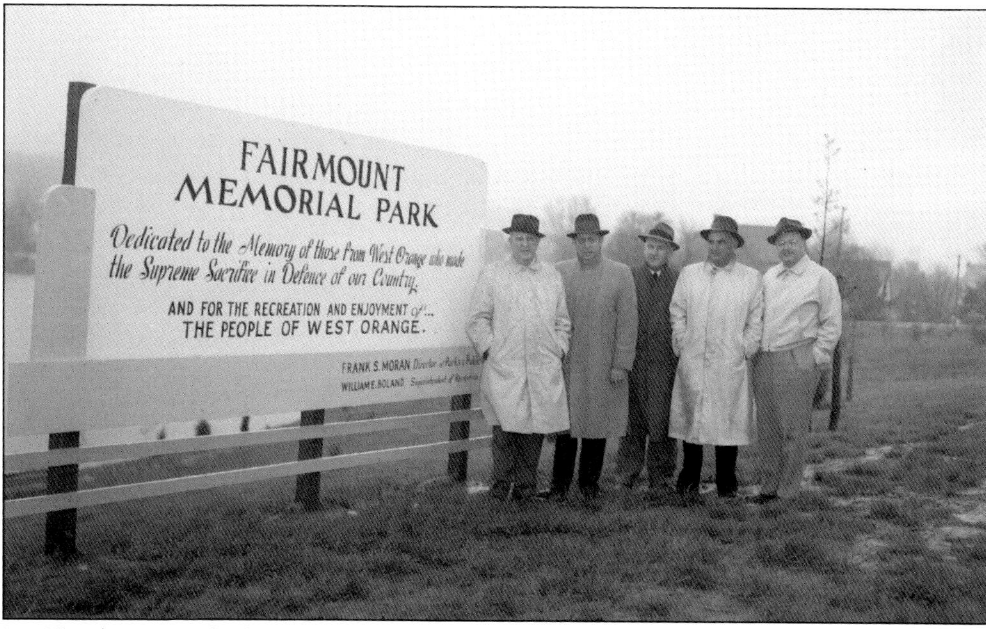

In 1958, the name of Lake Vincent Park was officially changed to Fairmont Memorial Park. Seen unveiling a new sign at the dedication ceremonies on May 1, 1958, are town officials, from left to right, Frank Moran, Edward Roos, William Kennedy, Lefty Boland, and John Berger. Today, the park has been upgraded and is known as Bernard Degnan Memorial Park, named for a former town mayor who served from 1938 to 1951.

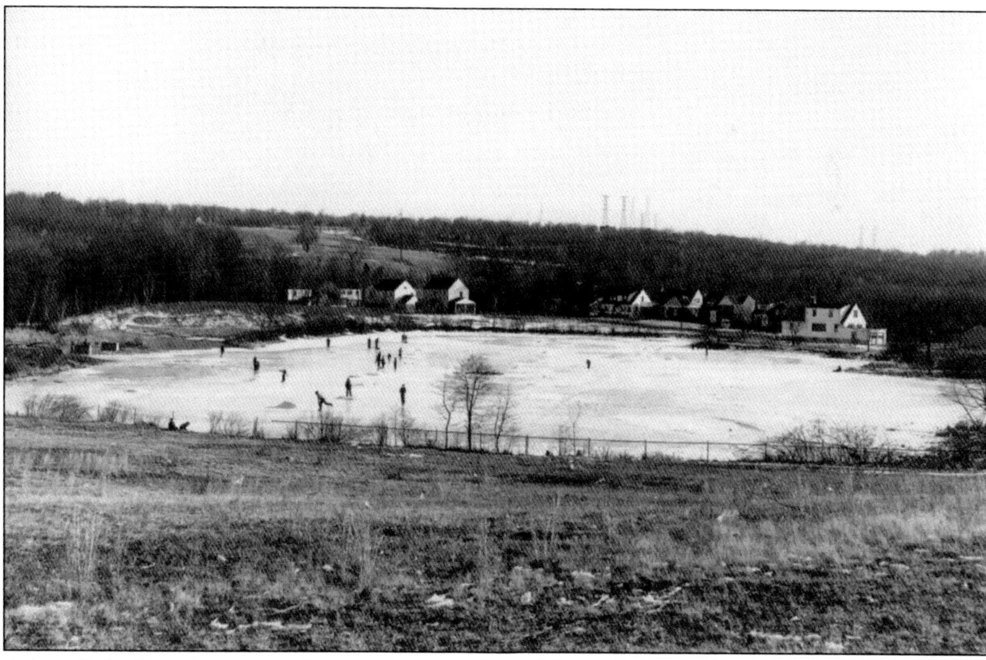

A handful of ice-skaters can be seen braving the cold weather at Lake Vincent Park during the winter of 1955. In the days before the field house was constructed, there was no inside shelter to retreat to in order to warm up or sip hot chocolate. Although ice-skating was offered at nearby Crystal Lake, this was the first town-owned park that offered ice-skating on a lake.

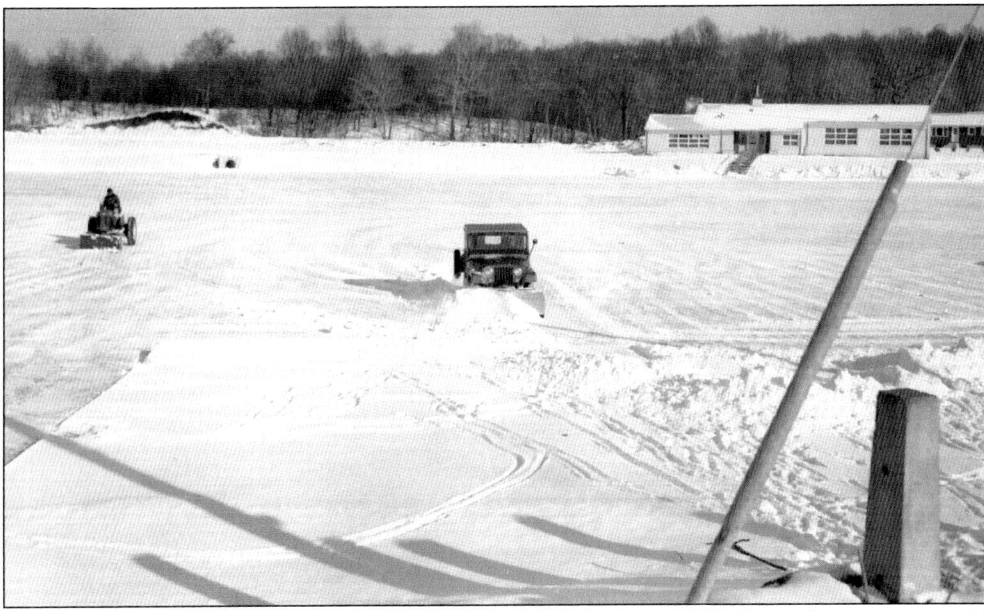

Town employees can be seen clearing the snow from Lake Vincent Park during the winter of 1956. The source of water for the lake is the West Branch of the Rahway River, which was widened here around 1850 to create a watering hole for cattle. The name Lake Vincent came from the Vincent family whose farm was once at this location.

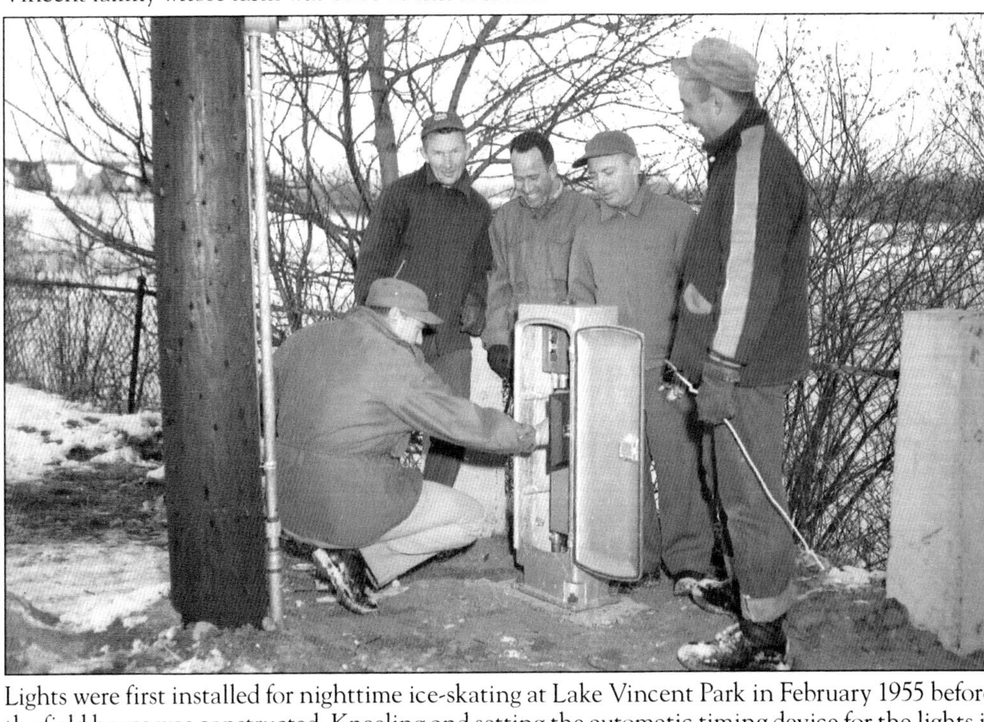

Lights were first installed for nighttime ice-skating at Lake Vincent Park in February 1955 before the field house was constructed. Kneeling and setting the automatic timing device for the lights is Ralph Curtis, captain of the fire department. Recreation department employees are seen receiving instructions on its operation. Standing are, from left to right, Joe Murphy, William Goldberg, Mike Gillen, and Jim Rogers.

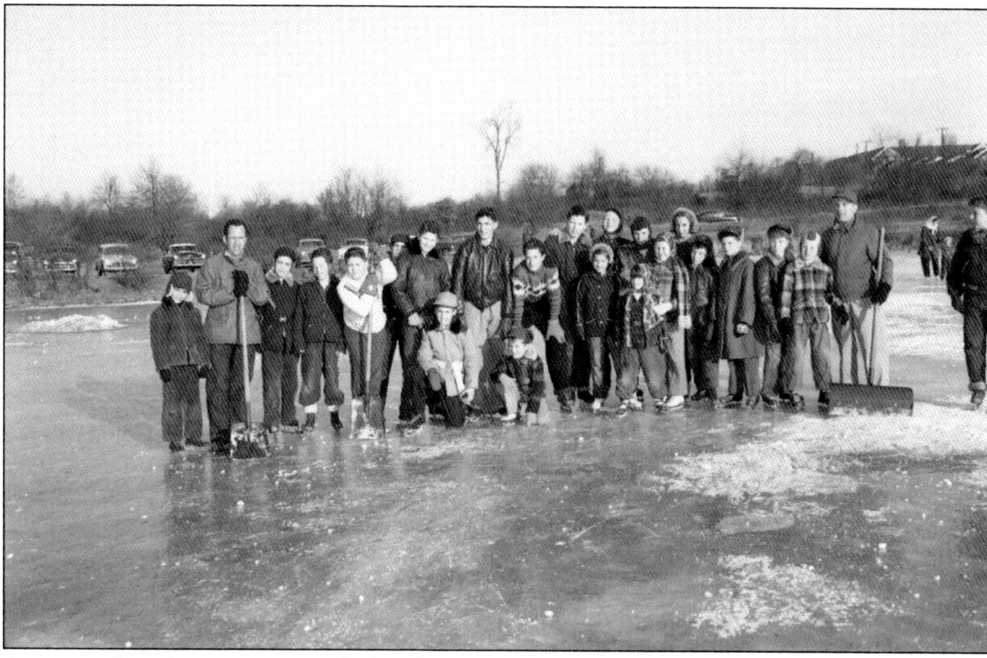

A group of ice-skaters is sandwiched in between two town employees—William Goldberg (left) and Mike Gillen (right)—holding shovels around 1955. Despite this park having undergone several name changes over the years, most older residents still simply refer to the location as Vincent's Pond and not the correct name, Bernard Degnan Memorial Park.

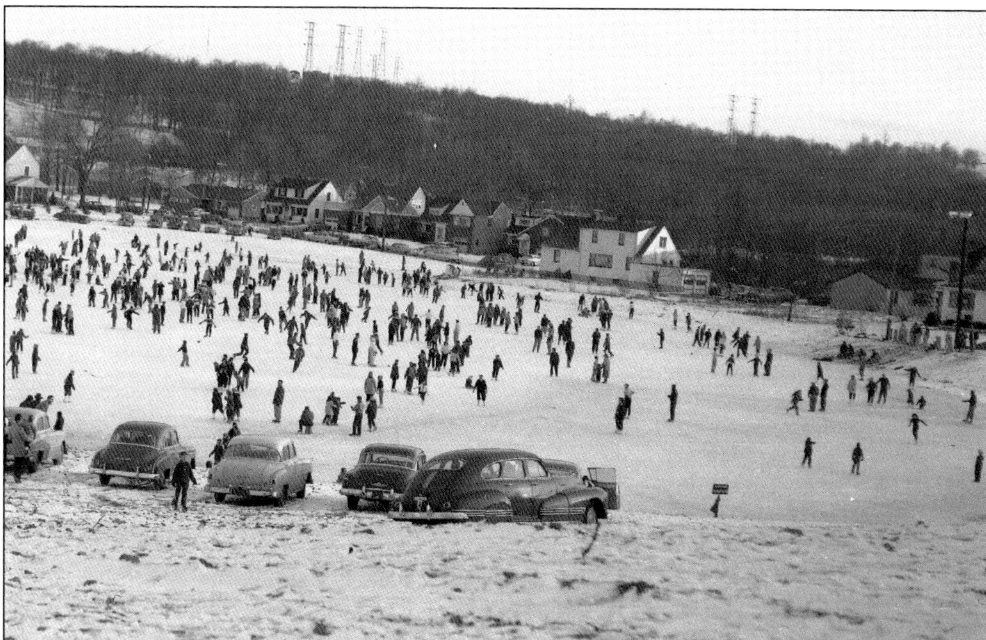

Another view of skaters at Lake Vincent during the winter of 1955 shows the popularity of ice-skating. It also illustrates how relaxed parking restrictions allowed cars to pull up right on the edge of the lake. The photograph offers an unobstructed view of houses along Hooper Avenue in the background.

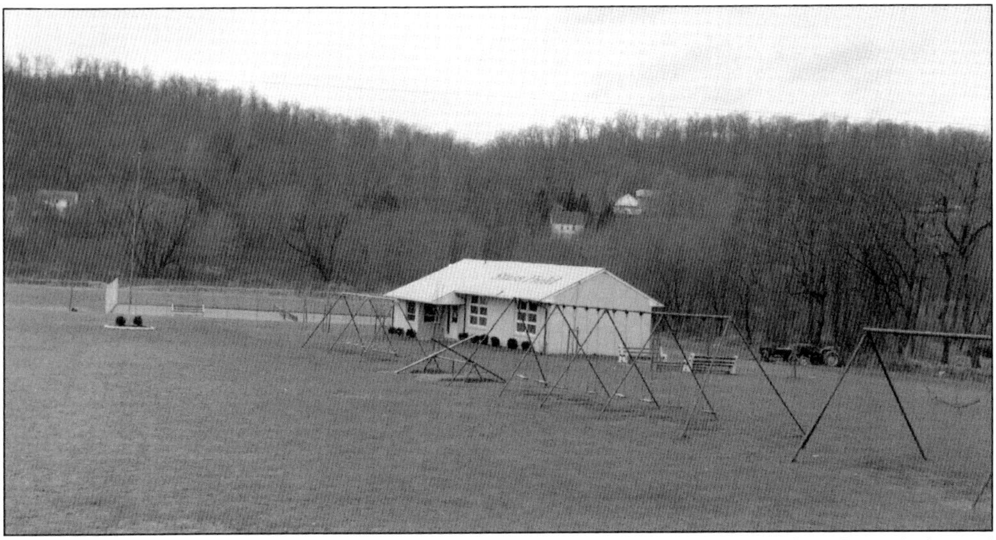

Stagg Field is a 13-acre playground named for Amos Alonzo Stagg (see page 46) and was dedicated on May 8, 1954. Stagg was a legendary college football coach and early innovator of the game. He was born on August 16, 1862, and grew up in West Orange. The original field house and playground equipment are seen here shortly after the playground opened in 1954.

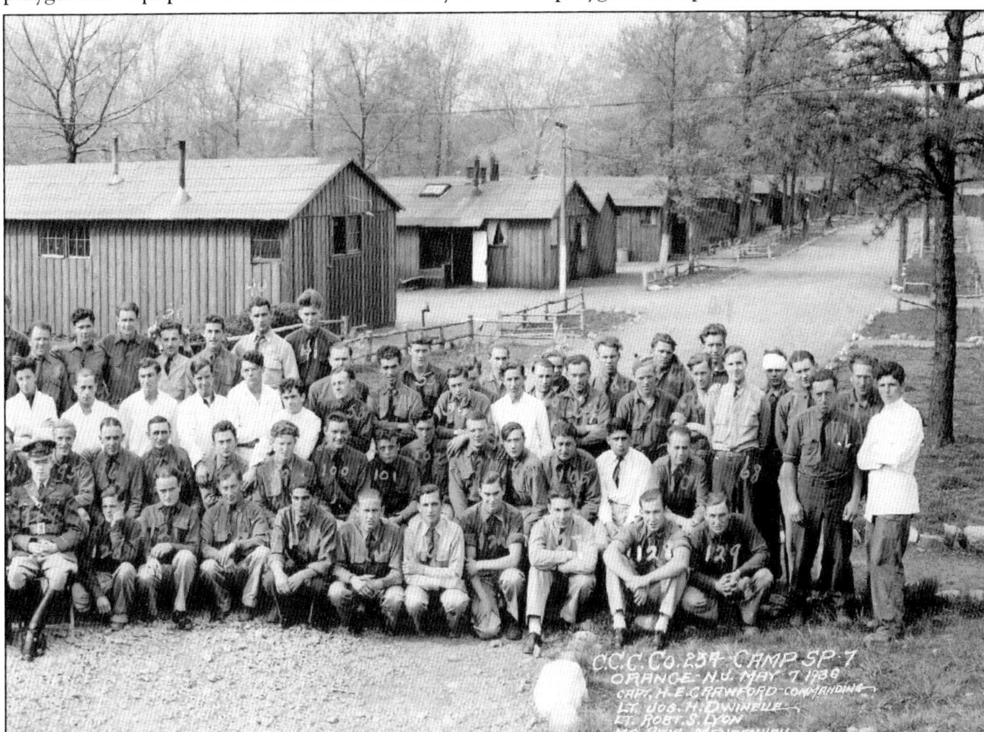

The Civilian Conservation Corps was created in 1933 by Pres. Franklin Roosevelt. Camp SP7 was one of 2,600 work camps scattered across the United States. It was officially listed in Orange but was actually located off Walker Road in West Orange. The young men seen here on May 7, 1936, came from across the country. They helped construct trails throughout West Orange in both the South Mountain and Eagle Rock Reservations.

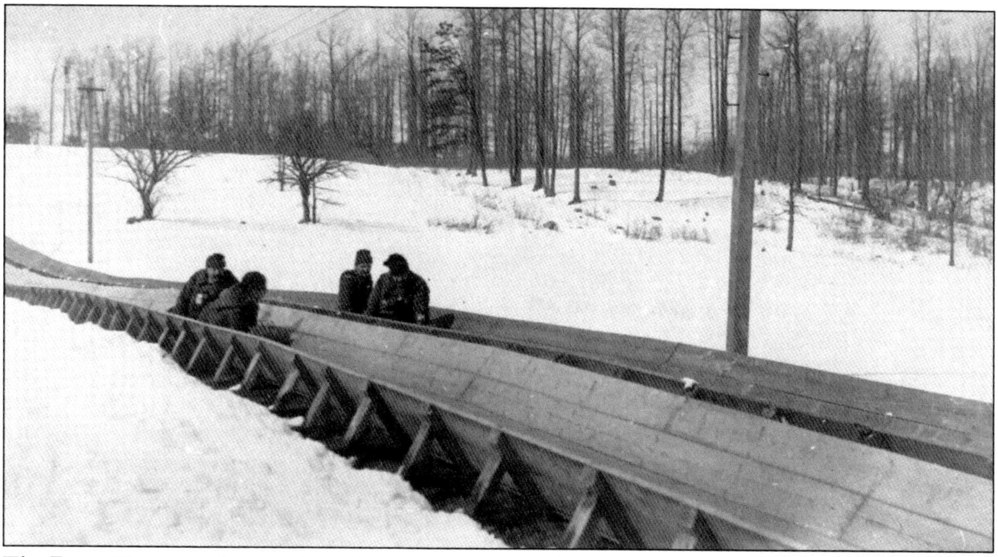

The Essex County Toboggan Club began operations in January 1886 on a toboggan slide, seen here in 1890, that closely paralleled the slope along present-day Hazel Avenue. Among the founders were Francis Tetrault and Francis O'Reilly. Tetrault was French Canadian, and toboggans were used regularly in his native Quebec. He was instrumental in making the winter sport of his home a popular attraction in West Orange for several years.

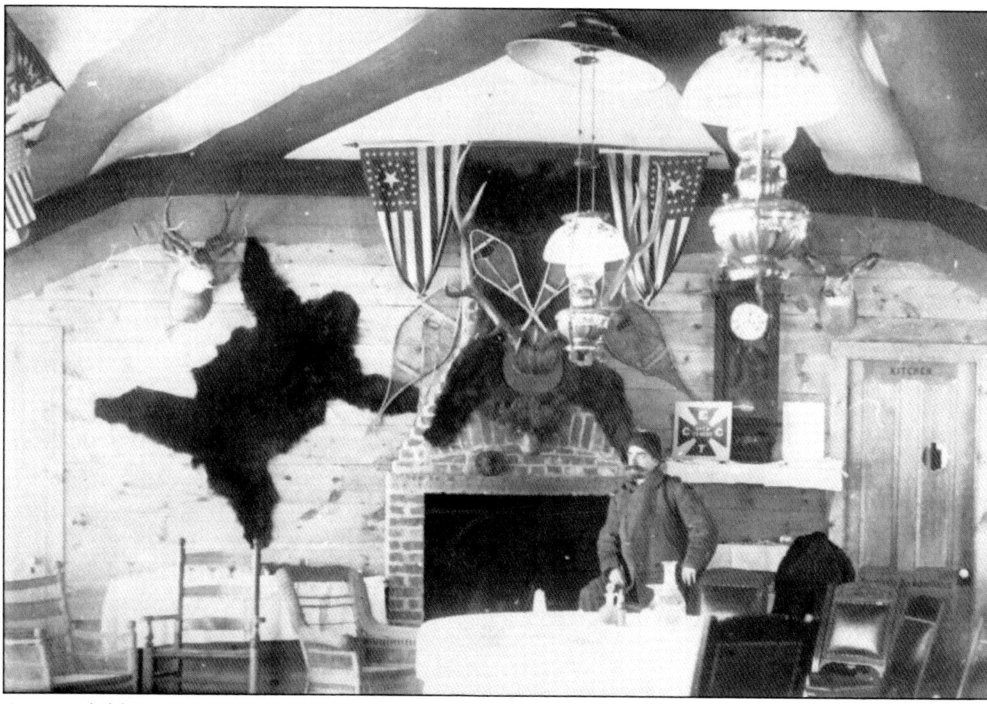

A new clubhouse was constructed near the current-day intersection of Hazel Avenue and Valley Road. Luna Stage Center is now located close to where the clubhouse once stood. An unidentified member is seen here inside the clubhouse in 1890. The bearskins and snowshoes hanging on the wall created a rugged atmosphere more typical of a winter lodge in Canada than suburban West Orange.

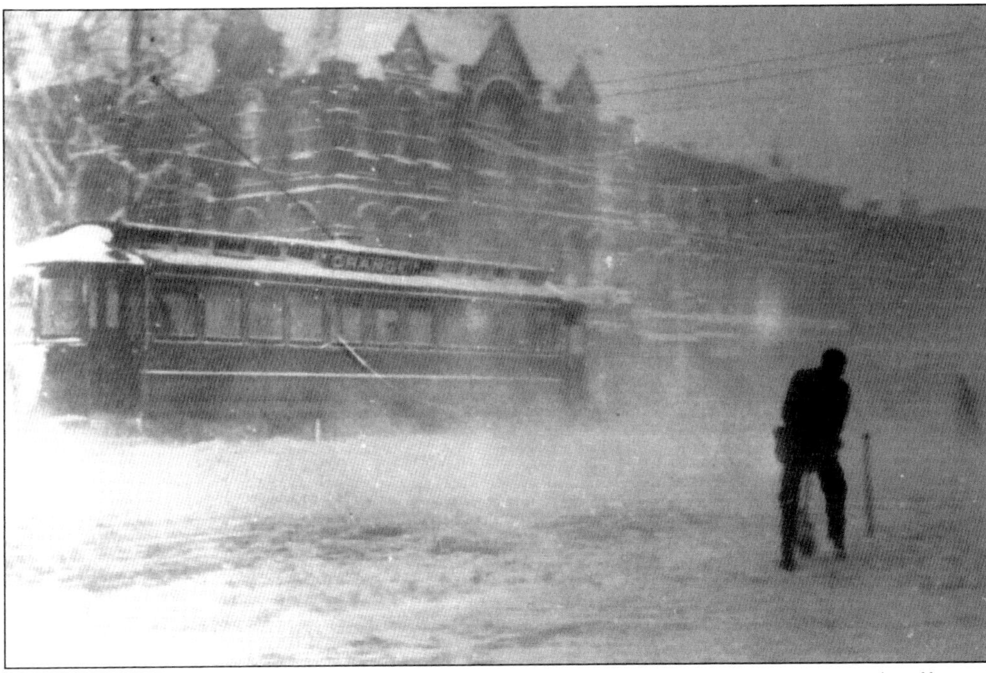

Shortly before midnight on March 12, 1888, snow began to fall and caught most people off guard while they slept. It fell constantly for a period of 36 hours and produced snowdrifts in excess of 50 feet. This photograph taken March 13, 1888, is perhaps the only photograph actually taken during the blizzard of 1888, showing a trolley stalled by the storm on Main Street in Orange.

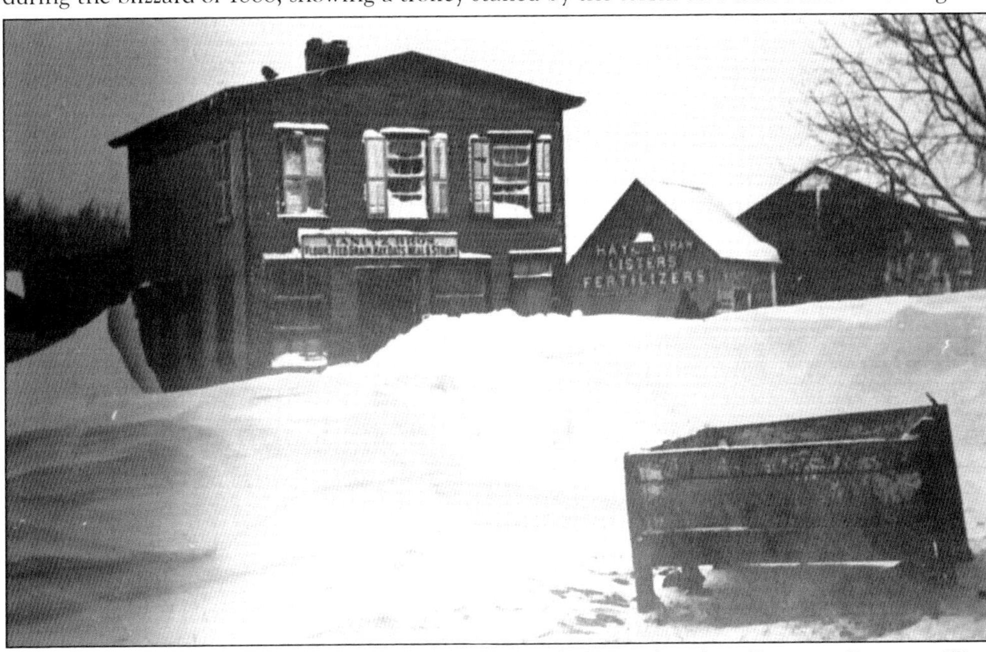

A picture taken after the storm shows the large snowdrifts produced on Freeman Street in West Orange by the blizzard of 1888. Snowfall amounts of 40 to 50 inches fell in parts of New Jersey with sustained winds of more than 45 miles per hour. All phone and telegraph communications from West Orange were cut off entirely for more then three days and mail service for five days.

Four

Legacy of Transportation

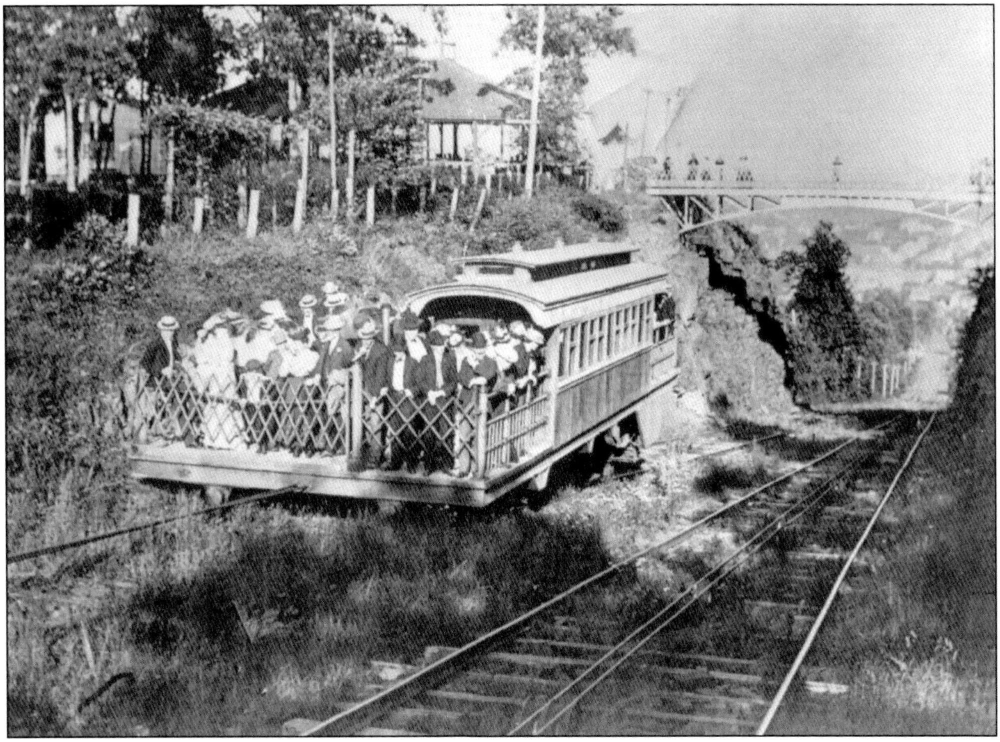

The Cable Road, seen here around 1900, was operated from 1892 to 1895 by the Orange Cable Company, which reorganized as the Orange Mountain Traction Company from 1898 to 1902. It was a cable railway using specially designed trolleys with platforms that were pulled by cables up the steep grade. It ran from South Valley Road to the mountaintop at Cable Lake at the present-day site of Rock Spring Country Club.

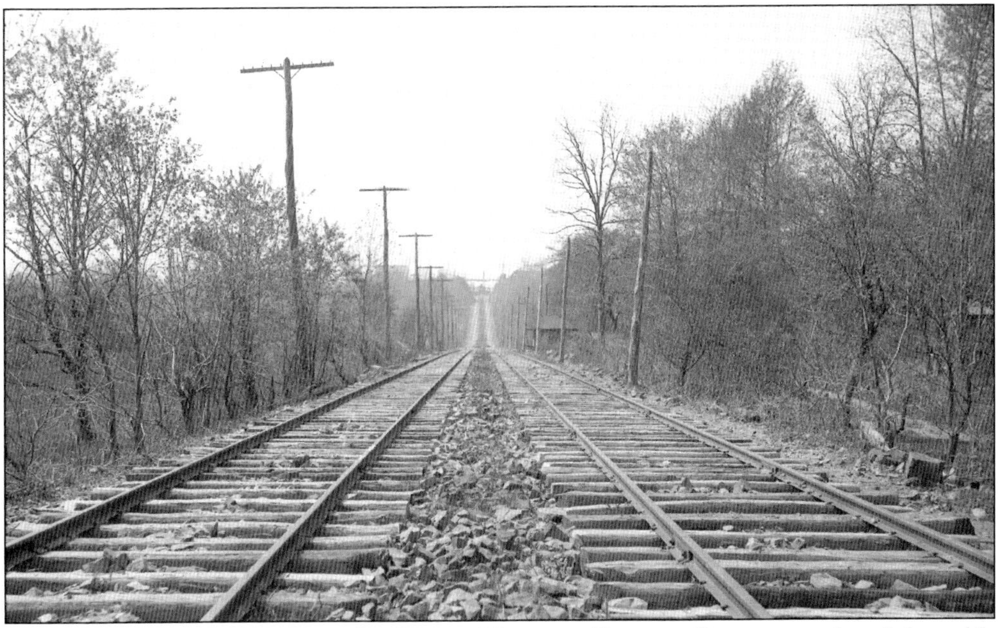

Four years after closing in 1902, the Orange Mountain Traction Company replaced the cable railway with two newly installed standard-gauge tracks up the mountain The company's plan was to use regular trolleys powered by overhead wires to climb the steep grade. The tracks are seen here on May 4, 1906, in a view looking west toward the summit with Gregory Avenue, the only public street that the line crossed, barely visible about midway. (ID.)

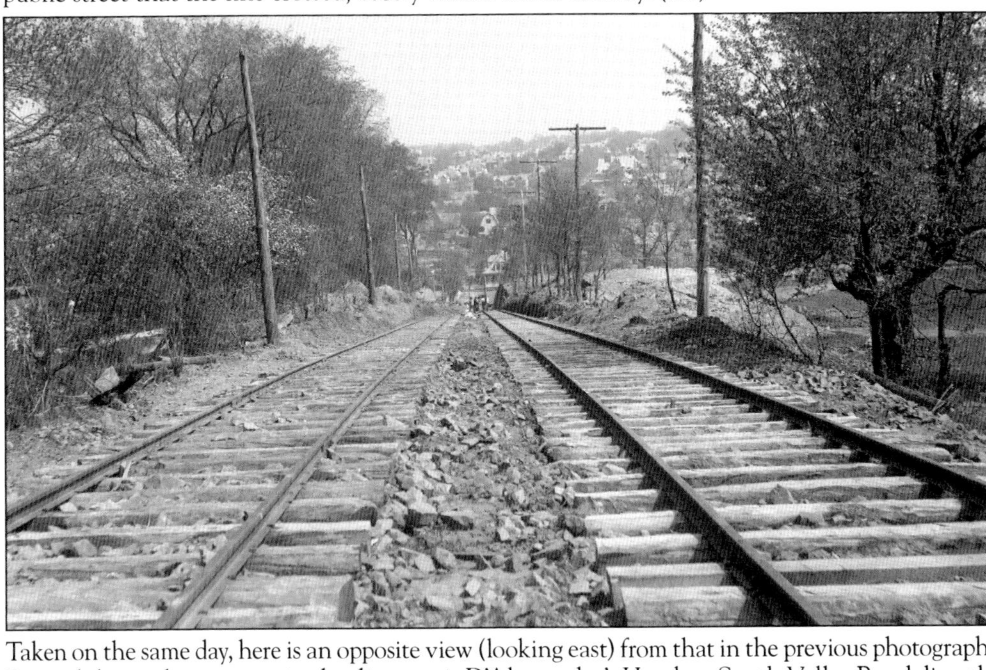

Taken on the same day, here is an opposite view (looking east) from that in the previous photograph. Beyond the work crew seen in the distance is D'Alessandro's Hotel on South Valley Road directly opposite the eastern terminus; it is still standing today as Suzy Que's Restaurant. Many concerns were raised that the grade was too steep for conventional trolleys to negotiate, but it was believed a new patented braking system was adequate. (ID.)

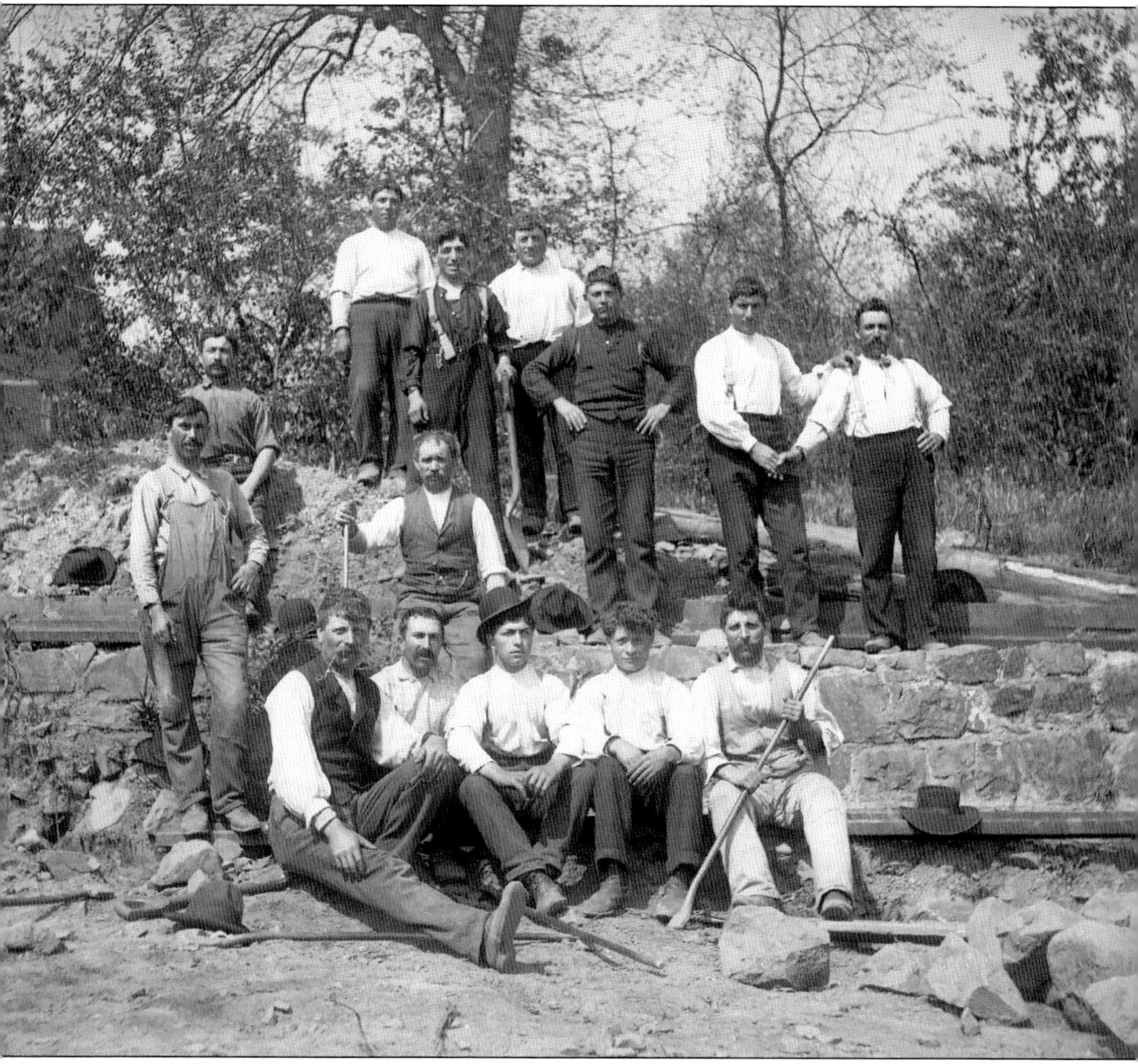

On May 4, 1906, these laborers taking a break are the same men seen in the picture on the bottom of the opposite page. Although taking a picture is commonplace in all aspects of life today, it likely was a novel idea at this time to have a photographer visit them while working. They were busy laying the last section of rails for the new trolley line that would run up the mountain over the route of the old cable cars. The inaugural run for the Orange Mountain Traction Company was planned for June, and the operators of the line were hopeful for a more successful venture than the financial failures of the cable cars. Despite repeated safety concerns from the public about the steep incline of the grade, company officials were confident their new trolleys were equal to the task. (ID.)

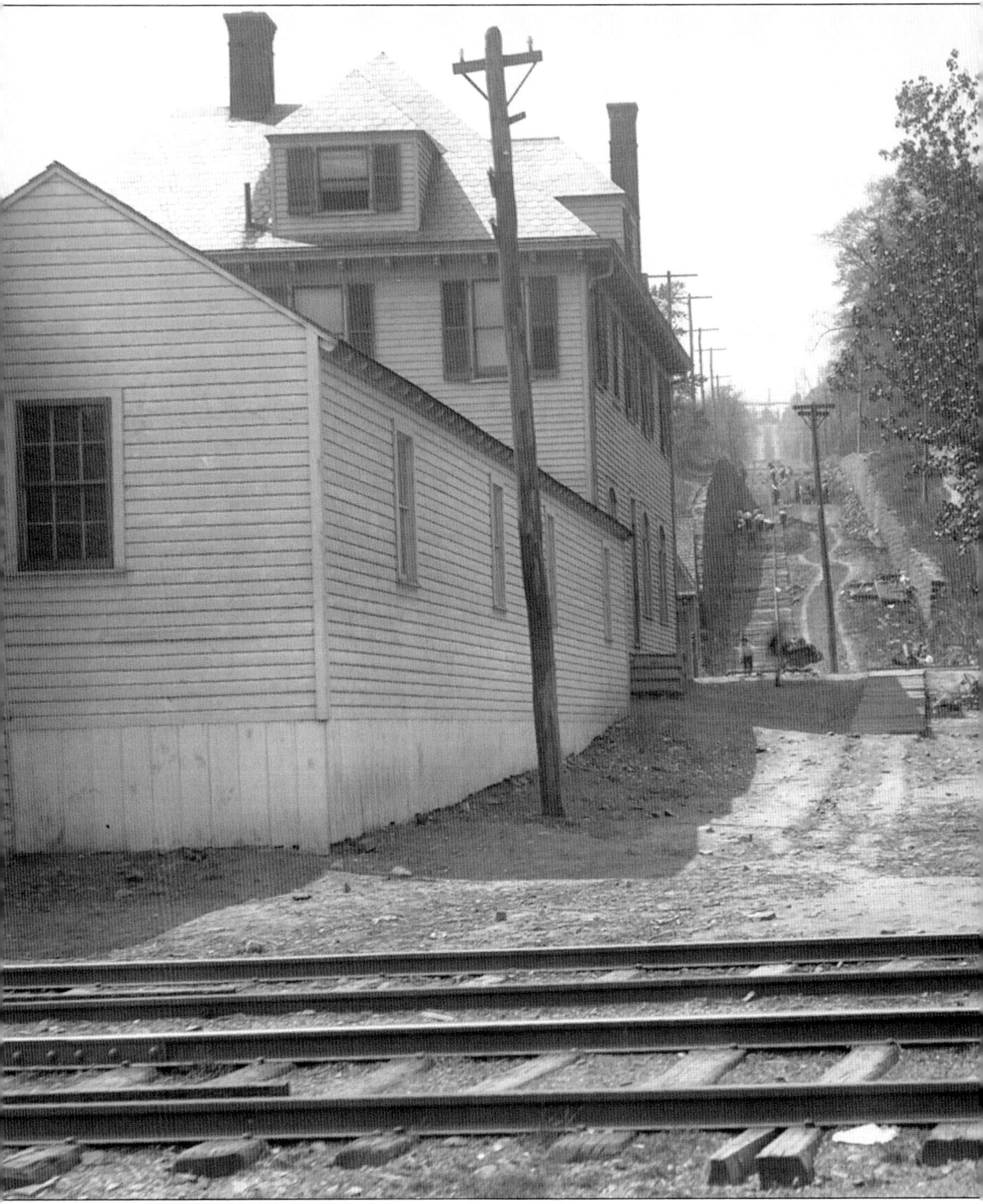

The last of four pictures taken on May 4, 1906, shows work progressing in the distance to lay new rails as seen from behind D'Alessandro's Hotel, the building to the left. This view is looking across South Valley Road from the current-day parking lot of Suzy Que's Restaurant. The work crew seen on the previous page can be spotted. The tracks in the foreground are those of the South Orange and Maplewood Traction Company, also known as the Montrose Line and "Swamp Line,"

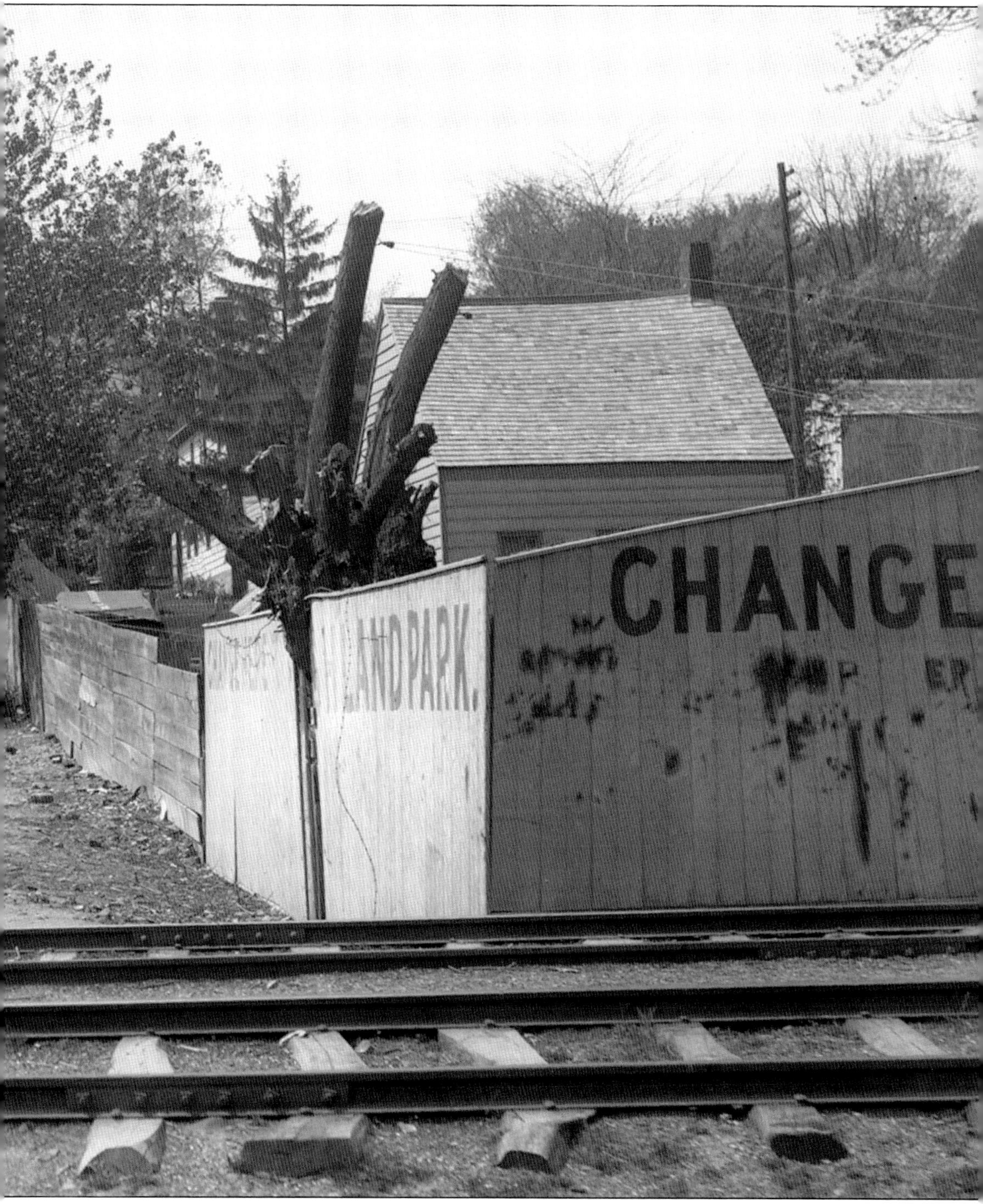

which ran from 1894 to 1927. At this location, passengers could transfer to the Orange Mountain Traction Company. The message on the fence reads, "Change here for Highland Park," which was a failed amusement park operated at Cable Lake on the top of the mountain during the days of the cable cars from 1898 to 1902. (ID.)

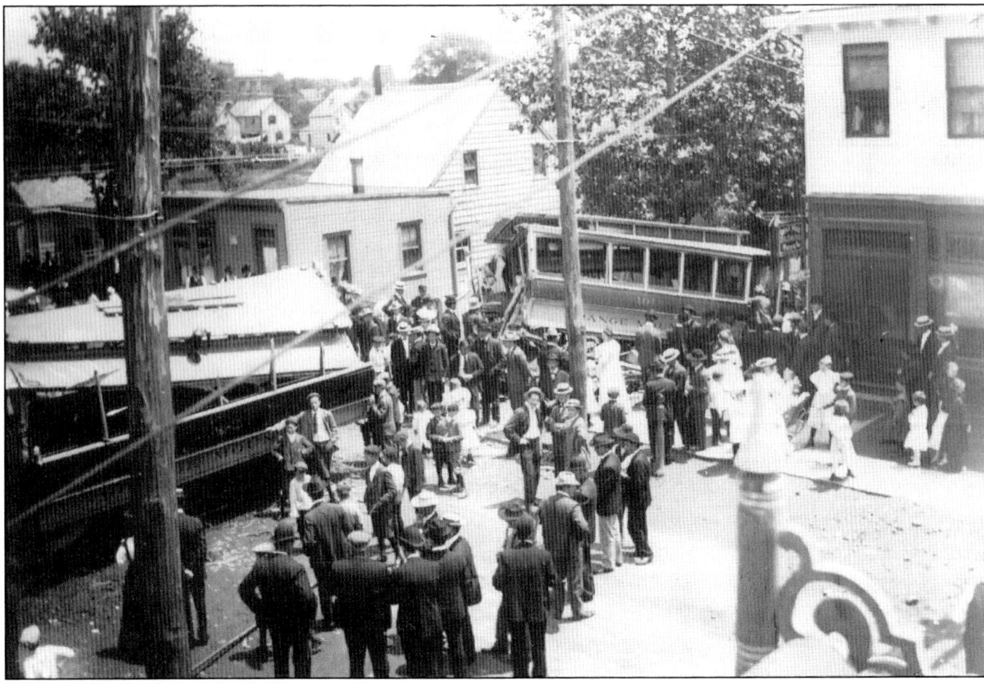

On June 24, 1906, disaster struck during the inaugural test run for the Orange Mountain Traction Company. As car No. 102 approached the steepest part of the grade, the wheels slipped and the brakes failed, and it began rolling back down the hill out of control. It crashed into car No. 101 parked at the bottom, hurling it airborne across South Valley Road into an empty lot adjacent to D'Alessandro's Hotel. (FS.)

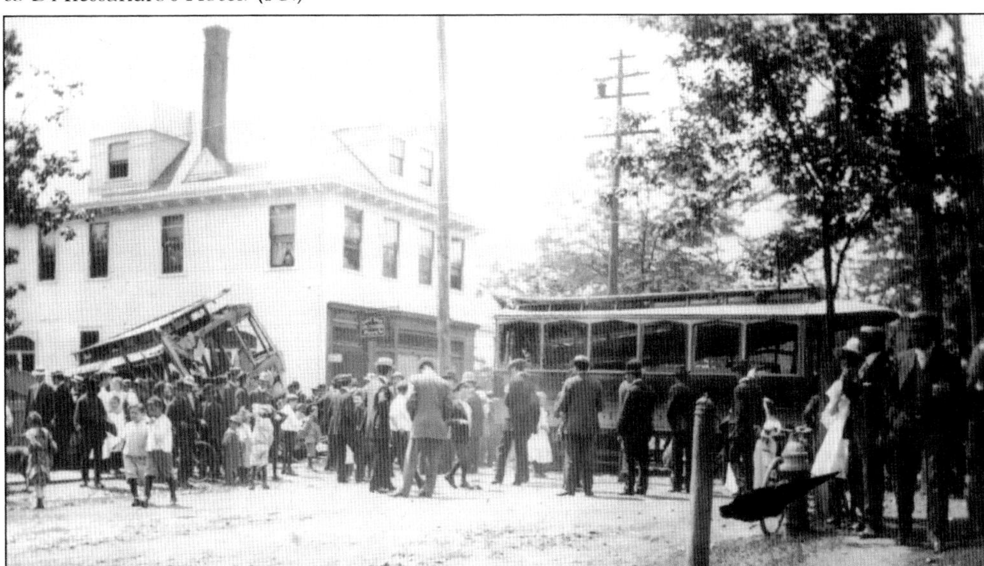

Both trolley cars were completely destroyed in the accident, resulting in one death and several serious injures. June 24, 1906, was the first and last day of operations for the ill-fated Orange Mountain Traction Company. This scene on South Valley Road across from D'Alessandro's Hotel shows the extent of the destruction and the fortunate near miss for the hotel. (FS.)

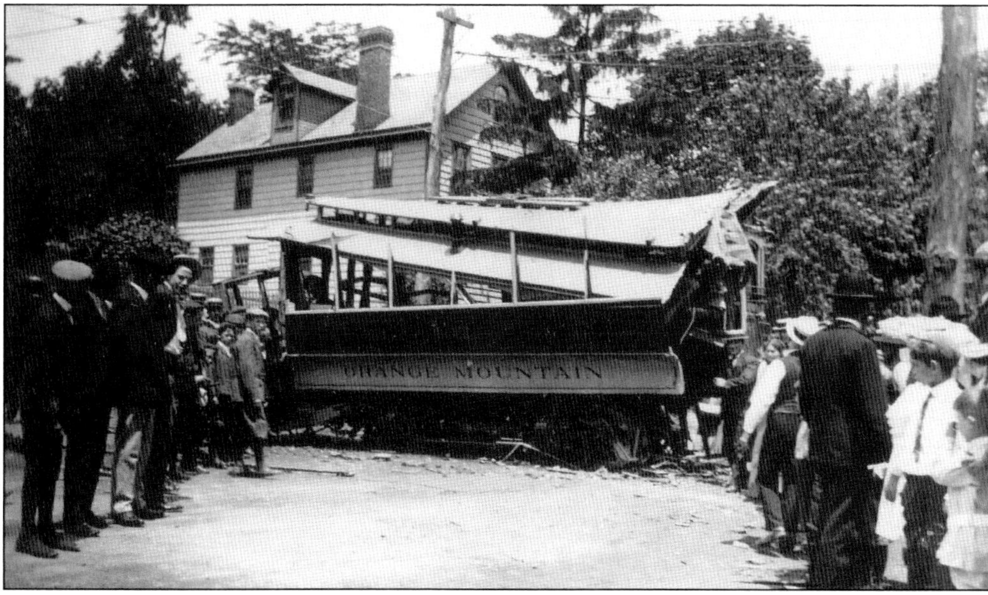

A reverse-angle view shows car No. 102, which came flying down the mountain out of control. Its momentum upon impact with car No. 101 carried it nearly across South Valley Road. The news spread quickly, and crowds of curious onlookers soon gathered, with untethered access to the scene. The house seen in the background, like the hotel building, is still standing. (FS.)

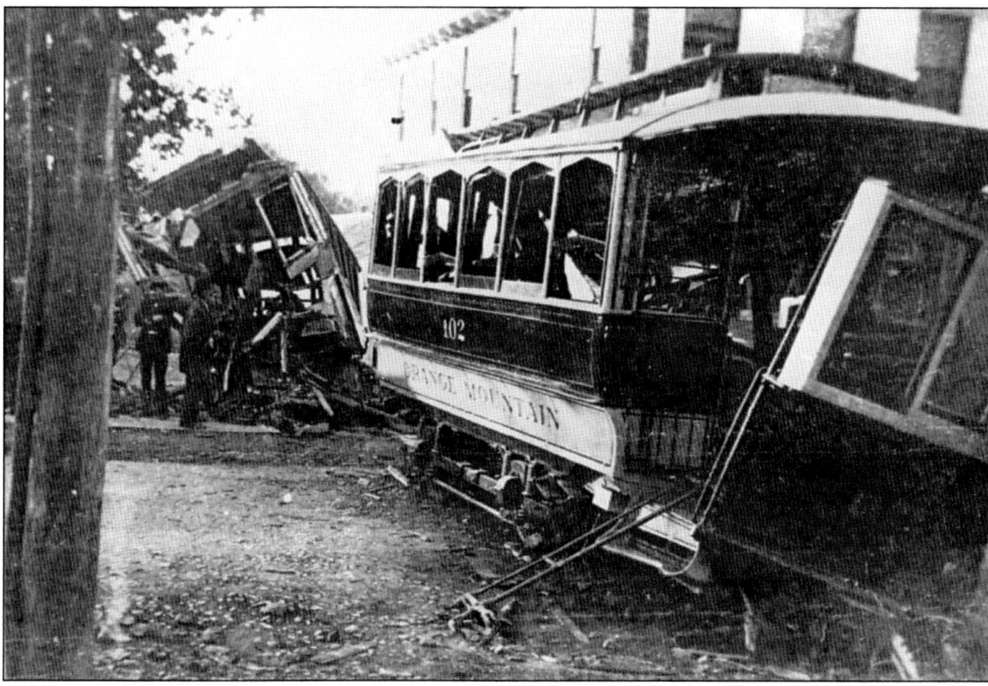

Following the accident, the Orange Mountain Traction Company abandoned plans for running conventional trolley cars up the route once used by cable cars. But organizers did not give up entirely on the idea of reaching the top of the mountain with a trolley line. Two years following the 1906 mishap, they ran a new line using a safer switchback route only crossing paths with the old line at a few locations.

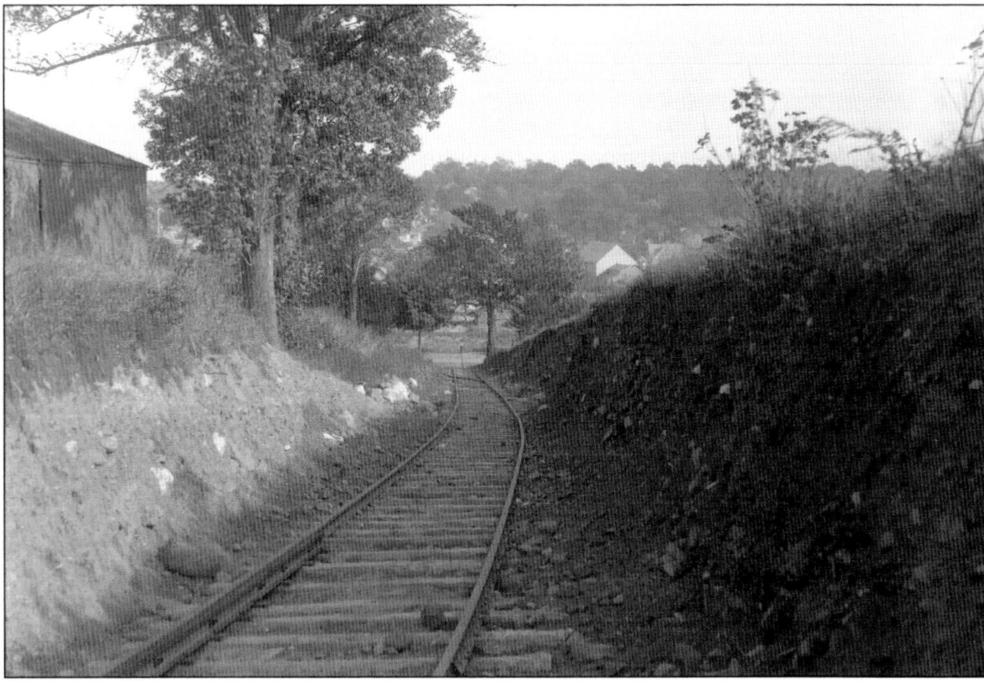

A new company, the Orange Mountain Railway, was formed and began a new rail line a short distance south of the previous line. It opened in 1908 and, unlike its predecessor, crossed South Valley Road on its route up the mountain. Taken October 15, 1907, this photograph shows the cut through the Freeman farm bordering Walker Road, in a view looking east with South Valley Road seen in the distance. (ID.)

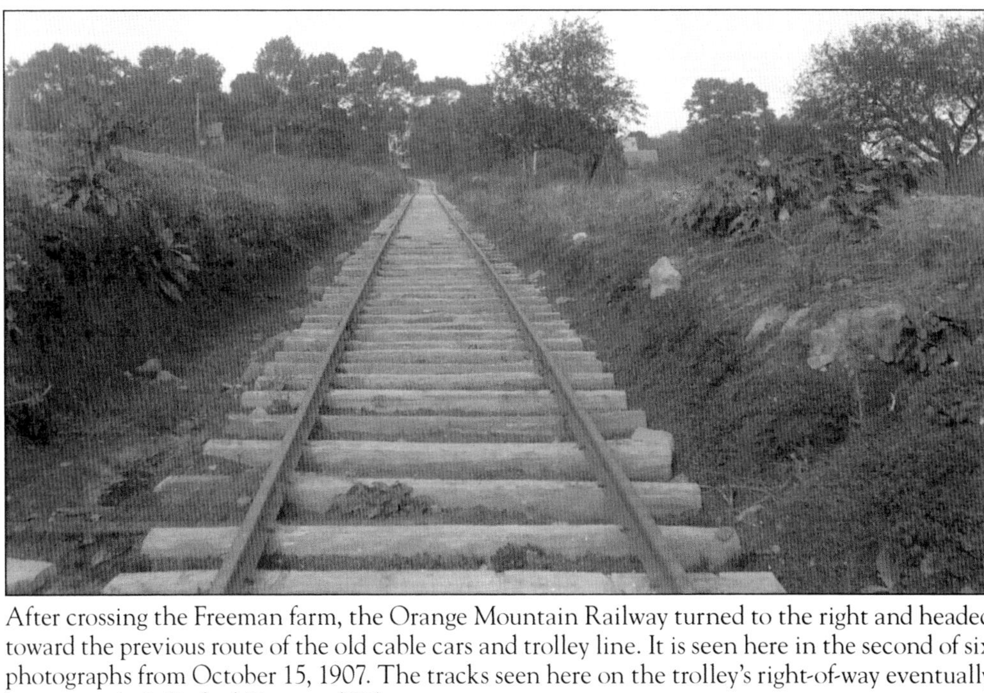

After crossing the Freeman farm, the Orange Mountain Railway turned to the right and headed toward the previous route of the old cable cars and trolley line. It is seen here in the second of six photographs from October 15, 1907. The tracks seen here on the trolley's right-of-way eventually became today's Oxford Terrace. (ID.)

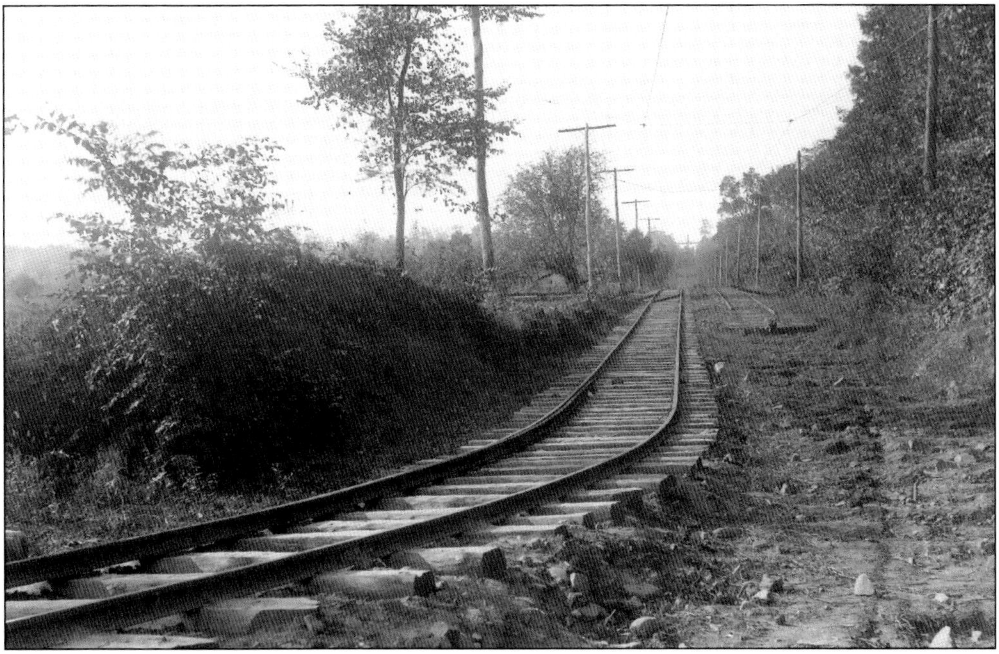

The Orange Mountain Railway was a new single-track line and is seen here in 1907 turning onto the roadbed of the old cable car line. It only traveled up the mountain over the old route for a short distance before breaking away on a safer zigzag route using a series of three switchbacks. Remnants of the failed 1906 line can be seen to the right. (ID.)

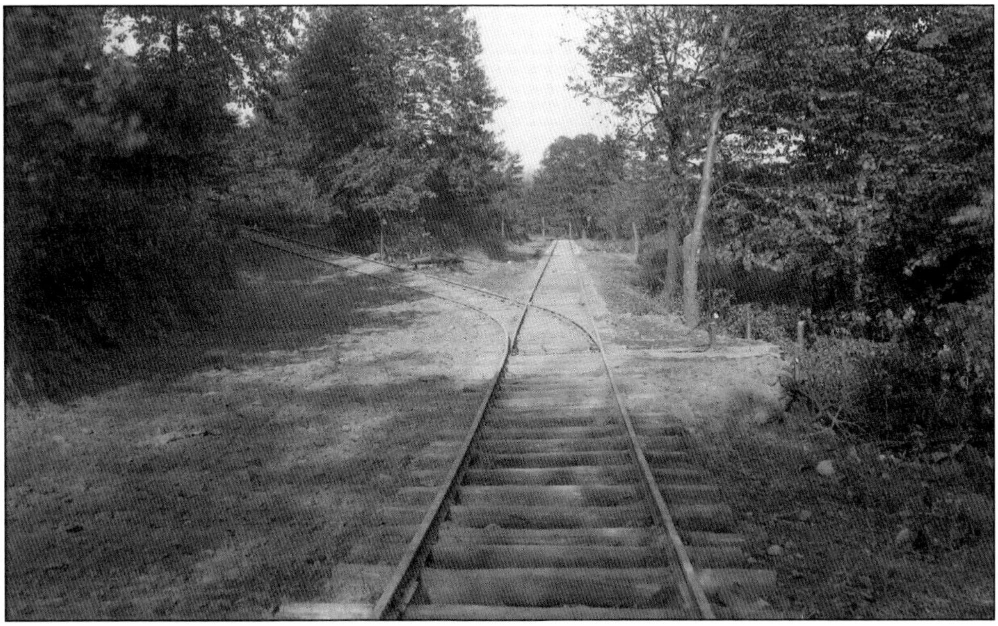

Pictured here on October 15, 1907, is the third of three switchbacks used on the Orange Mountain Railway. Each switchback had a short counter grade to stop a trolley if it should lose control and run away down the mountain, as happened on the 1906 route. These precautions ultimately proved unnecessary since no trolley ever went out of control on the gentler grades of the new line. (ID.)

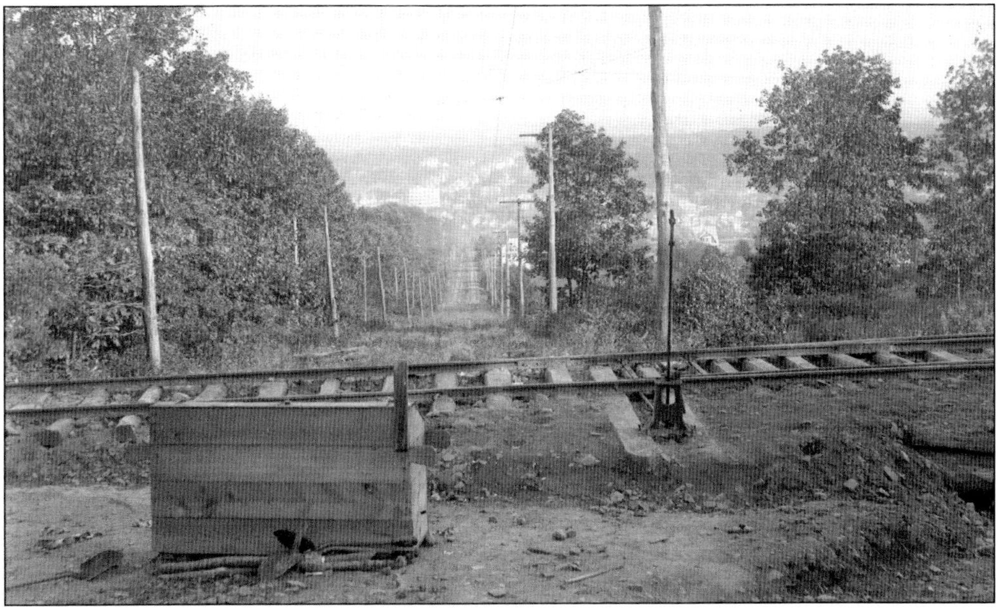

This 1907 view shows the new line passing left to right, in a view looking east down the old cable route toward the Orange Valley. The middle switchback is out of view to the right. This line opened in 1908 and ran as far west as the Rock Spring Inn on Northfield Avenue until it closed in 1914. (ID.)

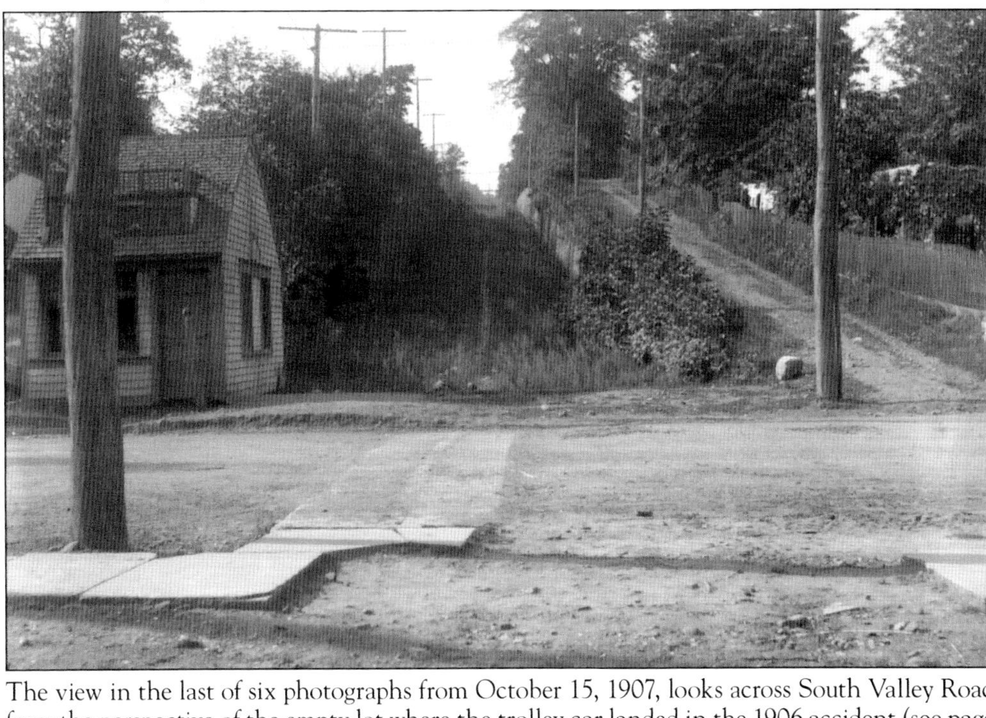

The view in the last of six photographs from October 15, 1907, looks across South Valley Road from the perspective of the empty lot where the trolley car landed in the 1906 accident (see page 110). It shows the abandoned ticket office on the left that once used by the Orange Mountain Cable Company in 1892 and the overgrown remains behind of the original cable car route, which is now part of Wheatland Avenue. (ID.)

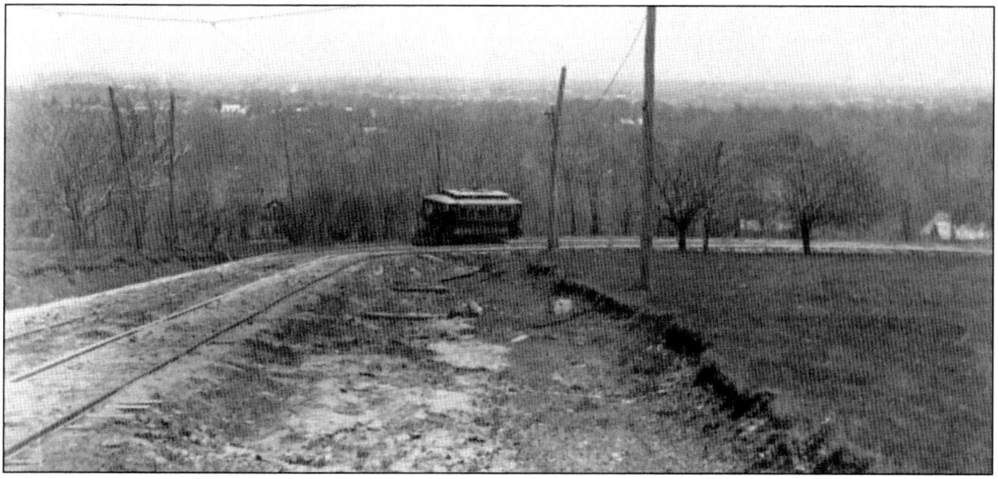

The Eagle Rock trolley line had replaced a stagecoach line dating to the 1870s and began operations in July 1894, originating on Washington Street and terminating on Mountain Avenue just below Eagle Rock. It is seen here in 1898 rounding the double-track curve at the bottom of what is current-day Nutwold Avenue. Today, this former right-of-way connects the bottom of Nutwold Avenue with Moore Terrace.

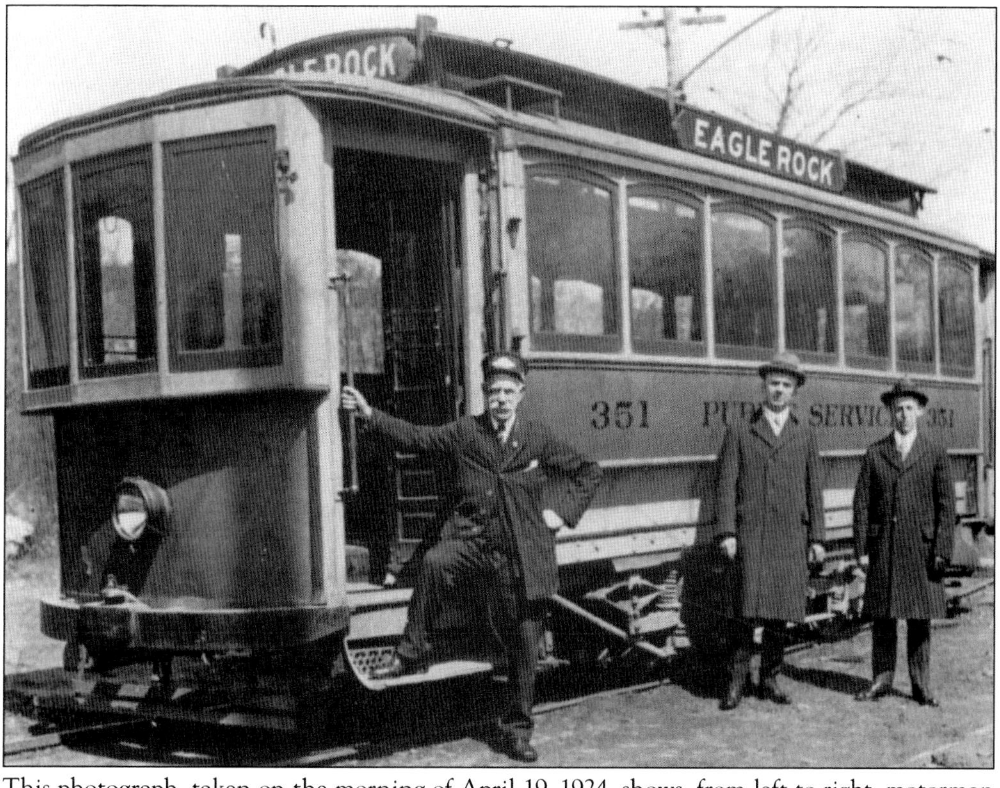

This photograph, taken on the morning of April 19, 1924, shows, from left to right, motorman James Costigan, William Pierce, and an unidentified person at an unspecified location on the last run of the Eagle Rock trolley. Four years after trolley service was discontinued, an attempt was made to provide bus service to Eagle Rock, but it only lasted until 1932, finally ending nearly 62 years of public transportation to Eagle Rock.

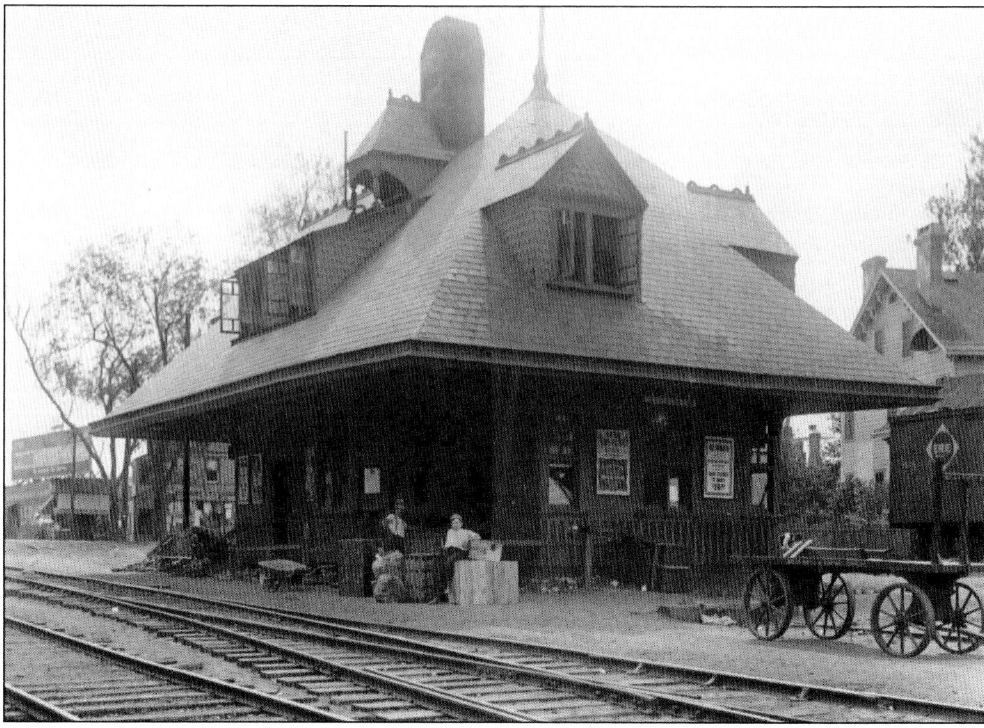

In 1874, a spur line on the Erie Railroad's Greenwood Lake Division entered West Orange. The Watchung, or Orange Branch as it was also known, began operations in 1876 to Llewellyn Station on Park Avenue. In 1881, the line was extended to Main Street, and a second West Orange station was built. It is seen here in 1901, and St. Mark's Church is out of view to the right.

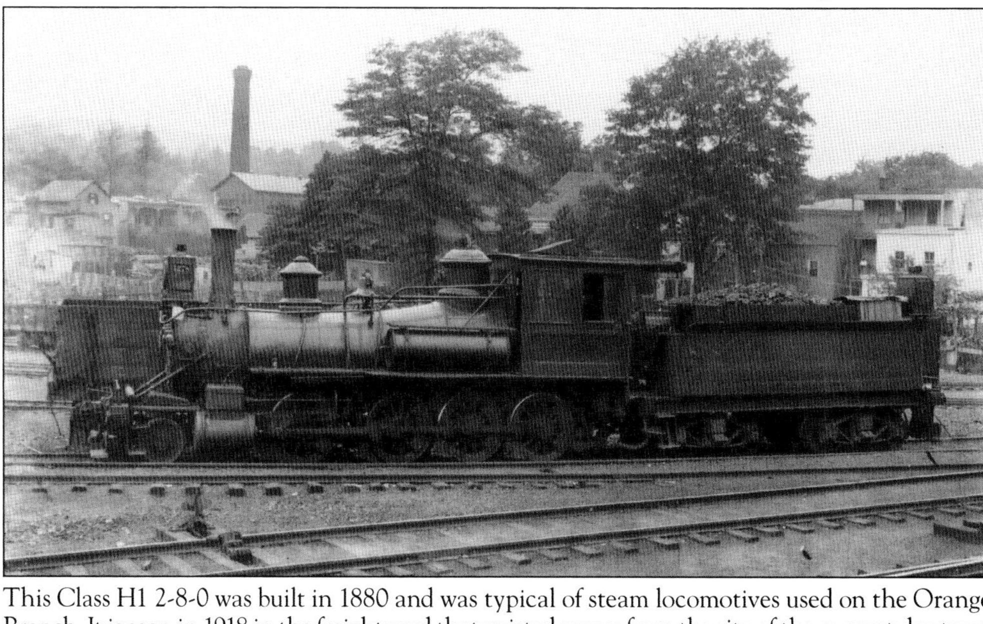

This Class H1 2-8-0 was built in 1880 and was typical of steam locomotives used on the Orange Branch. It is seen in 1918 in the freight yard that existed across from the site of the current-day town hall on Main Street. The tall chimney belongs to the hat factory that once stood near the corner of Main Street and Mount Pleasant Avenue, and the houses to the right are on White Street.

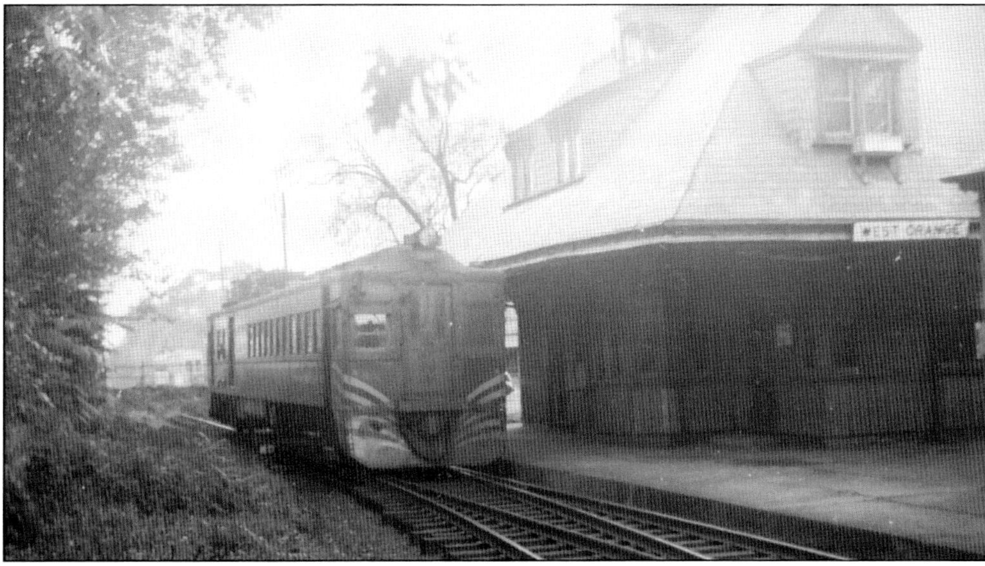

By 1936, steam locomotives had been replaced by self-propelled railcars, commonly referred to as doodlebugs, that had a gasoline-powered engine that turned a generator, which provided electricity to traction motors. The train station is seen here in the 1940s. Service using this type of motive power was discontinued in 1953 on the Orange Branch serving West Orange.

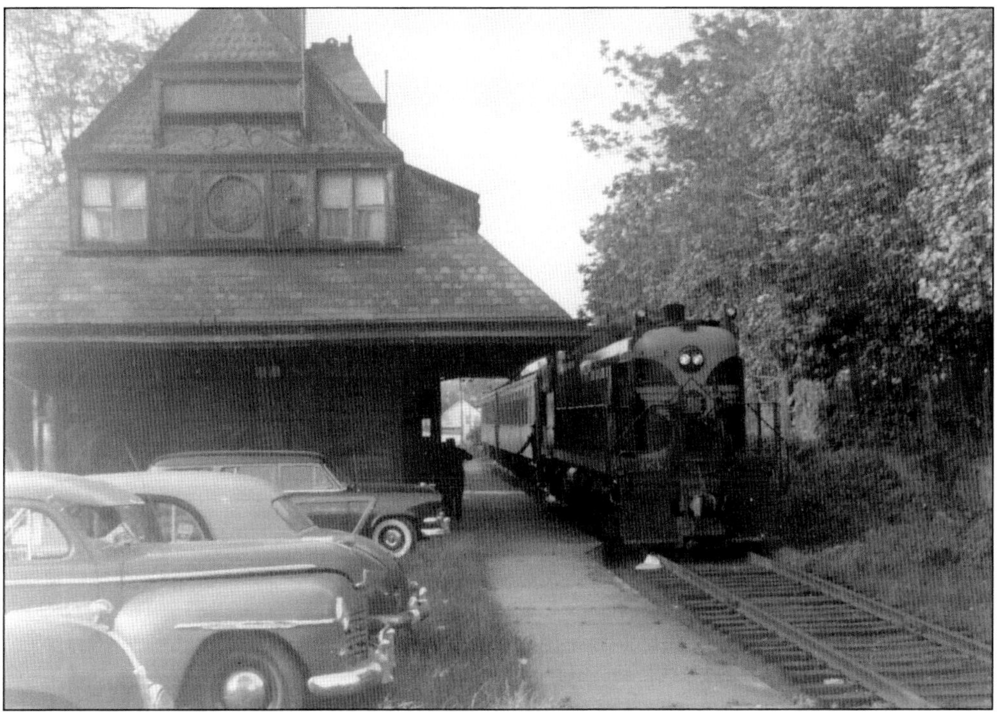

Passenger service to the train station on Main Street, seen here around 1955, continued, using diesel-electric locomotives manufactured by the American Locomotive Company (ALCO). The last passenger train left West Orange on May 20, 1955, and both West Orange train stations were torn down in the 1960s. Freight service continued on the line until the early 1980s, when all the rails of the former Orange Branch were ripped up.

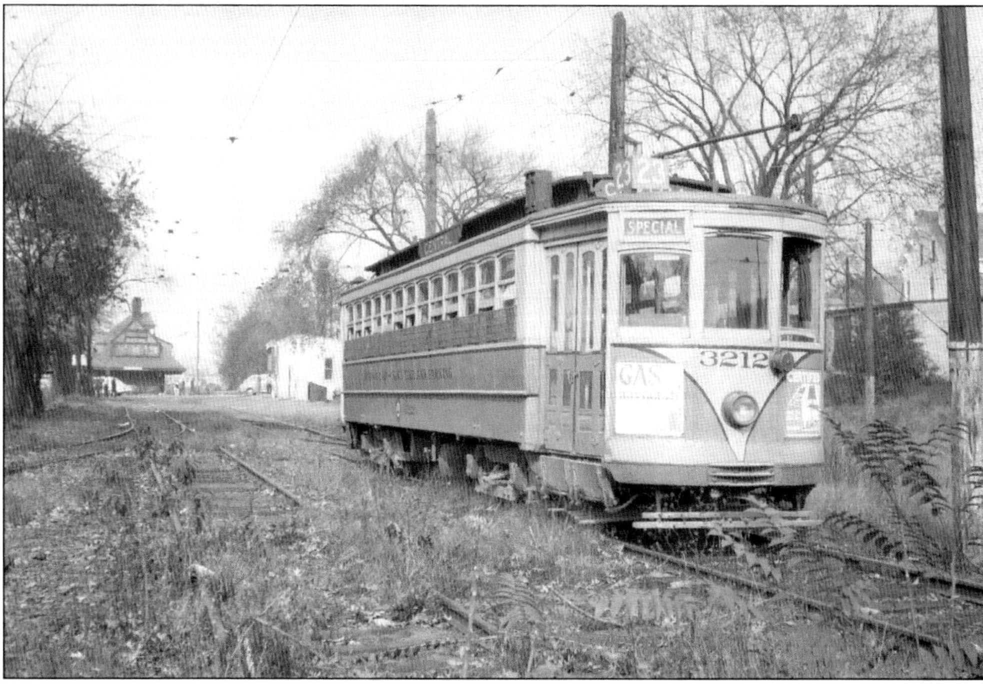

The South Orange and Maplewood Traction Company, also known as the Montrose Line and "Swamp Line," operated from 1894 to 1927. It began directly across from the Main Street West Orange train station, seen in the distance to the left. When the line closed the tracks directly opposite the West Orange train station, seen here in 1947, the area was reconfigured and became known as the Erie Loop, where trolleys turned around.

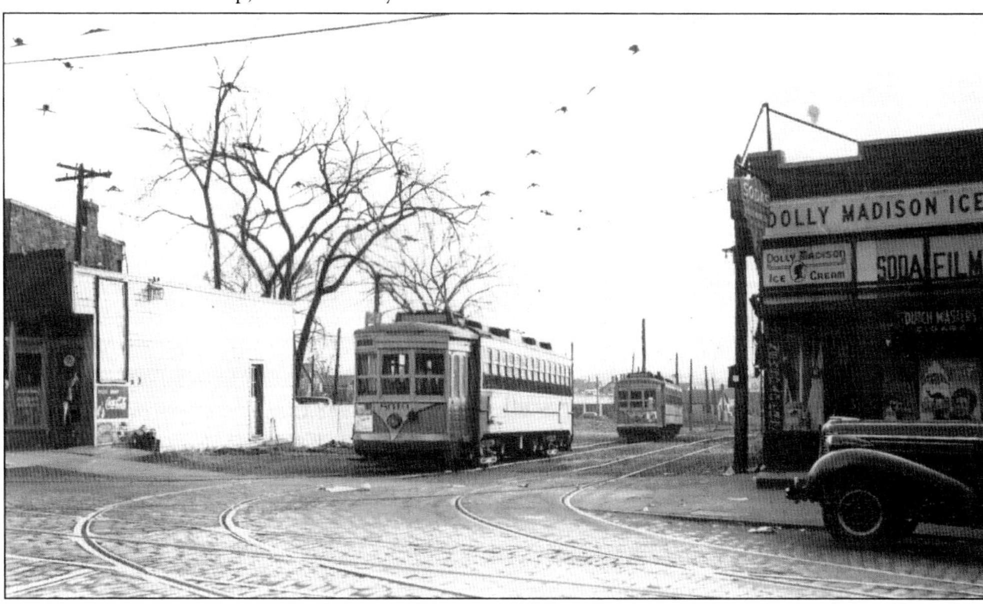

Trolleys can be seen entering the Erie Loop on Main Street in November 1946 across from the West Orange train station. All the tracks were removed in the 1950s, and this area is now a large municipal parking lot. Buses operated by New Jersey Transit on Main Street today still use the Erie Loop as a designated stop on the line.

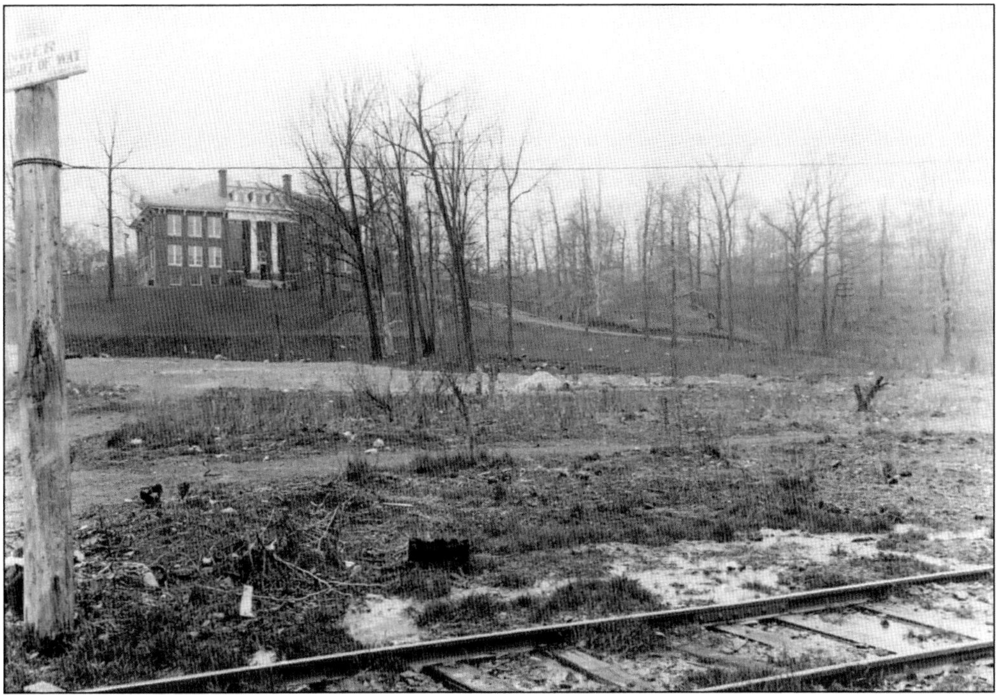

A single track of the "Swamp Line" trolley can be seen passing the Hazel Avenue school on April 15, 1913, on the first anniversary of the sinking of the *Titanic*. The sign barely visible in the upper left of the photograph reads, "Danger Trolley Right of Way." It apparently was the only preventive safety measure warning schoolchildren to stay away.

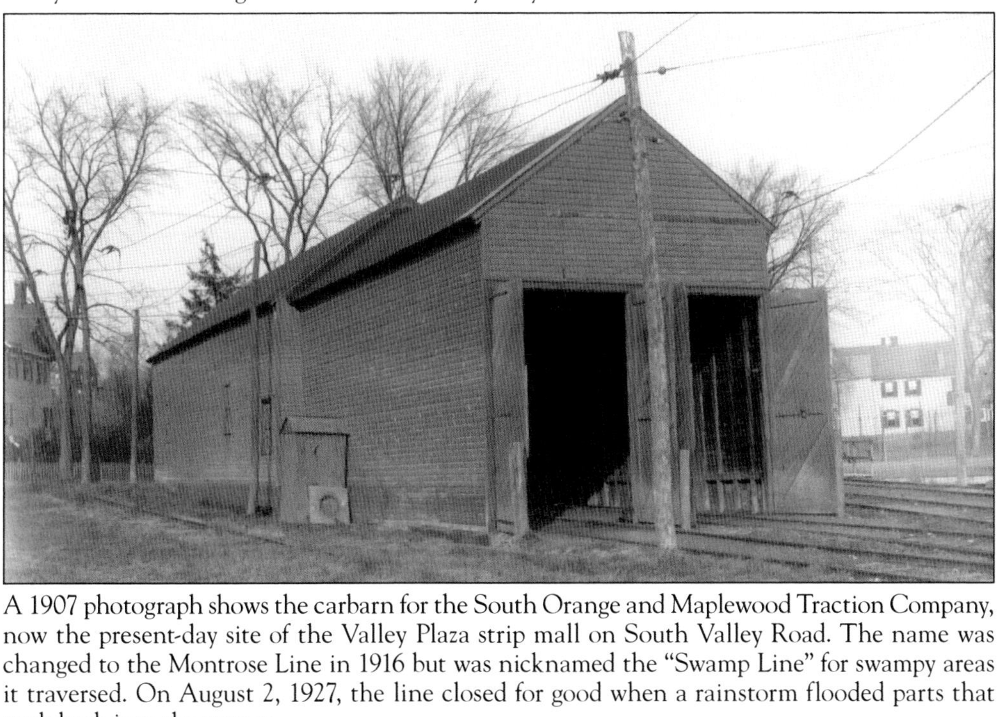

A 1907 photograph shows the carbarn for the South Orange and Maplewood Traction Company, now the present-day site of the Valley Plaza strip mall on South Valley Road. The name was changed to the Montrose Line in 1916 but was nicknamed the "Swamp Line" for swampy areas it traversed. On August 2, 1927, the line closed for good when a rainstorm flooded parts that sank back into the swamp.

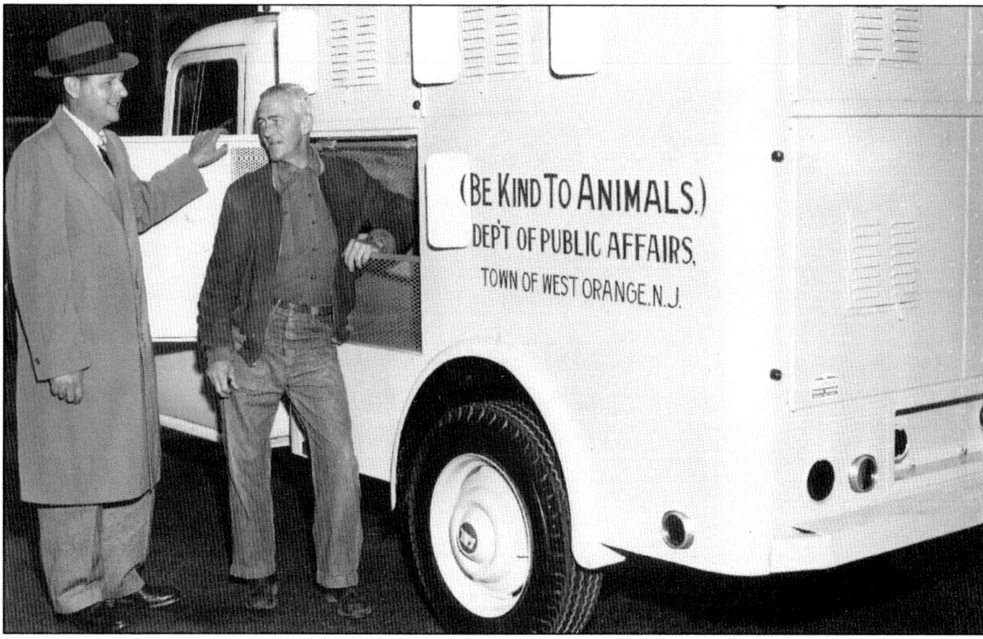

West Orange mayor Walter Quinn (left) can be seen talking with dog warden Ralph Parks about the newly arrived animal control truck on April 16, 1956. Purchased from General Motors at a cost of $3,600, it was the most up-to-date vehicle at the time. It was paid for with revenue generated by the sale of dog licenses and replaced an outdated 1952 model.

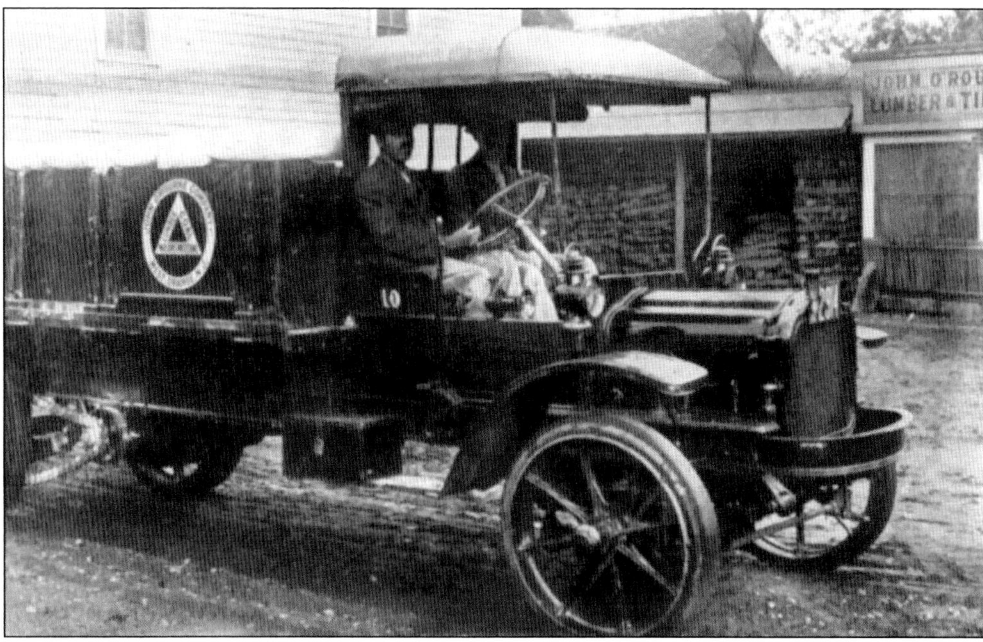

This delivery truck manufactured by the White Company for the John O'Rourke Company at 17 Park Avenue is seen in 1915. It had a three-ton capacity and replaced three teams of horse-drawn delivery wagons with greater efficiency and versatility. O'Rourke sold lumber, coal, and mason materials, and in 1943 this business became the E.L. Congdon Lumber Company, which still operates at the same location.

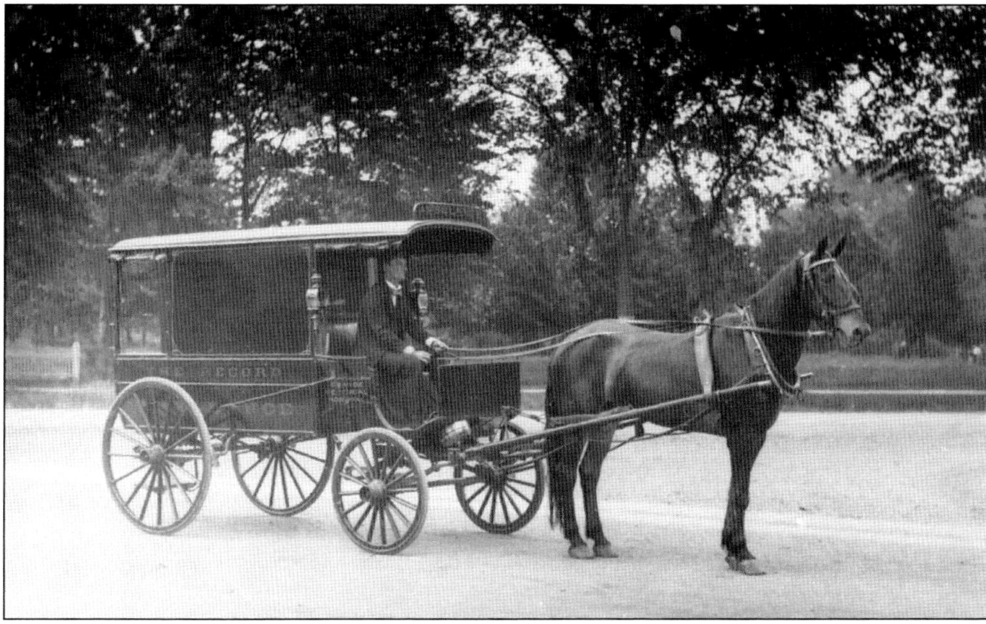

On June 15, 1888, a player was injured during a polo match on a field located near the intersection of Mount Pleasant and Gregory Avenues. There was no way to transport him to a hospital, which led to the founding of Record Ambulance, the first in the Oranges. The company's new horse-drawn ambulance is seen here in 1889. The ambulance service closed in 1987 after 99 years in business.

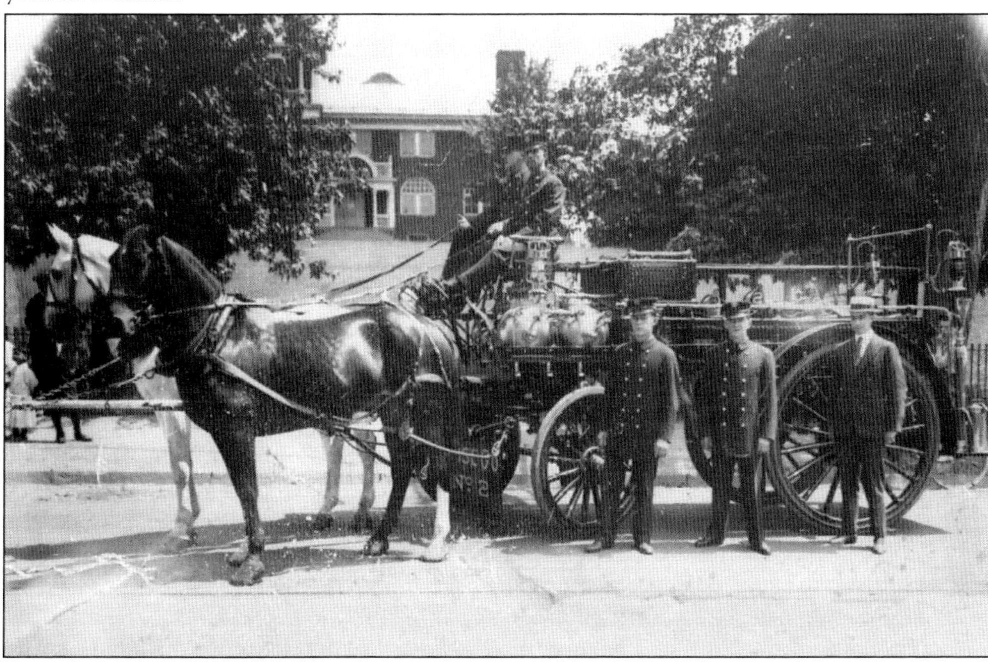

The horse-drawn wagon of West Orange Fire Company No. 2 is seen on July 4, 1915, in front of the Washington Street School across from the firehouse. Seated are, from left to right, William Bauer and Martin Kennedy. Standing are, from left to right, Timothy Conners, Joseph Allerton, and West Orange councilman Julius Weigel. The white horse is Dan, and the dark horse is Bill.

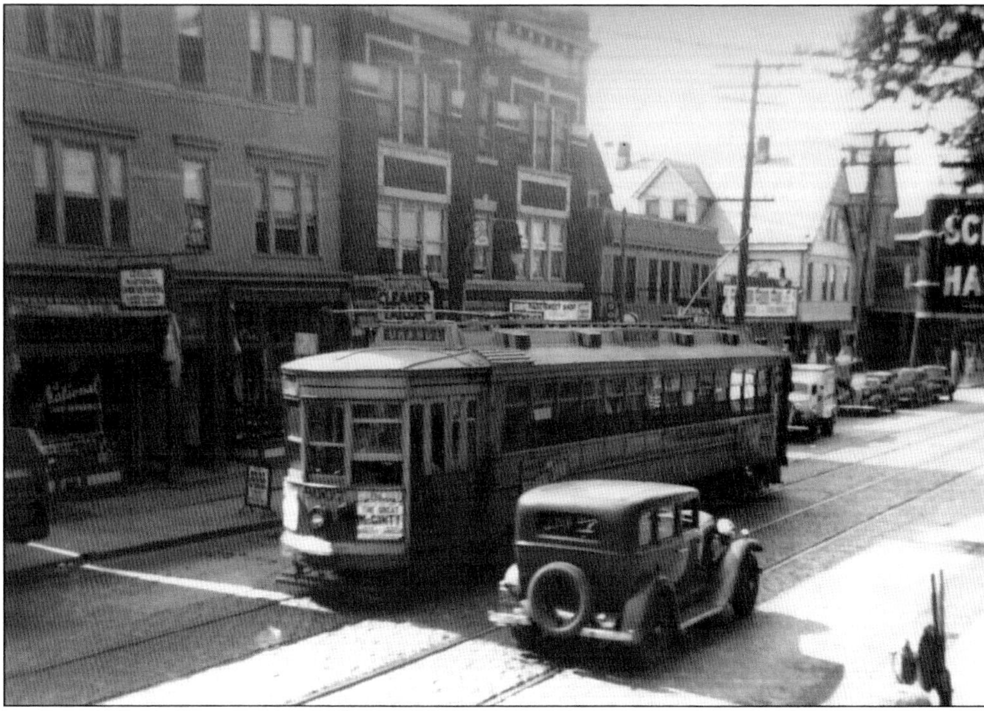

A trolley can be seen during the 1940s passing buildings still recognizable on Main Street today. A sign for Schneider's Hardware store is partially visible to the right. A trolley line from Newark first reached West Orange at this exact spot on February 1, 1892, and terminated at a hotel that once stood opposite this location.

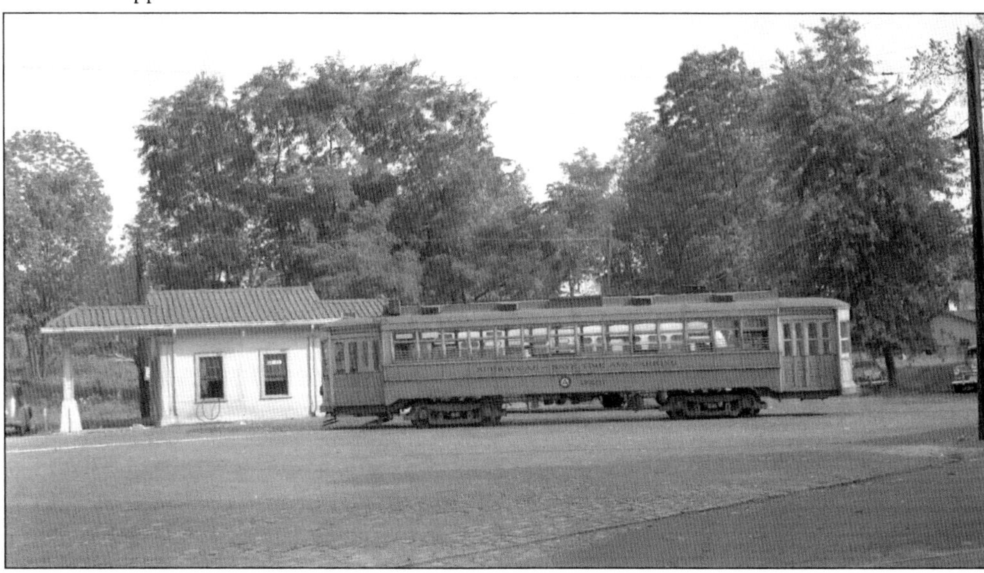

On March 4, 1892, the trolley line reached the end of Main Street opposite Harrison Avenue where a wye configuration turned trolleys around. In 1927, the line extended onto Mississippi Avenue, seen in 1947, to turn trolleys around on the new Mississippi Loop. It is still known by that name and now used by the buses of New Jersey Transit, and the shelter building seen here has since been replaced.

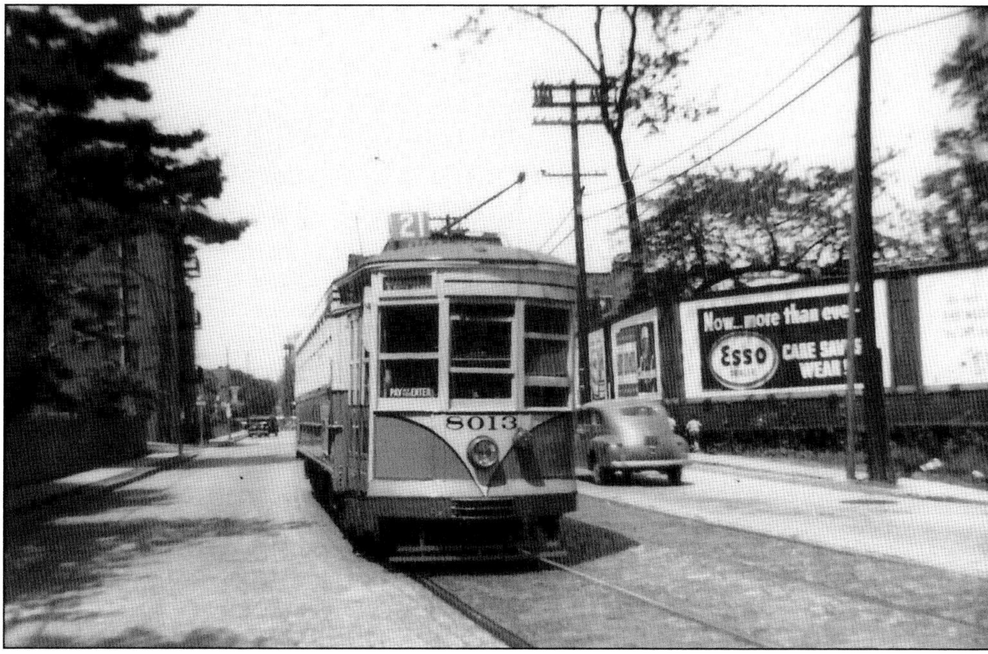

On March 31, 1947, Kathleen Morris, age three, and Jerome Nichols, age six, ran out from behind a parked car into the oncoming path of a trolley at the bottom of North Park Drive on Main Street, seen here around the time of the accident. They were struck by the trolley head-on, instantly killing Morris. Nichols never recovered consciences following the accident and died 10 days later.

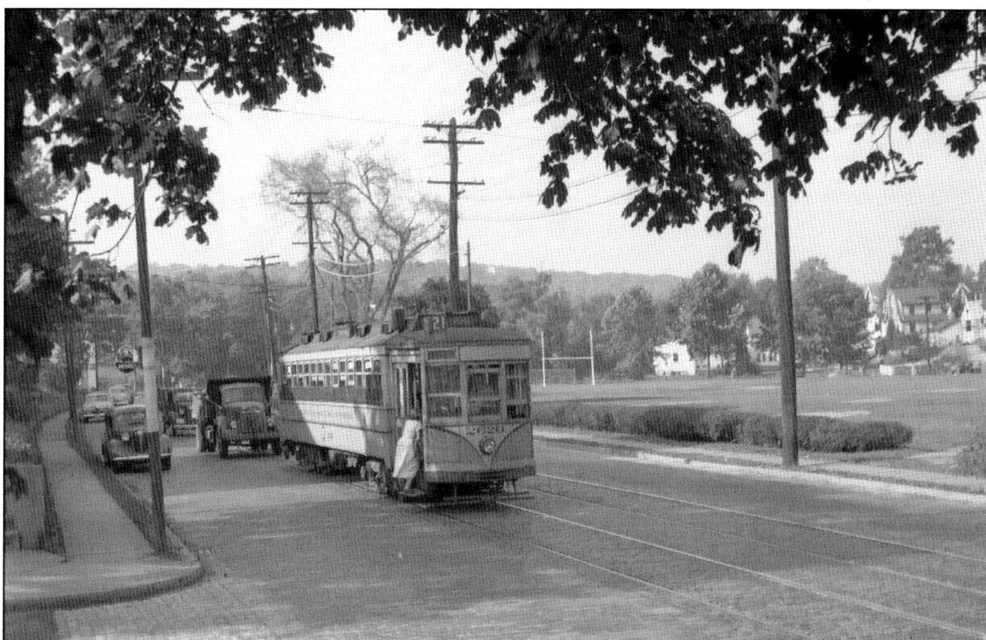

In July 1947, the football field and old-style goalposts of Thomas A. Edison Junior High School are visible to the right, opposite the trolley stop at McKinley Avenue and Main Street. In October 1945, a crowd of 20,000 spectators converged on this field following a World War II victory parade. The field is still in use but now completely fenced in and used solely for youth baseball.

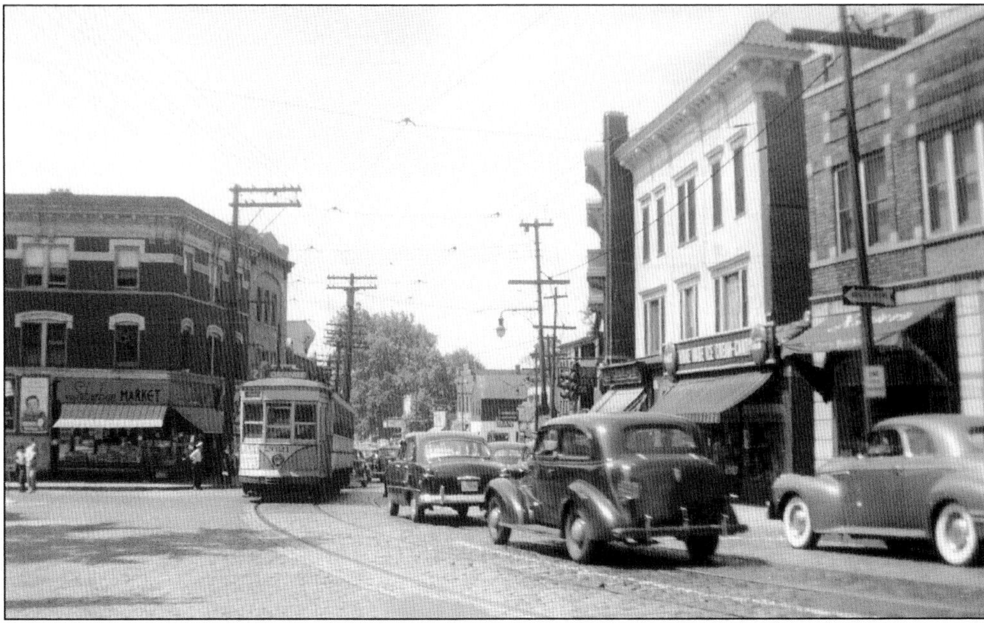

The trolley is seen passing Tory Corner at the end of Washington Street in the 1950s and shows how congested the street could be with the ever-increasing presence of the automobile. All the buildings seen in this photograph are still standing, and only the businesses have changed. The Suburban Market seen to the left is now Purchased Possessions clothing store selling men's fine apparel.

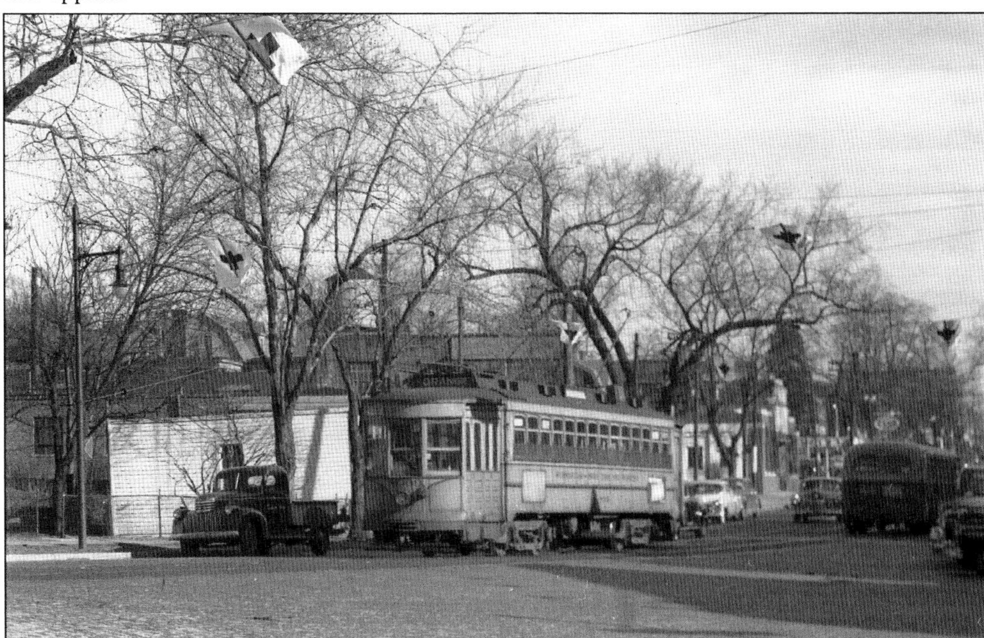

A photograph from February 27, 1951, shows one of the last trolleys leaving West Orange at the end of Main Street in West Orange. Service ceased two days later and had run for a total of 59 years, making the No. 21 line one of New Jersey's longest-running trolley lines. New Jersey Transit now operates buses along the former trolley route and still uses the designation No. 21 line.

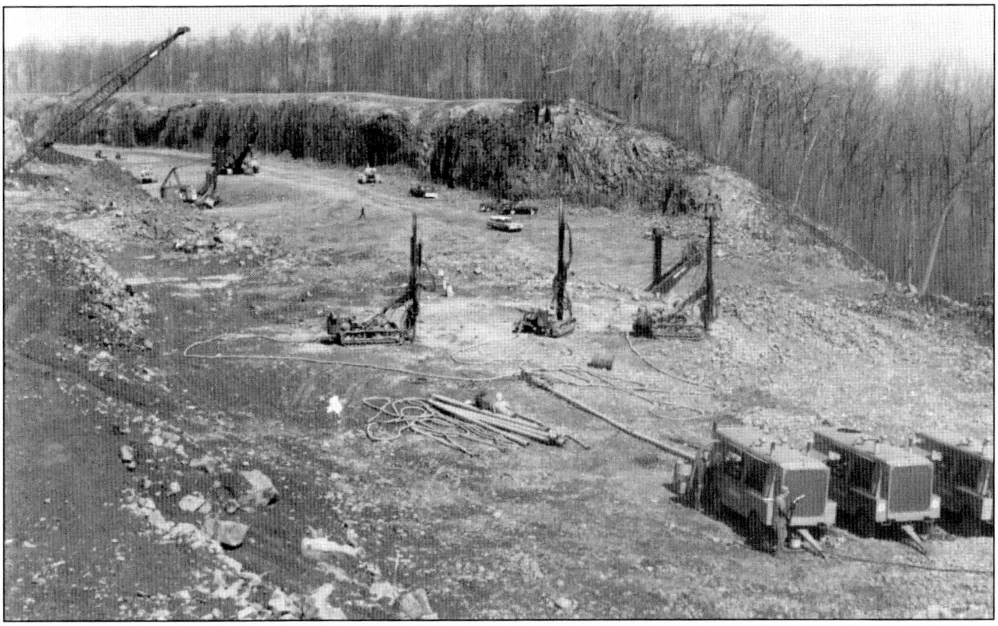

Ingersoll-Rand crawl drills are seen around 1969 drilling through the first mountain during the construction of Interstate 280 near the Prospect Avenue interchange. A tunnel had been proposed but was ultimately deemed too expensive. Each drill averaged 400 feet of hole per day, presplitting rock before inserting blasting caps, resulting in smooth cuts with steep sides. Remnants of drilling are still visible today along the sides of the deep rock cut.

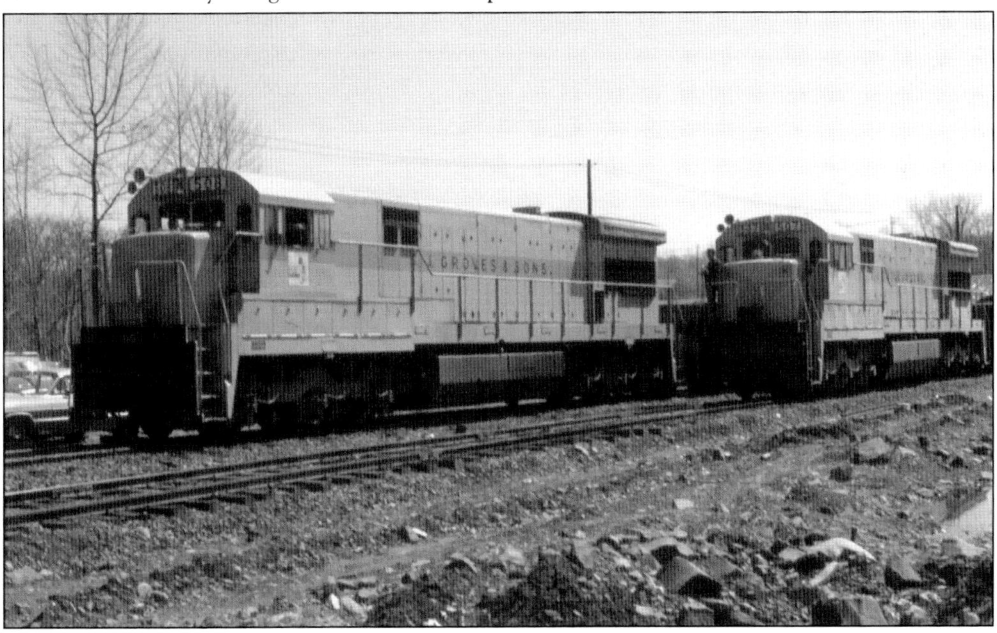

The contractor for this section of highway was S.J. Groves & Sons. The company determined that a temporary railroad was the most economical solution to move excavated rock between West Orange and the low-lying sections of Morris County where fill was needed. The two General Electric U33 diesel locomotives built specially for the task are seen in West Orange on April 9, 1971.

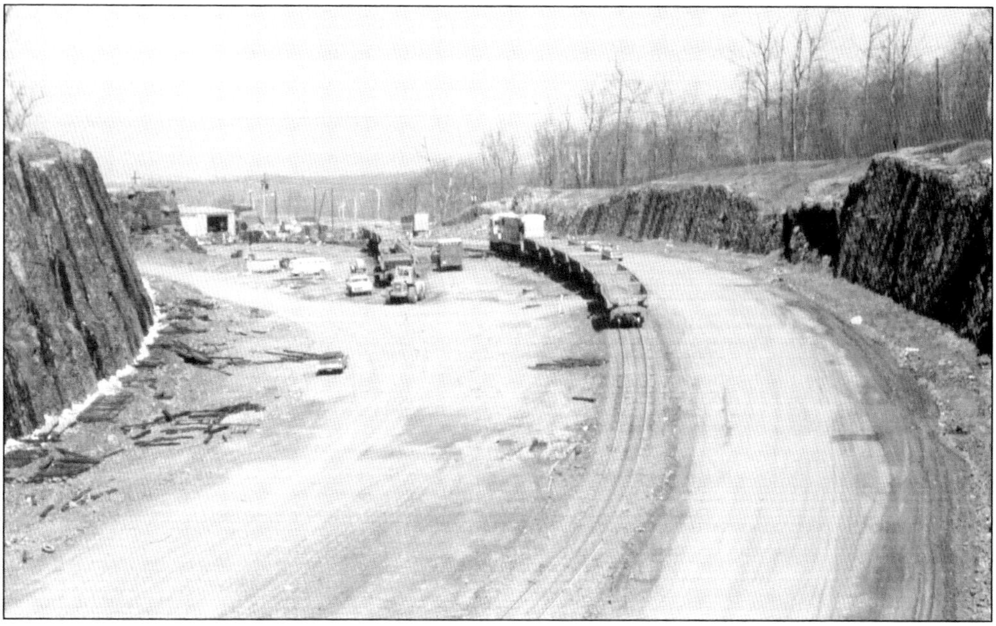

One of the work trains on the temporary railroad can be seen on April 9, 1971, in this view looking west just before the Prospect Avenue interchange. By this time, most of the rock from the top of the first mountain had been removed, and this scene, less the railroad, is totally recognizable today. The length of the railroad eventually extended more then 11.5 miles as progress moved westward.

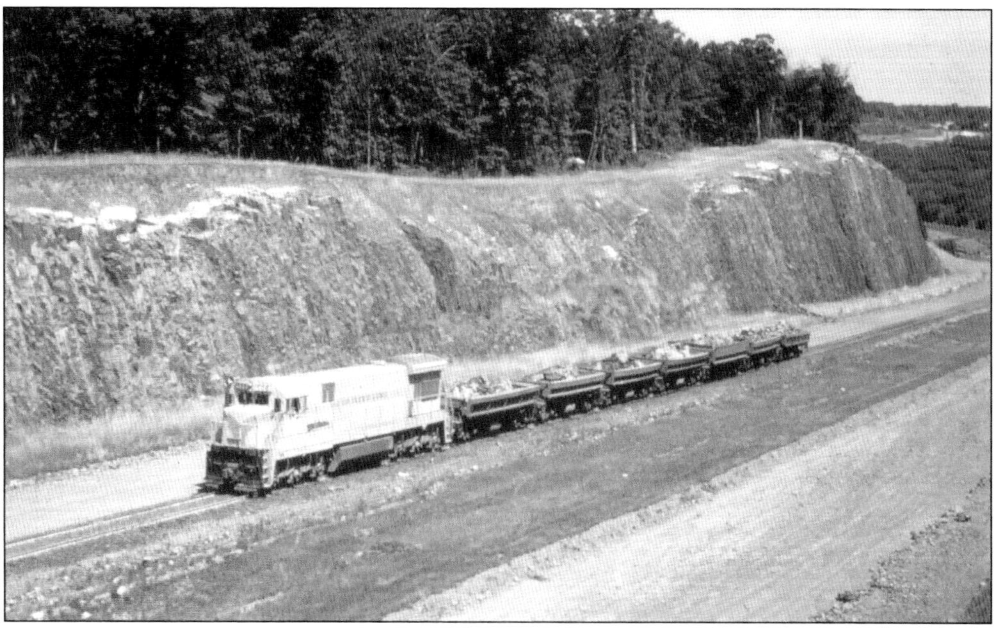

A typical work train consisted of seven cars, like this one seen in West Orange on July 21, 1970, fully loaded with rock. Most highway contractors would have considered a fleet of dump trucks to move the rock but the operating costs were staggering, considering they would have to run constantly. A feasibility study conducted by the McDowell-Wellman Company of Cleveland determined the railroad to be more cost-effective.

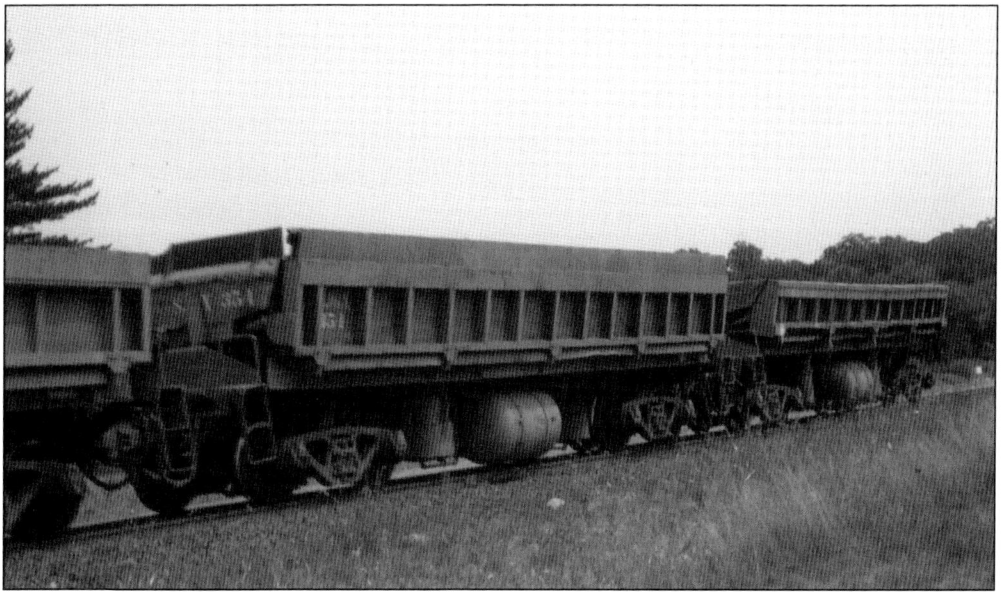

A closer look shows the specially designed side dump cars in August 1970. Each one was capable of holding 35 cubic yard of rock. A total of 21 cars were divided into three trains of seven cars each. The plan was to have one set in the loading zone, one set on a train in the dump zone, and one set on a train in transit at all times.

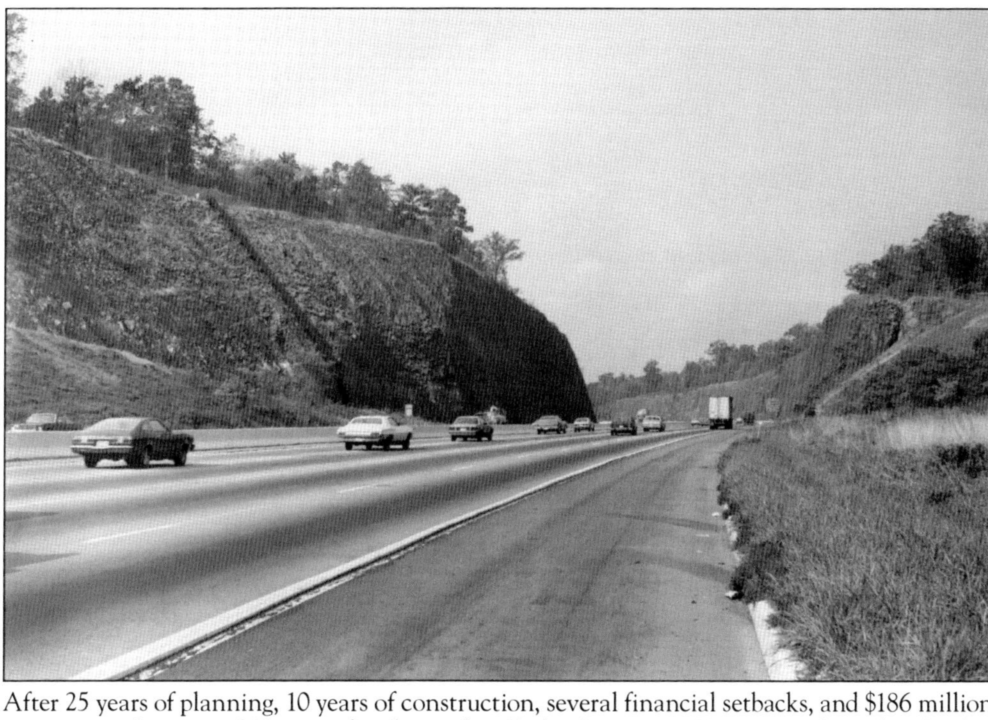

After 25 years of planning, 10 years of construction, several financial setbacks, and $186 million in expenses, Interstate 280 opened end to end on Friday, June 22, 1973. It is seen here shortly after it opened, in a view looking west through the deep rock cut on the first mountain. The Orange Mountains proved to be no obstacle for an interstate highway that now permanently defines the landscape of West Orange.